The Other Side of the World: Vision and Reality

Selected Reflections of India 44's Peace Corps Volunteers

Developed by
Mary Jo Clark
Thomas Corbett
Michael Simonds
Haywood Turrentine

A GROUP PROJECT OF INDIA 44 A & B

Strategic Book Group

Strategic Book Group
P.O. Box 333
Durham CT 06422
www.StrategicBookClub.com

ISBN: 978-1-61204-438-5

Book Design: Suzanne Kelly

Dedication

We dedicate this work to President John F. Kennedy, who inspired the concept of service to country, and to Sargent Shriver, who made this concept a reality. We also dedicate it to fellow volunteers who are no longer with us—Gary Gruber and Robert Proffit. Their legacy, and ours, is a better understanding between people, even on the small scale we were able to achieve. If we could multiply that legacy by the number of people on earth, we would achieve the ultimate mission of the Peace Corps—peace and progress. We also dedicate this work to future volunteers who choose to brave worlds they barely know in order to make this world a slightly better place. Finally, this is dedicated to our spouses and significant others who graciously submitted to the reliving of adventures acted out over four decades ago. Their patience and forbearing is greatly appreciated.

Acknowledgments

We want to acknowledge all of the dedicated Peace Corps staff who took a group of unskilled and naïve college students and helped them negotiate the trials of volunteering for two years in India. In particular, we thank Dennis Conta, our Peace Corps training director. We wish to express our appreciation to the many Indian officials who put up with us so long ago, as well as the many villagers who extended courtesy and friendship to the well-intentioned, but not always competent, volunteers who landed in their villages. In addition, we extend our thanks to our fellow volunteers who contributed to this work through either formal contributions or the sharing of memories and stories. Several individuals read early versions of selected chapters and were enthusiastic supporters in bringing this project to publication, including Jennifer L. Noyes (Associate Director of the Institute for Research on Poverty at the University of Wisconsin) and Ellen Turgasen, who has done extensive volunteer work in South America. Our final thanks go to Elisabeth Garofalo, whose scrupulous and sensitive editing made this a far better book.

Preface

This volume encompasses the thoughts and feelings of a group of young men and women who served as Peace Corps volunteers as part of India 44 A & B in the late 1960s. Some four decades after their return to the States, many of those volunteers gathered for a reunion in Oakland California. That get-together inspired a sharing that tapped deeply held feelings never before fully expressed. Out of this intimate sharing and mutual enlightenment grew a desire, among some at least, to put their more compelling sentiments to paper. This work is the expression and product of that desire.

The chapters prepared by individual volunteers capture much of what was important to them. Each chapter is unique in both style and content. Some are linear and narrative in character, providing an overview of personal motivations for going to India, describing seminal experiences there, and suggesting the longer-term implications of their India experience for their adult lives. Other contributors focus on specific events or issues, narrower perceptions, and emotions that remained integral parts of their subsequent life stories. Some are quite lyrical and evocative. Others are humorous, yet touching. All of the stories are moving in one way or another.

Despite this variation in style and content, certain universal themes emerge. We all felt unprepared for what we were asked to do. We all felt that we failed in one way or another, perhaps because we set our standards for success too high. We all left India sobered by its challenges and the extraordinary complexity of this ancient society. Yet, despite our self-imposed shortcomings, there is an almost universal feeling that what we tried was worth it. Each of us grew as humans and as contributing members of society. Each of us matured and evolved in the face of the personal privations and cultural frictions that we all confronted in our attempt to survive in rural India. Moreover, maybe, just maybe, each of us contributed to our villages in big and small ways, contributions that, for many of us, escaped our notice at the time. In the end, none of us, despite all the difficulties described in these chapters, concluded that volunteering was a waste of time. On the 50th anniversary of the launching of the Peace Corps experiment, we offer these reflections as a testament to the power of the idea of personal commitment and the gift of self.

Table of Contents

When you cease to make a contribution, you begin to die...

— *Eleanor Roosevelt*

MEMBERS OF PEACE CORPS GROUP 44 A & B[1]

Carolyn (Watanabe) Adler (A)
David Bauer (B)
Mary Jo (Dummer) Clark (A)
Carolyn (Jones) Cullen (A)
Tom Corbett (B)
Sheryl (Taub) Dale (A)
David Dell (B)
Roger Edwards (B)
Lynne Graham (A)
Michael Goldberg (B)
Gary Gruber (B) (Deceased)
Cheryl Hanks (A)
Diane (Hamilton) Jeffcott (A)
Pat (Gorski) Johnson (A)
Sylvia (Bray) Larque (A)
Diane (Logefiel) Lauro (A)
Mary (Welch) Krackenberger (A)
John Lievore (A)
David Lubbs (B)
Gareth Loy (B)
Tom McDermott (B)
Terry Merriman (A)
William Muhler (B)
Don Nordin (B)
Harry 'Hap' Pedigo (B)
Robert Proffit (B) (Deceased)
Sam Rankin (A)
Robin (Schatzberg) Samsel (A)
Donnie Schatzberg (A)
Michael Simonds (B)
Nancy Simuel (A)
Kathy (Kelleher) Sohn (A)
Susie Spence (A)
Randall Stoklas (B)
Marilyn Topp (A)
Haywood Turrentine (B)
Jerold (Jerry) Weiss (B)
William (Bill) Whitesell (B)
Gerald (George) Wilson (B)
Susan Krawiec Young (A)

A Reunion

Jerry Weiss

I honestly never thought I'd see them again. More accurately, I hardly ever think about those days, so I didn't think about them either. I tend to leave the past behind. But here they all were, all those Peace Corps Volunteers (PCVs) of 1967... the reunion.

Sorry, man. For me, it's weird to visit the past. I avoid reunions. But this was different, somehow comforting—like climbing back into the bed I slept in as a teenager.

Like a teenager, I walked reluctantly up the front porch steps that Sunday afternoon. I introduced myself to the man standing by the door. He said. "I know you." I looked at him, and I knew him, too. Then I walked through the door.

A man in his mid-sixties threw open his arms and said my name—more warmly than I'd ever heard it said anywhere outside my own home. I walked full-tilt into his embrace, and we held each other—he and I, men who barely knew each other—men who knew each other intimately.

Yes, indeed, Peace Corps changed everything for me.

Plucked from bicycling down Western Avenue in Chicago, I was suddenly living in a village in India in the nineteenth century. Well, maybe it was the twentieth, or it could've been the sixteenth. It didn't really matter—different ruler in the same castle. But in Bhawa, it was the same water in the same well drawn by the same women bearing the same pots on their heads. By mid-day everyone was out in the same fields they had been in every day since no one remembers when.

Oh yes, Peace Corps changed everything.

But tomorrow has its own demands…

The truth is I have already lived longer than any person I met in that village, except for one. Everyone else was dead by age 55. I avoid reunions.

There was just one person in the village that had lived longer than I have now lived. I can still see her—that one mystical person, face weathered and wrinkled, blind eyes looking directly into the sun—the one with the look of eternity. Mother India.

CHAPTER 1

Vision and Reality: Reflections of India 44's Volunteers

The purpose of a writer is to keep civilization from destroying itself.

Albert Camus

Those of us who came of age in the 1960s recall a special age. It was a period of great expectations and some bitter disappointments. It was a time of experimentation and adventure, one might even say bizarre excess. It was also an age of extraordinary caring and sacrifice, an era when all things seemed possible and where constraints were barely appreciated. We brazenly looked out upon a world that appeared to await our singular imprint with open anticipation. If putting a man on the moon could be realistically contemplated, then solving mundane social and economic challenges surely would not be far behind. We were just the people to do it, although you had to be there to fully appreciate the sentiment.

It was in this aura of anticipation and possibility that the Peace Corps concept emerged in 1961. In many ways, it was a classic expression of the zeitgeist of an age. From the moment of President Kennedy's iconic call to "… ask not what your country can do for you; ask what you can do for your country," over 200,000 idealistic young men and woman looked for a way to express their commitment to create a better country and a better world. What more appropriate venue for pursuing such lofty ideals existed than to serve in the Peace Corps?

Not surprisingly, given the tenor of the times, the ranks of the Peace Corps swelled in those early years. Fifty years ago, in 1961, the first volunteers arrived in five host countries. By 1966 it had grown to some 14,500 volunteers in forty-five countries. Buoyed by early successes and a favorable public response, ambitious plans evolved to expand the program to a peak of over 15,000 volunteers by 1969. The India initiative was one of the largest efforts with over 700 volunteers. By 1968, it was anticipated that over 1,000 volunteers would be in the field. A half-a-century later, some 8,500 volunteers continue to serve in seventy-seven nations.

At one point ambitions were even grander, perhaps even a bit over the top. There is an apocryphal story that President Johnson, in one of his more grandiose moments, even for him, told Indian Prime Minister Indira Gandhi that the U.S. would commit as many as 10,000 volunteers to India in the coming years. It was never clear whether this was a promise or a threat and, fortunately, nothing came of this purported 'vision.'

In any case, pure idealism was touching against power politics. In her post-colonial years, India steered a political path between the United States and the Soviet Union—the two superpowers, pleasing neither. Several U.S. Presidents wanted to draw this critically important country closer into their spheres of influence. Naively, perhaps, it was thought that the youthful idealism of the 1960s might be melded with the real-politick perspective of an older generation.

By any political metric, Peace Corps was and (arguably) still is a success as public programs go. It has endured for some five decades and celebrates its golden anniversary in 2011. Although the size and visibility of the program has diminished, the underlying popularity of the concept has never totally waned. Peace Corps apparently appeals to the country's finer instincts with an emphasis on volunteerism and service to others. It taps the nation's nobler sentiments and provides an outlet for those seeking some way to make a broader contribution to society.

There have always been critics, to be sure. Senator Daniel Patrick Moynihan, once described the Peace Corps as "...a rip-off by the upper-middle classes. Fortunes spent to send Amherst boys for an interesting learning experience in Venezuela." Experiences paid for by "…men equally young pumping gas on the New Jersey Turnpike."[2] Others, we are sure, feel it is merely another ineffective government program that costs the taxpayers money and yields little in return.

Our stories will not settle such a debate nor quell doubts about the program as it is structured. It will not satisfy concerns about whether public dollars should support such altruistic endeavors. Frankly, it is not our intent to defend Peace Corps or provide evidence of its utility. We seek neither to demonstrate effectiveness nor to suggest a basis for moving forward in the years ahead. We leave such tasks to the many policy and political wonks who perpetually agonize over such matters.

Ours, rather, is a much more individual quest. In the reflections that follow, we express our personal, and often very private, experiences associated with our Peace Corps tenure some forty plus years ago. Our view of Peace Corps is from the ground up as refracted through the perspective and subsequent experiences of our adult lives. In some important ways, though not necessarily by design, we temper exaggerated hopes with a dose of unromantic honesty.

The stories we tell through our reflections are sometimes touching, occasionally humorous, and often tinged with sadness and a pesky sense of sobering frankness. This is not a simple picture of idealistic young men and women changing the world for the better. At the same time, it is not a tale of failure or regret. What we present in our subsequent stories are memories and feelings shared in ways that can help us make sense of our own experiences and pasts. While each contributing author is spurred by very personal motivations, our collective story telling helps all of us deal with issues and feelings that often endured long after our service.

In the end, Peace Corps for the actual volunteers was not about the numbers involved, social or economic ends realized, or any political visions satisfied. It was about our individual experiences in the program and about our relationships with our fellow volunteers and others. While we all had some notion of the larger purposes associated with our efforts, the reality of Peace Corps for each of us emanated from our internal struggles to accommodate high hopes and unrealistic expectations to the gritty realities we faced on a daily basis.

Few other countries in the Peace Corps world posed as many challenges for the volunteers. India, particularly for recent college graduates with so little real world experience and so few of the personal skills and confidence we would later possess, revealed herself as a stern mistress. In truth, for only partially formed kids, she proved to be a harsh, often inflexible, testing ground for our ideals and our immaturity. Yet India also proved to be a marvelous petri dish within which to grow and become the adults we are today. We are getting ahead of ourselves here, though. Let us start with an overview of our introduction to Peace Corps almost 45 years ago.

India 44

It was in the confusing and conflicted context of the 1960s that over 100 of us reported to the University of Wisconsin in Milwaukee during the summer of 1966. We were about to become what would be designated as "India 44," the 44th distinct group to be sent to the world's largest democracy.

Our group, in fact, was unusual in two ways. First of all it was actually two separate projects combined to save, in theory at least, some training costs through a form of economy of scale. India 44-A, primarily but not exclusively female, was destined for community health work in the Indian state of Maharashtra, outside of Bombay (now Mumbai). India 44-B, primarily but not exclusively male (at first), was originally designated to work in poultry (later agriculture) in the Indian state of Rajasthan.

The second unusual feature of India 44 was that we were part of an experimental "Advanced Training Program" (ATP). The concept behind this experiment was to recruit those completing their junior college year. They would return, after an initial summer of training, to their respective institutions where

6

India 44A/B, Peace Corps Training, University of Wisconsin, Milwaukee, Summer 1966

they could continue to receive additional language and cultural preparation. Those remaining in the program would return for a second phase of US-side training before being sent overseas. In theory, the ATP approach would provide volunteers with opportunities for more intensive training and the utilization of resources during their final academic year to prepare for the eventual overseas experience. It was an interesting concept that did not work out quite as well as envisioned.

Our training was long and, at points, arduous. As a result, many fell by the wayside. The first phase of the training took place on the campus of the University of Wisconsin-Milwaukee from June 24th to August 26th 1966. This part of our training regimen included intensive language preparation, technical preparation for future in-country work, exposure to some of the social and cultural challenges we might face, and even some physical training to harden our bodies for the rigors ahead.

That first summer also included a field trip during the first two weeks of August to American Indian Reservations in either

South Dakota or Northern Wisconsin. This on-site experience was seen as a way to expose us to a different culture and perhaps acquaint us with the rigors that awaited us overseas. These sites were remote, and the living conditions primitive. For some, the overall experience presented a degree of hardship not previously encountered in our young, urban-oriented, and generally privileged lives.

At the end of the first phase of training there was a round of evaluations that resulted in the "deselection" of a number of trainees whom the staff concluded, wisely or not, might not be well suited for two years in rural India. At this point, the 44-B group lost ten of the 44 trainees who completed the initial two months of training.

To sustain the commitment of the remaining volunteers, a week-long session was held between semesters in Houston, Texas. For many of the northern volunteers, spending any time in the southern U.S. during the 1960s was an eye-opening experience and certainly an exposure to a different, if not alien, 'culture.'

Our group continued to shrink. During the school year that followed, another seven of the remaining 34 trainees of the poultry group (44-B) resigned. This twenty percent attrition rate was actually much lower than that of most Advanced Training Programs. According to Peace Corps records, only 551 trainees out a total of 880 enrolled in the ATP program returned for the final phase of training (a 37% attrition rate). It was this attrition rate, combined with the increased cost of the ATP program that caused Peace Corps to substantially reduce the program in the following year (down to 238 trainees) and then eliminate the concept entirely.

During the transition phase of the ATP program, the decision was made to change the focus of India 44-B from poultry to agriculture. The change in direction had little impact on those of us in the program. Virtually none of us had any experience in either poultry or agriculture. Having made this decision, Peace Corps also transferred the four remaining women from 44-B to 44-A (the Community Health Program), leaving 44-B as an all male contingent from that point on.

Only 23 of us remained in 44-B when the group returned for the last phase of training, which included another four weeks at the University of Wisconsin (this time at the Madison campus) and a final four weeks of training in India. There was a final process of self-initiated resignations and staff-initiated trainee deselections that eliminated another five trainees. At the finish line, only eighteen of the original 44 trainees for India 44-B were sworn in as volunteers. The companion group, India 44-A, had a similar attrition rate. Presumably, only the most committed, or those most in need of being committed to some institute for the pathetically deluded, would embark on the adventure of their lives in the summer of 1967.

India circa 1967

India in the summer of 1967 was a far cry from today's "India Inc." with its rapid economic growth based largely on corporate outsourcing and technological savvy. Today, the country enjoys the availability of a sizable technically competent workforce that is also fluent in English, the international language of business. Recognizing its emerging status as a world power, President Obama recently argued that India should have a permanent seat on the United Nations Security Council, surely a signal that the country has come of age.

Two generations ago, things were quite different. The country was not fully 20 years into its independence. India, freshly emerged from yet another brief war with Pakistan, was still trying to forge a national identity from a patchwork of ethnic and religious communities. At the same time, India was struggling to remain independent of the political and economic maneuvering of the superpowers of that era.

Internally, it was overwhelmingly rural and agriculturally focused. In many parts of the country, life had not changed much in centuries, with rural families trying desperately to eke out marginal livings on tiny plots of land. India then fully deserved its reputation as a "third-world country" with a precarious identity and an uncertain future.

Set up in villages outside of Bombay (now Mumbai) the volunteers of India 44-A found a community health care system in the earliest stages of development. The gap between the ambitious government plans and the reality on the ground was appalling. Facing primitive conditions and operating with little direction, those of us in 44-A struggled to have an impact with little in the way of resources while working with indigenous co-workers who sometimes lacked the most basic training and understanding of modern health issues.

Located in towns and villages around the city of Udaipur in the Indian state of Rajasthan, those of us in 44-B found most farmers working as they had for centuries, if not millennia, guiding a wooden plow behind a pair of bored bullocks. Rajasthan was located in the northwest corner of the country, bordering on Pakistan. It had a traditional reputation as an area where fierce warriors were bred to repel the many foreign invasions that rolled out of the northwest right through this harsh, unforgiving terrain into the heart of mother India. In some places, it had the look and feel of what the American wild west of circa 1880 must have been like.

Our living conditions varied widely, and with little apparent logic. Some of us were situated in towns with a rail or bus connection, electricity (sporadic), and a vibrant marketplace. Others were located in remote villages where the inhabitants spoke local dialects incomprehensible to Americans who had received all their language training in either Hindi or Marathi. Given the conditions, it is not surprising that we continued to lose members. Before our two years of service were completed, India 44-B lost five more of the eighteen volunteers that touched down in the summer of 1967.

Two factors were to make our India experience particularly challenging. First, despite an unprecedented investment in training and the stringent selection processes, we were woefully unprepared. The skill deficiency was certainly true of the 44-B volunteers who, with few exceptions, were urban, white kids that had recently graduated from liberal arts colleges. We may have been smart and well-meaning but doing agriculture well required far more experience than could be imparted in a few weeks of training, particularly when some of that training was in an entirely different field (poultry). The same might be said of the 44-A volunteers; only two were nurses and there were few with any real public health knowledge or experience.

Second, India was an overwhelmingly complex place with a culture that could not be more different from the one in which we had been raised. You can read about the differences in a book, be told about them in classes, and even do some role playing as a way to gain some exposure to a new set of rules. However, you cannot really know what you are getting into until you experience it. We quickly found that to avoid violating the myriad of rules emanating from diverse castes, religions, ethnic groups, and political affiliations demanded constant vigilance and a super-heightened sensitivity to this new world. Technical achievement in public health and agriculture quickly took second place to mere survival. Despite the challenges, you will see in the reflections contained in the chapters to follow that we did our best.

As suggested earlier, the India 44-A & B volunteers were part of the largest Peace Corps contingent ever assigned to a single country. However, this kind of ambitious investment of human talent was not destined to last. Under President Nixon, the overall scope of Peace Corps was to shrink to less than half the size it had been under President Johnson. More to the point, the government of India decided that it wanted less foreign influence to help shape its future development. Within five years of our departure in June 1969, the last Peace Corps volunteers would be gone from India.

Despite the cultural challenges, the primitive living conditions, and the real or perceived lack of preparedness, we emerged from our experience as better people. That was not necessarily apparent in the short term, as some of our stories illustrate with painful honesty. But with the subsequent testing of over four decades, our collective conclusion is unmistakable. For each of us, Peace Corps was a road well worth taking.

Making sense of it all.

In July, 1969, our India experience ended. After a series of debriefings, official ceremonies, and one last party in New Delhi, we embarked on our post Peace Corps lives. Returning to the States, some of us went East and some West as we sought to resume the remainder of our lives. Some subsequent contacts occurred among members of the groups but most of us went our own way. The experience of India and of each other faded, or so it seemed. Then, a funny thing happened. As the 40th anniversary of our return approached, a few of us residing on the West coast met to discuss the possibility of a reunion. Over time, this planning group found that most of those we were able to locate were, indeed, anxious to get together.

And so, some forty years after our tour of duty ended, more than two-thirds of those India 44 volunteers who could be located got together in Oakland, California over Memorial Day weekend in 2009. Not everyone who attended had completed the two-year tour in-country; however, that was irrelevant. Each of us had embraced the Peace Corps ideal. We had committed to the process and purpose of serving in India and had experienced India in that very real and personal way that the Peace Corps experience permits. Each of us had something to contribute to the dialogue that emerged over the course of the reunion.

During that three day event, we gradually began to open up to one another, perhaps in ways that the hubris or defensiveness of youth might never have allowed. Our sharing of past memories and feelings revealed just how little we knew of each other's experiences in that far away place to which we ventured when we were oh so young. Whatever the expectations might have been, the reality of the get-together proved remarkably personal and rewarding. It was as if 40 hours had passed since we had last been together, not 40 years.

The sharing over these three days evoked memories and emotions long muted by time and the demands of our frantic lives. For many of us, however, this all too brief get-together failed to quench a thirst for more of the same. It was as if we could only scratch the surface of a deeper, more persistent itch that could not be completely satisfied in such a short time. This lingering frustration, perhaps, pushed us toward the concept of individual written reflections.

Those who wished would put thoughts and reflections on paper: what brought them to Peace Corps; what they experienced during training and service; how those experiences shaped their subsequent life; and what that subsequent life looked like. Not all contributors would cover all these points, though some came very close. The point was never to satisfy some prescriptive list of topics. Rather, we wanted each contributor to touch upon whatever meant the most to them whether positive or negative, confusing or enlightening, profound or banal. For the author, each reflection was important enough to recall and express.

At the outset, we did not have a clear idea of what we might do with these reflections. Perhaps they might be woven into a publication, or shared with loved ones who might not have been able to embrace a portion of our lives that, by definition, was intensely personal. Perhaps they would simply be shared with our India 44 colleagues, serving as a way to fill in the blanks about our volunteer experiences and our lives. Or perhaps they will just be for ourselves, a way to express and understand a part of our lives that had such meaning for each of us.

Whatever their ultimate purpose or use, our reflections are found in the remainder of this work. They differ along many dimensions: length, focus, approach, and intent. Some contributions focus more on what the contributor saw and did. Others touch on the author's feelings and reactions to events. Each author chose his or her own unique approach to capture thoughts and feelings that may have long been unexpressed and perhaps inexpressible. Despite the variations, there exist a number of common themes that surface time and again, themes reflecting the dialogue that took place during the reunion.

For example, many of us carry within us a taste of failure, the sense that we did not do as much as we could or achieve as much as we wanted. We were not good enough, kind enough, smart enough, skilled enough, or compassionate enough. We carried that sense of deficit within us as a private, unspoken hell. The very act of talking about such feelings, articulating them, proved to be a welcome emotional purgative. Expressing our long-held private feelings in writing seemed like a reasonable next step.

Moreover, each of us found India both magnificent and daunting and carried elements of our struggle there back with us to the States. Each of us realized, on some fundamental level, that our experiences so long ago altered the trajectory of our lives and substantively influenced who and what we were to become. At the end of the day, each of us realized we were the better for our Peace Corps experience.

And so, these are our memories, our understandings, and our reflections on our commitment to India 44.

CHAPTER 2

India Remembered

Mike Simonds

Somewhere in the sky between London and Delhi I took out a notebook and scribbled my thoughts. It was July 29, 1967, and I was on a charter jet with over a hundred other volunteers on our way to postings in Iran and India.

The plane is largely dark now. In the passenger section only four lights burn. Four centers of activity in a sea of fatigue. In the slightly reclined seats figures bend themselves into some unusual positions to better entice the much needed and desired sleep.

The weariness is real. The product of many lost hours and many more miles traveled. The space we have traveled should not be measured in miles, however. It is from the New World to the Old, from the Old to the Ancient. Our plane moves through years as quickly as it moves through miles, from our world to theirs.

India? It is a collection of firmly held notions, a string of bright concepts tied together with care. The Real India is before us. How close the relationship will be to my India I cannot guess. A mystery made even deeper by a little knowledge.

The first surprise for us was the fact that we made it to India at all. Somewhere near the end of the flight, the charter Air India jet lost the covering on one of its outboard engines. I remember a lot of crowding at the window and excited conversation, along the lines of "It's not supposed to be like that, is it?" As far as I can remember there was no explanation from the cockpit, no

acknowledgement of the incident at all. I remember going back to my seat and looking down at the Indian countryside, all cut up into tiny farm plots, wondering if we were going to end up making a big crater there.

In the end we landed without incident, and again, as far as I can remember, nothing was ever said officially about the whole affair. But touring through Old Delhi the next day I remember seeing a headline in the *Hindustani Times* that read, in bold letters, "104 Peace Corps Volunteers Narrowly Escape Death!" I have always regretted that I didn't grab a copy when I had the chance, it would have made quite a souvenir. (Actually I don't think there were that many of us on the plane by then. The reporters probably used the original passenger list that included the Iran volunteers we had dropped off en route).

Sometimes I wonder if there is a parallel universe out there where we didn't make it to the runway. I'm sure that President Lyndon Johnson himself would have attended our Memorial Service, and it would have been a grand affair. At the very least though, it does seem to me that it is worthwhile thinking of the last 42 years as a gift that all of us have, that simply might never have been. It helps put everything else in perspective.

In this universe, of course, we made it to India alive and well. To a certain degree, I would be surprised at how familiar it seemed. We had, after all, been given a long introduction with endless lectures, pictures, movies and personal stories from returned volunteers. Yet much of it was surprising. At the end of the first week, I wrote down a list of the incidents that stood out most vividly in my mind.

The sight of camels pulling plows outside of Delhi.

The sad little man with the bag of chicken heads that he tried to sell to Gareth.

The soldier who chased the beggars from our train.

The beggars and the train.

The "Zoo Feeling" of being on display at every train station as people peeked through the window to watch us eat the unfamiliar food.

The three porters at the station who struggled to get my trunk onto the head of this one scrawny porter.

The little girl who came down out of the house while we sat on our bikes in front of the hospital, smiled at us, turned around, pulled up her dress, squatted, and defecated in the gutter.

Yes, India was going to be full of surprises. But the biggest surprise of all was the simple fact that I was there! How the hell had that happened? The simple answer was the most superficial. I had made the decision to apply to the Peace Corps on November 22, 1963. I still remember that moment I stood at the bus stop trying to get home after the campus had been shut down by the news of Kennedy's assassination. Lost in a bewildering flood of conflicting emotions, pain, anger, frustration, grief, the only gesture I could think of that made sense was the Peace Corps.

The reader will note, however, that I said I decided "to apply" to the Peace Corps. I don't think I ever imagined I would actually go overseas. At that time, the Peace Corps had a reputation for a rigorous selection process which I doubted I would survive. So I'm really not sure I thought this would ever go beyond a heartfelt, largely symbolic, gesture.

India? That would have never entered my mind. On the application form I expressed a preference for Thailand. The reason was simple. I thought Thai women were the most beautiful in the world (okay, so I was not a complete idealist). But when the Peace Corps came back to me to say that they had more than enough volunteers for Thailand but would I consider India, I was surprised at my reaction. There was actually an almost unconscious attraction to the spiritual reputation that country held for me, and I accepted the invitation immediately.

To understand this attraction, it is necessary to take a step back and understand my beginnings. I was the archetypical war baby (circa World War II). My father was from a mixed Portuguese and Greek ethnic neighborhood in Oakland, California. My mother was a WASP farm girl from Montana. Nothing short of a world-wide conflagration could have brought them together.

The result was an inter-cultural family that also implied a mixed religious household. Since there were to be four children, it was easy to divide us up equally, with me and sister number one attending my mother's Presbyterian church while my brother and kid sister started out as Catholics. While equitable, this arrangement was a logistical nightmare that ended only when the Protestant side of the family capitulated and converted. I was never sure that my father didn't regret this development because converts tend to be very rigorous in their religious observations. Henceforth, he would often find himself taken to task for not always practicing what he preached.

The important point for me, however, is that, because my conversion happened in adolescence, I grew up knowing that there was more than one point of view. I always knew that people held quite different beliefs and practices, which caused me to hold some part of my own beliefs with a healthy dose of skepticism.

The next big step came for me when I read *The Razor's Edge* in high school. It is a story by Somerset Maugham about Larry Darrell, a young man of some privilege who is deeply shaken by an experience during the First World War. A close friend is killed saving his life. This trauma prompts him to ponder some of the basic questions of existence, a need to know the meaning of life, as one was lost to save his. He travels around Europe, living in Paris and working in the coal mines of Germany. Eventually, he ends up in India where he meets a guru and has an "awakening."

An important part of the story, however, is what happens after that experience. He does not stay in India, but returns and reunites with his circle of friends in postwar Paris. He has changed dramatically, and yet Maugham shows that it is a tricky thing trying to live a spiritually meaningful life in the modern world, even after such a transformative experience.

I've found that this novel had an impact on many boys of my generation. If it somehow came up in conversation, the mere mention of *The Razor's Edge* would be enough to identify a kindred soul. Interestingly, it doesn't seem to have had the same kind of impact on the girls who read it. I do have a theory about that. I think that there are very few spiritual handles in our culture available to an adolescent boy. The theme of this book worked well because it validated that kind of spiritual longing. It did so within the context of a macho story (it was the result of the experience of war), and conveyed that it was possible to be a *man* and still have these kinds of feelings.

The Razor's Edge was my introduction to eastern religions. It sparked my curiosity, but the book is not really about the beliefs of Hinduism, as much as it is about the nature of the spiritual quest. Still, I have to say that it planted some seeds that would only come to fruition when I did learn more about the source of Larry's enlightenment.

The Peace Corps training program I was invited to join was an experimental project that involved an initial training period in the summer between our junior and senior years of college. This experiment was soon to be discontinued as the training costs and the drop-out rate were much higher than for other programs. This approach, however, gave me the opportunity to take some courses related to India in my senior year, one of them being a comparative religion course. That course was a life-changing event for me.

Eastern religions have a completely different worldview from the Judeo-Christian understanding of the universe. Jews, Christians, and Moslems all believe in a Supreme Being who created the universe and the individual souls that inhabit the Earth. In that sense, we are all God's creatures.

At its core, Hinduism differs in that it believes that we are all manifestations of God. Every spark of consciousness is a part of God, just as the drops in the spray from a wave are really part of the ocean, despite their momentary existence as separate entities.

Or, to use another analogy, we all become characters in our own dreams. Usually when we are dreaming, we are not aware of it. There are other characters in our dreams, and sometimes we can even become those other characters. Of course, none of that really exists. So, in a way, it's as if God is dreaming and has yet to wake up. Enlightenment is coming to an understanding of the oneness of the universe. The world as we know it is *Maya*, or illusion, and all the appearances are part of the dream. The only reality is the ultimate reality behind the dream, and that is the dreamer. When a person realizes this, they can blend back into that reality, as the drop does when it rejoins the ocean.

It was not that I accepted this cosmic world view in its entirety, but I did find it to be a fascinating new way to look at life. It's one of those fundamental changes in perspective that makes you see everything from a new angle, and when you do that, you embrace things in a way you haven't done before.

It would make a good story to say that this fascination with Eastern philosophy led me to a new level of spirituality during my time in India, but that was not the case. The India I served in was a far cry from today's "India Inc." with a growing economy based on technological outsourcing. We were there barely 20 years after independence, and, at that point, India had a well-earned reputation as a classic example of an underdeveloped country.

We often heard about the spiritualism of India as contrasted to the materialism of the West, especially from educated, middle-class Indians. I couldn't help but feel that there was more than a little defensiveness in their positions.

One incident that sticks in my mind was a dinner that a couple of us volunteers were invited to by a village notable. We sat at a table in a courtyard while we were served a virtual feast. Our host discoursed at some length about the superiority of Indian spirituality and the shortcomings of the materialism of the West. I remember looking over at a line of the village poor squatting against the wall of the compound waiting patiently for the leftovers that would be distributed after we left. I couldn't help but think that if they had a little more of our materialism maybe there wouldn't be so many poor depending on a handout for their basic nutrition.

I did visit a number of religious sites while I was in India, including one that plays a significant role in *The Razor's Edge*, the Ajunta Caves. And I often found these sites moved me to contemplation; however, that all seemed outweighed by the grinding poverty I saw all around me.

One aspect of the Hindu belief system that had always given me a problem was the idea of reincarnation. While in India, I was surrounded by people who accepted reincarnation as a fact of life. I had a number of conversations with upper class Hindu students in which they used the idea of reincarnation and karma to justify the social order. Obviously they were leading privileged lives because they were being rewarded for something they had done in a previous life. It was equally clear to them that the poor around them were being punished for past life transgressions. It made no sense to them to try and help those less fortunate or talk about reform. Attempting to change the calculus of life was futile at best, since they would have to work through their karma no matter how much effort you put into helping them. And, of course, it was hardly worth trying because the fact of their life now simply proved how unworthy they were in the first place.

India, in the late 1960's, was a challenge for a young, idealistic American in any case. But in the end it just seemed to me that the famous Eastern spirituality was part of the problem. Because of this I probably returned from India more materialistic than when I left. The next several decades of my life were devoted to building a career and raising a family. The books on spirituality gathered dust in the bookcase while I indulged my other reading interests such as history. It wasn't until I found myself in the midst of a painful divorce that I found myself drawn back to that area of the bookstore again. But that's a later part of my story.

—⟋⟍—

I don't want to make it sound like my only reason for going to India was a spiritual quest. I was also interested in the cultural experience. I had learned all about "cultural relativism" in college, and I was really interested in finding out if there was anything universal in terms of what human beings value, regardless of their culture. It seemed to me that an Indian village would be as far removed from my own background as possible, so it would be the place to look for that common ground.

Actually, college itself had been something of a cross-cultural experience for me. Growing up in a working class family, college had never been in my plans. After high school my father's union found me a job in a new factory that was just opening for business. It was an ideal blue-collar job since I was one of the first hired and would have the protective blanket of seniority as long as I wanted to work there.

There was a problem, though. A family friend had given me a course catalog from San Francisco State College and I was fascinated by what I found there. There were courses that explained philosophy, psychology, physics, metaphysics, economics, and sociology. How could I turn that down? I had no ambition to graduate with a degree, but I did outline the half-dozen courses I would need to take in order to fully understand life. I could then return to the factory and live out my life as a blue-collar philosopher. Now, how sweet would that be?

The only reason I was even able to go to college was the terrific bargain higher education used to be in California. If I remember correctly, a semester's tuition was $48.50. That was not per credit; that was for a full course load! At that rate I could make it with a summer job and a small loan with some work-study thrown in.

Still, going to what was essentially a middle class college was a cross-cultural experience for this blue collar lad. And it was just full of surprises! I'll never forget my first day of class. Taking my seat, I waited eagerly for my first experience of a college level lecture. In walked a distinguished gentleman with a touch of grey in his hair, wearing a suit and tie, and carrying a briefcase. To my surprise he sat down next to me in the classroom. Next, this young chick walks in with long hair and an appearance I would have described as classic "hippie", who went up to the podium and began giving the lecture! This was not going to be the college experience I'd come to expect from all those Hollywood movies!

In the end things didn't work out the way I'd planned. To begin with, my faculty advisor didn't understand my grand design any better than my parents did when I quit what they thought was the perfect job. My advisor made me take all these required courses that didn't interest me. More importantly, however, was the fact that the dozen courses I had chosen did much more to undermine what I thought I knew about the world than they did in helping me understand it. So, before I knew it, I had enough credits to graduate, and it seemed silly not to do it. By that time, of course, I was committed to going to India, so there was no question about the next step.

There was one place that India completely met my expectations. It did teach me a lot about being an American and my own values, as well as giving me a sense about what is universal in the human experience.

The incident that first comes to mind was one where I was invited by Gary Gruber, another India 44B volunteer, to come to his village during the inauguration of a 4-H club program. The kick-off ceremony revolved around a speech by an American official. I never was sure whether he worked for the American International Development (A.I.D.) program or was there as part of the international 4-H movement or something. I know that he had been a successful farmer in the Midwest before this current assignment.

What I remember most vividly is that the speech he gave was the best example I had ever seen of the concept of the "Ugly American". It was full of clichés and platitudes that had no relevance at all to the culture of the villagers assembled for the event. At one point, I remember him saying "Your parents want you to be good little Indians and good little farmers. Your government needs you to be good little Indians and good little farmers". Yes, he did use the phrase "good little Indians".

I would have been completely mortified if the villagers had understood any of this. Fortunately, his speech was "translated" by an assistant who totally ignored what he was saying. To the uninformed it looked like he was translating the remarks, because he waited patiently for the speaker to finish a phrase before speaking himself. Instead of relaying the "good little Indian" nonsense he gave out very practical information "We are going to give each of you six packets of seeds" then he waited for the next pause from the speaker "and a set of tools", and so on.

The climax, however, came at the end of the speech. When the American was wrapping up, the translator turned to the audience and announced in the most serious tone:

"Okay you backwards peckerwoods! Don't screw this up and embarrass your country. This is a real *Pukka Sahib* who has come all the way from America! This man" he said, pointing at the speaker "makes 30,000 rupees a month! And he is here just to help you, so don't bring shame on the village."

At this announcement, a hush came over the crowd and you could see the jaws drop. Thirty thousand rupees was more cash than everyone in the village combined would see in several lifetimes. The idea of one human being earning that in a month strained the wildest imagination.

The speaker, unaware of what was actually being said, undoubtedly was very satisfied with the respect that his speech had earned him since a heightened level of deference was immediately apparent as he walked off to greet each village elder. Thirty thousand rupees a month will do that for a person.

After the speech, the plan was to clear an area to plant several garden plots. At this point, all chaos broke loose as the kids grabbed the tools being handed out and started digging and raking in every conceivable corner of the field. Gary tried to establish some sense of order, but couldn't get more than the six or seven kids nearest him to pay any attention to his calls.

At this point I heard our American *Pukka Sahib* shout "No! No! No! That's not how you do it!" He then grabbed a rake, cleared a patch of ground for eager, if incompetent, future farmers and began showing them how you properly prepared a garden plot.

If there had been stunned amazement when this guy's salary had been announced, there was utter disbelief at the vision that now presented itself. Every volunteer had encountered the Indian cultural aversion to physical labor. We all had stories about some government official who would ring a bell to bring in a servant to hand him a folder that was just out of reach on his desk, rather than get up to get it himself. Avoiding physical labor was a key indication of success and status. But here was this 30,000 rupee-a-month *Pukka Sahib* not only digging in the dirt, but apparently enjoying himself!

For me this was probably the best, single example I had of the two sides of American culture on display in India. Yes, this guy had a certain cultural arrogance. Yes, he was ignorant of local culture and unaware that his remarks were being totally misquoted by his assistant. But it also is true that in America hard work is not devalued, and even relatively wealthy people are not above getting their hands dirty in order to get the job done.

My main interaction with Indian culture, I must admit, was through my cook, Kassem Ali. A Moslem in his forties, he pretty much adopted me. He didn't speak a word of English, so this forced me to improve my own Hindi language skills since dinner depended on it. We communicated well enough that at one point I even attempted to describe for him a wedding ceremony I had attended in Bombay for Jerry Weiss and Sylvia Bray using my chess set to represent the parties.

Kassem was very conscientious about his duties and insisted that we sit down once a month and go over his account book so he could explain each and every expenditure from the monthly food allowance I gave him. He made me write each one down and add it up separately from his account, and, if the two didn't match by as much as a penny, we had to go back over the whole month's list. I dreaded these sessions and assured him I trusted his accounting but he would have none of it. He was being given a responsibility and wanted to be sure that I had a full accounting.

It was from Kassem that I learned most of what was going on in the village and how the locals thought and reacted to the things I said and did. What I discovered is that many human values, in fact, are universal. The people in the village were judged as to whether they were trustworthy, reliable, honest, generous, or grasping. The big contrast with life in the U.S. was that people in India lived out their entire lives in the same village. So if someone got a reputation for untrustworthiness it followed them all of their days.

It seemed to me that the main difference in ethics revolved around attitudes toward sexuality. And here the obvious explanation was that the family was of such importance in a society without a social safety net that sex outside of marriage was simply too much of a threat.

I found that most young Indian males tended to have an image of American society as one of extreme sexual liberation (not to say promiscuity?). Of course, since most of their impressions came from Hollywood movies, this was not surprising. Even the farmers in the villages had often seen one or two American movies shown on Sunday morning in the theater in Udaipur, sometimes even with the reels played in the correct order!

I remember that when Bill Whitesell and I were in our training village, we came upon a group of farmers sitting around a campfire. They were delighted to hear that we were Americans because they thought we might be able to settle a debate they were having.

"In America, does a man have to buy a woman dinner before she will sleep with him? Or is it that sometimes you can get a woman to have sex without the dinner?" The speaker was convinced that in his understanding of American culture the dinner was required, but one of the group insisted he had seen a movie where the woman had gone cheerfully to bed without demanding to be fed first. The consensus, however, seemed to be that even in America only an absolute slut would surrender her body without first demanding the ceremonial dinner that was her due.

Bill and I tried, with our then limited Hindi, to convince them that the situation was a great deal more complicated than it appeared in the movies. But they knew what they had seen, and dismissed our explanations as a kind of cultural defensiveness.

This is not to say that the cultural attitude in India was at all puritanical. They greatly appreciated the value of sex, but just confined its expression to marriage, (for women at least). Since they tended to marry young by our standards, sex was a part of most of their adult lives.

In fact, they were often very curious as to why we were not married at our advanced ages (early 20s), and how we could manage two full years of celibacy. I know that there was a great deal of speculation in my village as to whether I was seeking appropriate release on the various holidays I took away from the site.

I didn't help matters with my imperfect Hindi. Unfortunately, the word in Hindi for "holiday" is very similar to the crude word for "intercourse" (think of a foreigner who has trouble mixing the sound of "f" and "l" in English explaining that he is looking forward to having "good luck"). While sitting with a group of Indian students one day, I told them I was planning on going up to Delhi for a week long holiday. Their jaws dropped in amazement until one of them laughed "Oh, he means 'holiday'" whereupon they all collapsed in hysterical laughter. The joke was on me, of course. But for one minute, I had been their God!

—ᄴ—

The Peace Corps didn't send us to India for the intercultural experience or to complete a spiritual quest. They actually expected us to accomplish something worthwhile in terms of development. However, they seemed to be a bit confused as to exactly what that was supposed to be for our group, 44B.

In our first summer of training, we were designated as a poultry group. I was actually quite comfortable with that. My parents had kept a chicken coop in the backyard in our working class neighborhood in Oakland, so I was familiar with the whole process of raising chickens. My grandmother, who had moved in with us, was assigned the responsibility of turning those chickens into Sunday dinner based on her experience on the farm in Montana. I was allowed to sit in on the process from the moment she whacked their heads off with an axe to gutting and plucking them. I can tell you it is a lot of work to turn a live bird into a meal.

Somewhere during that year back at college, the powers that be decided that India needed agriculture experts more than they needed poultry farmers, and we were so notified. Although my parents also had a vegetable garden that included corn, this was the extent of my knowledge in this area.

Certainly, the focus on agriculture made sense, and the plan that the Peace Corps had developed for us looked good on paper. We were sent to a farm in Wisconsin to spend four weeks learning about agriculture (we even got to set up some practice demonstration plots). Then we were off to India where we were sent to an Agricultural Institute to learn more about how farming worked there. As I said, the plan made a lot of sense on paper.

The main flaw in the plan was in the nature of the instruction we received in India.

The staff at the agricultural institute were more interested in what was going on in international research than what was happening in the villages nearby. For some reason, they seemed to think we were American experts (or at least serious agricultural students) and were mainly concerned with impressing us with their theoretical knowledge of the subject.

There is one lecture that I remember most clearly. An Indian instructor, quite comfortable with the King's English, did a

very thorough job expounding at length about the virtues of a new form of pesticide. All of us were taking detailed notes on a subject that was clearly going to be vital to our work. We were brought up short, however, by his closing comment.

"However, despite all these advantages, I don't think you should recommend this approach to the farmers you will be working with".

"Why not?' several of us asked in unison.

"First of all it's too expensive. Secondly, it's not available in India."

I remember going back and drawing a line across several pages of notes.

The Peace Corps realized that they could not make us into agricultural experts in the few weeks of training that were available. However, they thought if we could master the basics on the new hybrid varieties of wheat and corn we might be able to make some contribution to getting these new crops adopted, even if our general knowledge was sketchy. It was a dubious proposition at best.

My reputation as an agricultural expert suffered during my first weeks in the village. While touring one farmer's field, I congratulated him on his good crop of lettuce only to be told it was tobacco. I tried to bluff my way out of this by explaining that in American slang we often referred to tobacco as "lettuce" but I don't think he bought it. Anyway he always seemed dubious about my hybrid proposals after that.

I remember going on one tour with the local Agriculture Extension Officer (AEO). We stopped at a field recently planted with wheat and after quick examination he noted that it had very good germination. At the time, I thought this was a perfect example of what was wrong with our program. I had a handbook that told me that "X percent" of seeds germinating should be considered a successful planting, but I had no clue as to what that looked like in the field. In fact, I was surprised to find out that wheat looks like grass when it first sprouts. The field looked like a poorly seeded lawn to me.

I never did accomplish much in the area of agriculture. I never felt confident enough about my knowledge to push people into doing something I really didn't understand. Moreover, my fluency in Hindi wasn't adequate to make me persuasive even if I did.

We were supposed to be part of a team with the Block Development Officer (BDO) and the various Agriculture Extension Workers. I remember a meeting we had near the end of my tour. The BDO was collecting our reports to forward up the chain of command. At that meeting I told him that unfortunately I couldn't say that I had accomplished any of the goals in the plan as I understood them.

"Well, you can't say that" he responded.

"But it's the truth".

"But it's unacceptable" he went on as if trying to explain to a child: "The government sets the goals and then we have to report how we accomplished them. It is unacceptable to report that the goals were not met."

I argued that if the government didn't receive accurate information about what was happening in the field they couldn't formulate policy correctly but he didn't see the relevance of that remark to our situation. It was clear we were at an impasse. Then he came up with a brilliant solution.

"Write up your report as you see fit in English" he told me "and then I will translate it into Hindi before it is submitted."

I had a good idea of what this meant in reality, but I was tired of fighting and realized that he did not make the rules. He was just playing the game as he did in order to survive. Besides, he was going to have to live within that system long after I had gone.

I am convinced that somewhere buried in a dusty archive is an official report in flawless Hindi that describes in quite glowing terms my many accomplishments in the field of agriculture during my tour in India. It is a fantasy of mine that sometime in the future an academic researcher delving into the history of the Green Revolution will uncover that document, and my accomplishments will become enshrined in an equally obscure doctoral dissertation on rural development. To my way of thinking, that would be a fitting end to my role as an agriculturist.

While my role in agriculture was largely one of frustration, I did leave a somewhat more enduring mark on rural Rajasthan in a very different area—two new schools. How I ended up working in those projects was really quite unintended.

My first visit to a local school had very mixed results. I was invited to attend the Mahatma Gandhi birthday celebration. The Headmaster suggested that I might want to say a few words if I was so inclined. I knew he expected me to give my remarks in English. I, however, was determined to exceed those expectations and say something appropriate in Hindi.

I made up a simple little speech appropriate to my limited vocabulary. It said something to the effect that while Gandhi was a national hero in India, his emphasis on non-violence made him a hero to the whole world. It was only five or six sentences long, yet simple and heartfelt.

When my turn came to speak, I got up and carefully recited the lines I had memorized. My presentation was greeted with a stone silence that continued even as I made my way back to my seat. I looked over to see the Headmaster's face contorted as if he was working through some unsolvable puzzle. Then suddenly he jumped up and announced: "I've got it! I know what he was trying to say!" He then repeated my speech in grammatical Hindi, and I finally received my well-deserved ovation.

As a result of my semi-successful presentation I was invited back at a later date to tour the school. Half way through the tour, I was invited to have tea with the Headmaster. He was very emphatic about the need for a new school building, which was, in fact, completely obvious. Classes in Fatehnager were held in a long hallway on the second floor of a local warehouse with nothing much in the way of partitions between the areas where the different classes were held.

The Headmaster asked me if I knew of any grant programs that could provide funding for a new school building. I had actually heard something about a Peace Corps program in this area. Did I know what resources were available? I wasn't sure, but the figure of a thousand dollars stuck in my head. I told him that I really didn't know much about how these programs worked. If he was interested, however, I would check into it and tell him what I found out. He said he would appreciate that.

After tea I finished the tour with a couple of the teachers. I was then ushered out into the common area where I found the entire school assembled. The Headmaster took the podium and solemnly announced that "Mr. Mike has promised to secure ten thousand rupees for a new school building!" The students erupted into cheers and the teachers crowded around to shake my hand.

"Oh Shit!" I thought "I guess I AM going to have to find out about this program!"

It turned out that the program was relatively simple. A school in the U.S. would raise a thousand dollars or so through a bake sale or a car wash. That money would be funneled through a Peace Corps volunteer to a community that met certain criteria. I don't remember much about the requirements, but they couldn't have been too onerous. My India diary mentions preparing for a visit from Peace Corps staff to meet with the local officials to ensure the money would be well spent. Truthfully, I remember nothing at all about this part of the process.

Once the project was approved, I was mainly involved in authorizing the transfer of funds to pay for the construction. All of the work would be done by locals making a mere pittance for this type of work. My main role at that point became the cultural interchange between the American students and the sponsored school. Letters and photos were to be exchanged, and I was the main channel of translation.

My Polaroid camera had been stolen soon after I got to India, so I was lucky to have Hap Pedigo, another India 44B volunteer, act as my official photographer. I enjoyed this part of the project, although it did involve a level of reverse culture shock. The American school actually sent a copy of their yearbook. I had become accustomed to the barebones Indian schools with their four cinderblock walls and students sitting cross-legged on the floor with their individual slate boards. How, exactly, was I going to explain the "student parking lot" or the "Olympic size swimming pool?"

In the end, this was another Indian surprise. When I showed the local teachers the yearbook they seemed most impressed by the quality of the print job! "American schools have such high

quality paper," they marveled. What they saw inside, I think, was just too far outside their imaginations to really register. However, the quality of the paper, that was something they could understand.

Unfortunately, delays in procuring some construction materials meant that the building was not completed before I left India. I never actually got to see that school with its roof!

The delay with this first school project didn't seem to damage my reputation as the School *Wala*. In my last six months in-country I was approached by a delegation from a neighboring village, Chunda-Wat-Khari, who wanted to know if I couldn't get a school project for their village. Since I had worked my way through the bureaucracy once, the second time was a piece of cake. The project was also much smaller (basically a two room school house, with a storage area) and was completed in record time. I was able to see at least one school completed before I left India.

Leaving India was going to have as many unanticipated twists as my tour in-country. Although I left at the same time as most of the other volunteers in India 44 A & B, I was not mustered out with them. I needed to be medevaced to Germany and I was damn lucky it happened that way!

It was on the train trip up to Delhi for our termination conference that I noted some odd problems with the vision in my left eye. There were repeated flashes of light, and it seemed as if I had lost some of the field of vision in that eye. A final health exam was required before we were mustered out of service, and I happened to mention this eye problem to Doc Hibbard when he asked if there were any issues he should be aware of.

I was sent to an Indian eye doctor who dilated my eyes and gave me a thorough examination. At the end of these tests, he treated me to a bit of classic Indian logic that I should have been used to if I had been thinking straight.

"The Peace Corps office is closed now, so I can't talk to your doctor" he explained to me in the utmost seriousness. "I think he should explain to you my findings. What you have is very serious but I don't want to tell you what it is because I don't want to worry you. You should go back to your hotel and not move any more than is absolutely necessary. You can talk to your doctor in the morning for a full explanation."

What? I have something so serious that he is afraid to tell me because I might get upset? Can you think of anything you could say to a person that could make them more upset?

In this situation I did what any healthy, well-adjusted young man would do. I went back to the hotel and got drunk. Fortunately, I had my good friends Bill Whitesell and Tom Corbett there to help me get *really* drunk. It was probably the wrong thing to do, but what the hell, I was obviously going to die soon anyway.

When I finally got a chance to talk to Doc the next morning and learned that I had a detached retina, I was actually quite relieved. There is nothing like thinking your days are numbered to put other problems in perspective.

The proper procedure at this point would have been to put me on the next plane to the U.S. I pleaded with Doc not to do that. One of the great benefits of being mustered out of the Peace Corps in India was the opportunity to travel on the way home. I remember other volunteers in our group debating whether to go home via Europe or Asia. I had made my plans for a westward return trip. While I knew that was not possible now, I wanted to salvage something of this opportunity.

The Peace Corps did have an arrangement through the State Department that allowed them to send volunteers to the main army hospital in Frankfurt Germany, although that was supposed to just be for volunteers who would be returning to the field. The Doc was a great guy and a former volunteer himself. When he learned that my sister was in Germany because her husband was stationed at the Air Force Base in Frankfurt, he pulled some strings, and I was on my way.

My experience in a military hospital was another episode of culture shock. Fortunately, since I was there under State Department auspices, I was given VIP treatment. I was in a room with two other patients awaiting eye surgery. Also there, courtesy of the State Department, was an Ethiopian army officer who had been partially blinded when a blasting cap went off in his hand. The other patient was a regular infantry sergeant. Every morning the top Sergeant on the floor would come in and check on us.

"Good morning, Mr. Simonds, did you sleep well? Good morning Lieutenant Mahaon, how are you feeling?" Then, turning to the infantry sergeant, he would shout, "Get out of bed, Jenkins, this floor needs to be mopped. Do you think you're on a #^\$@# vacation?"

It's good to be a VIP.

My eye operation was performed long before the days of laser surgery. I made the mistake of asking the surgeon what was involved in the operation. He was absolutely delighted to have the opportunity to explain his craft. Taking a football sized model of an eye out from his desk he explained in great detail the procedure they use to squeeze the eye so it will bulge out of its socket so they can make the incisions and begin peeling back the layers of tissue. I don't remember too much of the rest of the explanation as I was getting a bit woozy at the time. If ever there was a case of too much information, this was it!

Because of the intrusive nature of this style of surgery, I had both eyes patched to minimize eye movement. Moreover, my head was sandwiched between two sandbags to block any head movement at all. Telling this story over the last forty years, I have always explained that I was kept in this state for two full weeks. I was absolutely amazed when I did some fact checking for this piece in my diary and found out it was only two days! It sure as hell felt like two weeks!

On the third day, the patch was removed from my good eye so I could at least see what was going on around me. That same day Tom Corbett and Bill Whitesell showed up to visit me, taking a break from their homeward bound odyssey. Unfortunately, I was not in a place where they could get me *really* drunk again, which, at that moment, I sorely regretted.

I had one more fun moment with the top sergeant before I was discharged. Although he treated me with a grudging respect due to being a State Department designee, for some reason he really hated my beard. He used to tease me that he was going to sneak in and shave it some night when I was asleep.

He was there when the surgeon (a full colonel) took off the last eye patch and told me I could be discharged in a day or two.

"Good" announced the sergeant "then you can shave off that friggin' beard".

"No!" The surgeon cut him off. "No shaving! That's too much eye movement."

"Yes sir!" and with a 180 degree attitude pivot the top sergeant turned to me "You heard the colonel, Simonds! I'd better not ever catch you with a razor in your hand!"

I was going to miss him.

I stayed with my sister for a few weeks while I was recovering as an out-patient, and got to know my new niece. She pretty much saved my life, because I was not allowed to read or watch television because of the eye movement restrictions. (I did cheat once to watch the Moon landing.). I never knew how much I would miss reading. There were times when I found myself stealing quick glances at the back of cereal boxes.

My sister and her husband did take me on a couple of road trips up the Rhine River. And, when I was finally discharged, I took one of those "See Italy in Four Days" excursions. It wasn't much, but it was a lot better than missing Europe altogether.

—◊—

Coming home was rather anti-climatic. I flew into New York City and stayed in a hotel for a few days before flying down to Washington D.C. for a proper discharge from the Peace Corps. While in New York, I saw some newscasts about a strange event occurring in a place called Woodstock. It was strangely fascinating to see what was happening in the states at the time.

I remember that while I was in India, I used to wonder how I would ever explain what it was really like to the people back home. Once I got back home, I discovered that most people weren't all that interested. I guess it's like any veteran coming back from an intense experience in another world. If you can't share the memories, there is little to do but to bury them.

The first months back in California were very frustrating. Before leaving Germany, the surgeon had told me that I had "holes" in the retina of my other eye, and that they would need to be "plugged" if that retina was not going to detach as well. However, once I was back in this country there seemed to be a good deal of bureaucratic confusion over exactly who was going to pay for this procedure or where it should be done. I don't remember the details of this at all but it was finally determined that I would be sent to a VA hospital.

This was another major case of culture shock (this was at the height of the Vietnam War). This time the procedure called for a needle to be inserted into my right eye which would "freeze" the holes shut. The anesthesiologist didn't do a good job and I was fully aware of the needle penetrating my eye, a fact that I announced as emphatically as I could. There was a good deal of cursing and swearing, and I drifted off before the needle came back out.

Later, lying in my bed recovering, a nurse came by, tossed a clipboard on the bed and told me I needed to get downstairs for a doctor's appointment. I waited patiently for a wheelchair to appear, but instead it was the nurse who came back and demanded to know why I wasn't on my way. Her response to my explanation of waiting for a wheelchair was a "And who do you think you are?"

I used to be a VIP. I guess I wasn't anymore.

I felt so woozy that the only way I could make my way down the hallway was to walk sideways, holding on to the wall. I finally made it to the elevator, but when the doors opened I saw all these faces that seemed to float up towards me. So I did the only thing that seemed reasonable at the time, I threw up all over them.

After that, the nurse seemed convinced that I did need a wheelchair trip after all.

As a result of the time it took to get all this resolved, I just drifted along feeling like I couldn't make any real decisions about my future. After my eye was finally taken care of, I was talking to Whitesell, and he invited me to come east and give

Philadelphia a try. Since I was 26 years old and, at this point, had never seen snow, this seemed like a reasonable idea. On such slender threads were life decisions made at that age.

Bill was attending Wharton Business School at the time, working on his MBA. I slept on his floor for a few days before he introduced me to Les, another returned volunteer from India, who was organizing a group of business students to rent a house in West Philadelphia. With my housing situation settled, my next objective was to become employed. I quickly landed a job at the Van Pelt Library at the University of Pennsylvania, mainly because I typed 48 words per minute on their typing test. So much for all my valuable international experience!

I ended up working at the Van Pelt Library for the next seven years. They had a program where they paid half your tuition if you went to the library school down the block at Drexel for a Master's Degree in Library Science. I liked libraries, and that seemed like a good deal to me at the time.

One of the perks of working at the library was that I got to train the student assistants, who were predominantly bright young coeds. Each semester, the administration would send me a new batch of pretty and enthusiastic young things that were always very eager to be molded by my experienced hands. It was a situation that would never repeat itself in my life.

One way I found to break the ice with these young ladies was to offer to do their horoscopes, a skill I had developed after returning from India. In the days before computers, this was not an easy task, but it always provided a wealth of topics to talk about, and some inside information on their dating status if they took up the offer to do a compatibility reading.

One young woman who especially impressed me was Dale Shedd. However, when I did her chart, without even purposely looking at the compatibility ratings, I could not believe what a perfect match she was for Bill Whitesell. The next time I saw Bill (who was living in DC by this time), I told him there was a girl I really thought he should meet.

"Is this more of your astrology crap?" he asked. Admitting that it was, I had to endure a half hour tirade about how sad it made him to see such a fine mind wasting time on such drivel before he adamantly refused to ever meet her, just out of principle.

This was a setback. However, fate was not to be denied. Eventually Dale introduced me to her sister Lynne, whom I ended up marrying. At the wedding, Dale was a bridesmaid and Bill was my 'best man,' so they had to meet. They have been happily married for well over thirty years now.

This made Bill my brother-in-law and our kids cousins. Now that was a development that we wouldn't have anticipated in India. But then again, our cooks there were brothers, so maybe we were just following tradition.

After I got my library degree, I began looking for a professional job. At first I was convinced that I wanted to work in an academic library. That was where people pursued truth and knowledge, wasn't it? But by the end of my seven years, I was completely disillusioned. It seemed like the library existed for the faculty; graduate students were tolerated but undergraduates were treated as the scum of the earth.

When I did find a professional position, it was in a public library in Norwalk, Connecticut. I was much happier there. Public libraries are fundamentally democratic institutions, and everyone that walks through the door is treated equally.

I worked at the Norwalk Library for seven years. Toward the end of that time, the library joined a consortium of six libraries trying to develop a shared automation system so that each of the libraries did not have to reinvent the technology wheel. I represented my library on the governing board of this organization, and when we burned out our first two Executive Directors my fellow board members asked if I wanted to try to take this impossible position. I did and have been doing that job now for twenty-five years.

Over that quarter of a century this organization (Bibliomation) has grown from eight libraries to forty-eight libraries, and the staff from three to twelve. I have never been a "techie" and freely admit my limitations in this field. However, I understood the technology well enough to tease out the financial support and political questions that needed to be brought to a Board of Directors, and seemed to have a talent for explaining complex issues in terms that make sense to laymen.

—‍ɯ‍—

For most of the next thirty years my focus was on building a career and raising a family. My memories of India largely faded into the past, and there were very few occasions that stirred them from their resting place.

Ironically, this phase of my life seemed to become relevant again after my divorce when I became involved in the on-line dating scene. My time in the Peace Corps was just one element of the profile I created, but one that was unusual enough to often generate curiosity. I found myself dredging up old stories to satisfy the interest I had inadvertently sparked. Most of my misadventures had a humorous element to them and so they were easy to share. But one correspondent pushed me beyond that level, and forced me to confront a few of the memories I had tried hard to bury. In response to her genuine concern, I ended up reliving one of the most painful of these, and wrote it down for her

I was in Bombay, walking along the seawall away from The Gateway to India. It was a beautiful day, not too hot, and I was enjoying the view of the Arabian Sea. My mood changed quickly, however, the moment that I saw her.

She was still a ways from me when I saw her approach the first tourist for a handout. I tensed. I had been in India long enough to know how things worked. This was one of the prime tourist areas in the country. Real beggars did not make it here. Only organized gangs capable of paying off the police could work this area. I picked up my pace to see if I could slip by her unnoticed and without a confrontation.

As I got closer, however, my heart sank. She was carrying a small child. I had read about this in the Indian papers, but never had to confront it in person before. Gangs purchased small children from families so desperate in their poverty that they will trade the life of one child to save the rest. The purchased child

45

is starved, sometimes mutilated, in order to increase its market value as a begging tool. Their life spans are mercifully short. There will always be replacement children for sale.

I had to pass close to her in the street to slip by. As I did so my anger rose. Many people stopped to give her money. What was the matter with them? Were they blind? The child she held out in front of her was as pathetic a soul as I had ever seen, with stick arms and legs, a bloated belly and a hollow face. But the woman holding him was actually fat! There was no subtly here. Didn't they see her belly hanging over the knot in her sari? The extra folds of fat in her arms showed as she lifted the child? How could they look into her pudgy face and think that one cent would ever be spent on that child?

For a brief moment, I thought I was in the clear but then she spotted me. Looking like a typical Western tourist, I was a prime target for her. She changed course to intercept me.

A knot tightened in my stomach. I took the nearest turn to avoid her. Too late, I realized I had turned out into a small observation platform in the seawall. There was no place to go from here. I turned back to find her blocking the entrance. I tried to step past her but she was too fast.

She held up the child in front of me "Baksheesh, Sahib" she cried. The child, dutifully following its training strained to raise its emaciated arms in supplication. I tried to look away, but my eyes were drawn to the eyes of the child.

His eyes were like black holes to the soul, a soul wracked with more pain and suffering than any should ever endure. His eyes drew you in with their hopelessness, the bewilderment of the innocent in torment, the plea for mercy that would only come with the release of death.

I knew what I could not do...I could not feed the monster that enslaved him. But to avoid doing that I would have to look into those eyes and say "No". Deep inside me I was afraid that if I did that, something inside me that I valued, some important piece of me, would die.

I tried to look away, but his stare held me in a vice like grip. I knew I had no alternative. The first time I tried to utter the word it stuck in my throat. The second time it came out as a whisper...or as a prayer. Only on the third try was it loud enough for her to hear. "No".

She repeated her plea and stepped forward, thrusting the child up towards my face. It was a mistake. The spell was broken. The helplessness I felt instantly changed to rage, and I screamed at her in Hindi: "Get out of here you fucking bitch!"

She stepped back instantly, stunned as if I had struck her across the face. She realized she had overplayed her hand, and the curse in Hindi told her I was no tourist...I knew what was going on.

She took two more steps back, then turned and began to walk away. It was only then that my focus widened and I could look out at the street. Dozens of people had stopped, frozen at the incredible sight of a rich American screaming at a poor beggar woman. Most were already reaching for their pockets or their purses, either out of genuine sympathy, or to avoid a similar scene.

Half way across the street she turned her head and smiled at me in triumph. I had just made things easier for her. She knew it, and she wanted me to know that she knew that I knew it.

I turned back and leaned against the wall, and looked out at the sea. I felt sick to my stomach.

I think we would all like to pick and choose what parts of the past we want to carry with us in the present. But that is probably an illusion.

And we all had a glimpse at the dark side of India.

India and the Peace Corps were a large part of my life, but that was now just over forty years ago. I kept a diary while I was there, as well as a journal. But, for the most part, these memories have been kept on a shelf, gathering dust except when a *Slumdog Millionaire* experience comes along to scare them into life again.

This all changed for me in May of 2009, when a couple of dedicated members of my old Peace Corps group managed to pull together a reunion out in Oakland, California. This turned into a three-day affair, beginning with a dinner at an Indian restaurant in Berkeley and continuing with two nearly all-day sessions at the homes of two of the returned volunteers. On the second day, we sat in every available space in one crowded living room and each person was given five minutes to sum up their lives since India. After lunch, we returned, and people shared their favorite memories from those days. And as each story was recounted, it triggered long-forgotten memories among the listeners, creating its own dynamic.

I had not seen most of these people for forty years. Yet, at the end of the three days, it seemed like old times, and it was the last forty years that were but a dim illusion. It rekindled old relationships, and brought life back to dead memories.

So what did I learn in India? What did that experience teach me? Can I sum it up now, any better than I could when I was there?

The experience wasn't that neat. It doesn't fit into simple categories that can be cataloged along with life's lessons. But there is one moment that stands out, and comes back to me now as I try to put my feelings on paper.

There was one trip that many of our group took together to Agra where we got to see the Taj Mahal. It was magnificent when we toured it in daylight, but that was only the prologue. Fortunately, we had timed our visit to be there during the full moon. This is when the Taj is in its full glory, and the solid marble structure does actually seem to float about the landscape.

In all my travels, this is the one man-made monument that fully lived up to its advance billing, and did not disappoint in any way. But as I was sitting there gazing up in wonder, I got a very annoying mosquito bite on my foot. At first, I deeply resented this intrusion on such a transcendent moment. Then it occurred to me, that this is what life is all about. We are always looking up at a Taj while something drags us back to mundane reality.

The reunion gave me a chance to glimpse the Taj again. Now I'm back home and I need to scratch my foot.

CHAPTER 3

Journey to Myself

Mary Jo Dummer Clark

Prepping for Peace Corps

When I arrived at the University of San Francisco (USF) in the fall of 1963, student volunteerism was rapidly becoming an accepted part of the university's ethos. We were part of the Civil Rights era, and the university took an active role in promoting social justice, although we didn't call it that at the time. I don't remember ever being told of any expectation that we would make a difference in the world. That was simply what we set out to do and what we expected to accomplish.

My first adventure in the realm of social and political activism was as a reluctant tag-along. I was invited by one of my new nursing classmates to go with her, her boyfriend, and a freshman friend of his, to promote voter registration in what we then called the "Black" churches in San Francisco (SF). So, one Sunday morning the three of us boarded one of San Francisco's ubiquitous buses and went to a church in a rundown urban SF neighborhood.

That was my first exposure to a "culture" other than my own. As a cradle Catholic before Vatican II, I was used to the solemn, non-participatory rituals of Sunday Mass. Shouts of "Amen" and "Praise the Lord" were beyond my experience. I grew up in a lily white neighborhood and only encountered a few token Mexican kids in my Catholic high school. I knew nothing of any other religious groups (other than going to Methodist Sunday School with my cousins in Iowa). Frankly, all this exuberance terrified me.

Not only was I bewildered and frightened by people who were so boisterous about their religion, I was terrified of strangers. When I was not much younger, I would wander for hours in a store looking for something before I would ask a clerk, a stranger, for help. I drove my mother crazy because it could take me hours to run a simple errand.

I don't know why I was such a shy introvert in interactions with strangers. As a small child, I was outgoing and would chatter to anyone who would listen. Maybe it was changing schools at age ten, moving from a school where I was well known and liked to one where I was the stranger who didn't quite fit. At any rate, something happened along the way to make me fearful of anyone I didn't know. In high school, I was involved in a variety of activities but with people I already knew.

At the time, I considered myself unpopular. Looking back, though, that probably wasn't completely the case. I was definitely an "egghead" or "brain" (that was before the advent of "nerds" or that would have been the appropriate label) and was probably too open about my academic successes. I certainly didn't have any dates but I was elected girls' senior class president, was on the drill team (even the smaller, more prestigious drill team during basketball season), and held various leadership roles on campus. I guess I couldn't have really been the pariah I thought myself at the time. I remember my mother telling me that all teenagers had similar feelings of inadequacy, but when I compared myself to my "more popular" friends (those who had dates for the school dances or steady boyfriends), it didn't look that way to me. At any rate, I was an insecure and miserable adolescent. And, when it came to meeting strangers, I was a total wreck.

Back at the church in San Francisco, the pastor asked us to explain to the congregation why we were there. Fortunately, one of the guys gave our spiel about registering to vote. My thoughts at the time were along the lines of "Who are we, a pack of privileged white kids, telling these people they ought to vote?" Later in the service, the pastor asked if one of us would like to give our interpretation of the bible verse for the day. In those days, Catholics didn't spend much time with the bible, and I was verging on real panic. Again, one of the guys dealt with the situation, and we were finally able to leave. I have never been so glad to escape in my life.

Despite my anxiety provoking introduction to volunteerism, I got involved in SWAP, the Student Western Addition Project, initiated by Fr. Gene Shallert, S.J., one of the sociology professors on campus. The Western Addition was an area of town adjacent to (or maybe in, my SF geography wasn't very well developed at the time) the Tenderloin District and therefore located on the "wrong" side of Market Street. SWAP comprised a variety of social action initiatives and I was involved in two of them. One initiative was tutoring 7th grade kids in math, and the other involved helping with a recreation program. My naiveté was shaken to the core when my twelve-year-old students started telling me about their classmates who got suspended for having sex in the cloakroom. The kids thought it was cool; I was appalled. But I managed to stick with the program for a couple of years until my nursing class schedule interfered.

During my junior year, I went with some classmates to do intake histories at a home for unwed mothers. We were given the first name and last initial of the person we were to interview, and I was assigned to interview a girl (P), who was pointed out to me by the nun in charge. Fortunately, P hadn't seen me yet because she was a girl from my high school class. Like many pregnant teenagers at the time, she had gone 400 miles away to have the baby and hide her "disgrace." I had had the concept of confidentiality drummed into me in nursing school, and I knew she would be mortified if she recognized me, particularly since I was one of the "goody-two-shoes" in my class. She already had a reputation for being rather "fast" (mostly because she got caught smoking in the girls bathroom, I think). I told the nun I couldn't interview her and why. She agreed and gave me another client, a 26 year-old girl who had an affair with her married boss and was "reaping the consequences." I remember thinking, in similar circumstances that could have been me.

All in all, my volunteer activities served to disturb my complacent view of the world and leave me shocked and bewildered. How did such a parochial introvert come to join the Peace Corps?

It occurred mostly by accident, as have many of the greatest opportunities and experiences in my life. Peace Corps had never entered my consciousness (outside of knowing that it existed) until I was walking across campus in my junior year. Patty, the friend I was with, suggested we stop by the Peace Corps recruiting table and see what they had to say. I hadn't even realized they were on campus.

The idea of starting my nursing career somewhere outside of the U.S. appealed to me. I think, in large part, this was because I was a little frightened of going to work in a hospital after graduation. Despite my 3.98 GPA, I wasn't all that confident of my abilities in nursing. What if I did something wrong? I figured I could function effectively in a place where people wouldn't know any better and where no one was likely to sue me. I reasoned that whatever level of care I could provide would be better than none in an underdeveloped country.

Both Patty and I filled out the Peace Corps application. I think I put down Africa or some such place where they spoke English as my first choice. I guess I didn't want to face a different language as well as a different culture. I received an invitation to something called an Advanced Training Program group slated to go to India. I really thought about turning it down and waiting for someplace where they spoke English. I decided I might not get another chance, so I accepted. My friend, Patty, whom I saw as the epitome of a dedicated Peace Corps volunteer, was turned down. Go figure!

That First Summer

I don't even remember the trip to Milwaukee that first summer or how I got from the airport to UWM. My first coherent memory is being assigned to a dorm room in Holton Hall (the name of which I only remember because I wrote it on the pictures I took). My roommate was Robbie Lammons, another California girl, but from that decadent UC Berkeley. Remember, I was still a pretty naïve nursing student from a rather strict (where girls were concerned, anyway) Catholic university. Fortunately, Robbie and I hit it off well from the start.

I remember the first evening with all of us gathered in a large lounge area. One of the language instructors (Hindi, not Marathi, I think), shook hands with each of us and must have introduced himself in some foreign language that left me bewildered. I finally got the picture and told him my name. Language classes are some of my most vivid memories. I think our primary Marathi instructor was Mohan Limaye, a man with the patience of Job. He needed it to deal with many of us. Fortunately, my fears about having to learn another language were mostly unfounded, and I found I learned it fairly rapidly—with an accent that was not overly atrocious. I did engage in some bloopers, such as the time when I asked the male language instructor sent with us to the Indian reservation to "pass the vagina" (*yoni*) instead of the butter (*loni*). At first he wouldn't even explain my mistake, but I finally convinced him I needed to know what I had said so I wouldn't do it again.

I also remember sessions that, today, might be labeled as cultural sensitivity training. If I remember, correctly, though, they went beyond sensitivity training and picked at our brains to see how stable we might be in a foreign environment. I also remember the Peace Corps watchword of "flexibility," which, in our minds, translated to "wishy-washy."

Other memories involve evenings at Buddy Beeks. Drinking alcohol was another new experience for me. Was I alone in thinking that I was the only one who wasn't used to drinking? I certainly felt like a fish out of water and as if everyone else was far more sophisticated about that kind of stuff than me. I found it interesting at the reunion that one of the group members credited another with introducing her to marijuana, but that volunteer swears he didn't start using it until after Peace Corps. Personally, I could have sworn that there was a small group that was using the stuff even that first summer. Another shock for my sheltered self!

In addition to drinking, I learned a few other bad habits that summer. My dorm mates back at USF were shocked when I referred to one of our less favorite faculty as a "bitch." They even commented that they thought Peace Corps training might have had a less than salutary effect on me. I also stopped going to Mass regularly that year (not that I ever let my mother know that!—Catholic convert that she was) and engaged in as much of a belated adolescent rebellion as my sheltered upbringing would allow.

Going back to training memories, though, I also remember the chicken coops and gardens. As I recall (and then only because I still have pictures of it), even those of us in the health group planted a community garden—not that Carolyn and I ever planted anything when we got to India. We were too busy with activities in the health center and the village. I also have some pictures of us sitting around in the lounge at Holton hall. Some of us (Kathy Kelleher and Janet Lloyd, I think—definitely not me) were musically talented, and we sang around the piano. We also spent a lot of time discoursing on ideas of the day. On occasion we went out to places other than Buddy Beeks. Bill Whitesell always said he liked to go to movies with me because I was the only person he knew who cried more than he did.

At some point, several of us went shopping and bought six yards of soft fabrics that would drape relatively well. One of the women language instructors showed us how to drape a sari, but none of us were very accomplished at it. Somewhere I still

have that piece of fabric, which was as different from the saris I bought in India as night is from day.

The highlight of the summer and, based on the reminiscences shared at the reunion, one of the more memorable events for all of us, must have been the time spent on the Indian reservations. My group was sent as far north as one could get without swimming across Lake Superior. After we found out where we were going, John Lievore went around for a week saying "Odanah? Who ever heard of Odanah?"

The group of us who went to Odanah was a mixed bag—no one that I was particularly close to in the training group was included (probably another test of our "flexibility" on the part of the training staff). As closely as I can remember (and that's after having my memory jogged by pictures), my group consisted of Sunny Yadwarkar (our handsome, single, movie star wanabe language instructor), Lois Crean (training staff nurse), John Lievore, Diane Logefiel, Nancy Caughran, Roberta Gulkis, Alison Barnet, Judy (whose last name I can't remember and whose picture is not in the group directory), and myself. We were probably the most poorly matched assortment of people ever put together in a group of tents!

I had only been camping once in my entire life, so I was not of much help in getting our three tents set up. At least it wasn't raining the day we arrived. If I remember correctly, we weren't able to set up our tents until late in the day because there was some disagreement on where we were supposed to put them. Whoever was in charge at the tribal level finally decided to put us down by the river next to the youth center, essentially a run-down shack that was supposed to provide activities for tribal youth and keep them out of trouble. Our presence there certainly gave them an outlet for mischief!

Once we got the tents set up, we rigged an outdoor kitchen and John built us a rather rickety shower enclosure that never got used because we didn't see the sun again for the rest of our stay. Lois did most of the cooking, and I have to say that we ate fairly well while we were there.

Our first or second night there, the local youth "welcomed" us by sneaking into one of the tents. Sunny and John were sharing one tent, with Lois and the girls divided between the other two. The invaders got a surprise when they picked the guys' tent. We were none too thrilled to think of them coming into the girls' tents, so we reallocated ourselves between two tents with one guy in each until Peace Corps brought Sam Rankin up from another site. I haven't a clue how Lois notified them of our difficulties. That was in an era before cell phones, and there weren't many local homes with phones. Perhaps one of the tribal elders had a phone, or there might have been one in the community center.

When Sam got there, we went back to using all three tents, but with one guy in each. At that point, it started to rain and continued until we left. Our sloppy tent set up had its consequences, with rain collecting in the dips in the roofs and leaking through.

The incipient juvenile delinquents in the tribe weren't through with us either! One night in the pouring rain, they pulled up the stakes of the tent where I was sleeping, and it collapsed on us. John was in that tent and couldn't find his pants. I was trying to hold up the central tent post so the tent wouldn't completely engulf us, and none of us could find a flashlight in the dark. By the time anyone got out to see what was going on, the miscreants had disappeared.

After that, we gave up any attempt to accomplish anything in the local community (what can a group of outsiders accomplish in a week, anyway?) and spent days and nights inside soggy tents drinking Southern Comfort (straight out of the bottle). Due to the enforced proximity, we talked to each other more than we might otherwise have done. One of the things we learned was why one of the girls was so prickly that none of us really wanted to be around her. She was born out-of-wedlock and grew up in an era when that was definitely not accepted. Neither she nor her mother was accepted, and she was harassed by other kids at school with jibes that incorporated snide comments from their parents. After hearing her story, we were rather ashamed of the way we had tried to avoid her. Several of us shed a few tears of remorse, and I think all of us learned not to judge people solely by their actions, but to search for the underlying causes of behavior.

I learned another lesson from that experience that I now use when I'm teaching program planning to undergraduate and doc-toral nursing students. The "town" of Odanah was situated along a river emptying into Lake Superior. The town flooded every year with the advent of the spring rains. In its infinite wisdom, the Bureau of Indian Affairs had the Army Corps of Engineers build a nice new housing development up on the surrounding hills. The housing development remained there—empty. The local people didn't want to live in it. When their homes flooded each year, they dug themselves out of the mud and moved back in. They had lived by the river for generations, and they weren't about to move. The lesson—ask people what they want or need before trying to fix something they don't want fixed. Unfor-

tunately, the lesson didn't sink in very well, because many of us attempted to do the same thing in India, forging ahead with solutions that might or might not be something desired by people in the village. I think this is why many of the immunization campaigns our group initiated were less successful than we had hoped. I guess we thought if we provided the immunizations, of course, they would want them (a better mouse trap with a needle)!

Because of the rain, not only did we not use the shower enclosure that John rigged up but, after the first day or so, when we bathed (sort of) in the Bad River, we didn't clean up at all. It was just too cold to get undressed long enough to take even a sponge bath. By the end of our stint in Odanah, we were filthy and smelly. We were delighted to be the first group back to UWM because we got first dibs on the showers. We were freshly scrubbed and in clean clothes before the rest of the groups got back. None of us ever really figured out the Peace Corps' purpose for dumping us on the reservations in the first place. Maybe it was to see how we coped with adversity and frustration. For the most part, none of us **EVER** encountered such horrible conditions in India.

David Dell figures prominently in another memory from that first summer's training. He and Bill Whitesell needed a fourth for bridge, so they decided to teach me to play. Being semi-intelligent, one would think I could grasp the basic concepts of the game. Bill was a pretty good teacher, but Dave was an absolute tyrant. To a serious player like Dave, no mistake, no matter how minor, was forgivable! I don't think I have ever been subjected to such a tirade as I was as his partner. I have never again played bridge. I even refused my saintly Grandma when her bridge club needed someone to make up another table. No way am I ever going to subject myself to that again!!! (In case you haven't noticed, I don't respond all that well to criticism). I am, however, still speaking to Dave but I know better than to play bridge with him.

There is a picture of the whole double group of us (India 44 A & B) that I think was taken shortly before we left to go back to school for our senior year. That was the last time we saw some of the group because they didn't return the second summer and didn't end up going with us to India. Some were washed out (or "deselected" to use Peace Corps' terminology), for reasons the rest of us found callous or ridiculous. The two that I found hardest to accept were Paul, a California surfer type, and Asher, linked by rumor to the Communist party. Others simply found other directions for their lives (marriage, career opportunities, etc.). Like the trip to Milwaukee, I have no memory of the trip home but I do remember waiting for the cabs that took us to the Milwaukee airport.

We were supposed to continue our language and cultural training back at school. Robbie arranged for the two of us to be tutored in Marathi by a UC Berkeley graduate student, so I drove back and forth across the bridge (until my brother wrecked my car). We also kept in touch with Mike Simonds and Gareth Loy, who were in San Francisco.

Peace Corps was so much a part of my future plans that I thought everyone knew I was going to India after graduation. Certainly, my nursing classmates were aware of it, but seemed surprisingly uninterested in the prospect or in knowing about my training experiences. It came as something of a shock to the graduate student I dated in my senior year (yes, I did finally get a few dates) to find out that I was heading to India. He was an engineer turned theology student and an extremely talented photographer. We spent a significant portion of the year searching San Francisco for picturesque spots. He was particularly keen to find a place where the entirety of St. Ignatius (SI), the University's beautiful church, was visible. After several months of searching, he finally pinpointed a tiny green spot on a map of the city. It turned out to be a small park on top of a hill that offered an unobstructed view of SI. I still have one of the glorious pictures he took from there.

Jim didn't realize until graduation evening that I was leaving for India. Somehow my plans had never come up. I guess I just assumed he knew because everyone else did. He wrote to me for several months when I got to India, and his letters were as graphically descriptive as his photos. Eventually, he stopped writing, and a mutual friend told me he had found someone else. There was no real commitment on either of our parts, and I wasn't devastated. I did miss his letters, though.

Back to Milwaukee

After graduation, I went home to Whittier to await our departure to India. In the meantime, I met several of my classmates in Long Beach, where we took the RN state board licensing exam. That was about a week before I left for the second summer of training in Milwaukee.

I do remember the trip this time. I think it was more memorable because I was leaving home for two years. My parents were resigned, I think, and my middle brother didn't have an opinion one way or the other. On the other hand, my youngest brother and my favorite cousin were appalled. At one point, I had thought about Navy nursing as an option, but my cousin, a career officer, thought that was not a good place for a "nice" girl like me. So, I went even further into what he considered danger by joining the Peace Corps. Judging from the protective stance of Peace Corps, however, I was probably safer in India than I would have been in LA. My youngest brother and an old family friend concocted a plan to introduce me to some nice guy so I would get married and stay home. Given that neither of them knew any nice guys to introduce me to, that plan fell through, too, and off I went back to Milwaukee in late June of 1967.

We were pretty well split up during that second summer of training. Most of us in the health group (44A) were sent out to live with families in the "black" sections of Milwaukee. I was sent for an "internship" at the Inner City Development Project (ICDP), an Office of Economic Opportunity (OEO) agency. The director asked me to sort of evaluate the performance of the program. I gave him my fresh-out-of-school, know-nothing opinion that a couple of his outreach workers did too much for their clients—to the point that they were fostering clients' dependence rather than promoting their independence. Although I was right, I probably could have been more tactful in expressing myself. I got involved in several of the agency projects but don't remember now what they were.

I met a VISTA volunteer who also was assigned to ICDP. I remember thinking he got all of the bad parts of Peace Corps, working in an alien culture in frustrating circumstances, while trying to accomplish something without any resources. He didn't even get the adventure of traveling to another country.

I had somehow gotten over my almost paralyzing shyness by that second summer. This was a very good thing since I was going to be "on display" for the next two years. I think that was the most profound aspect of my Peace Corps experience. Although I still had some doubts about my abilities, I was much more confident. That confidence was only to grow throughout my time in India.

One other self-confidence-boosting assignment I had was being responsible (more or less) for the experience of others in my group during the couple of shifts we spent in the emergency department at Milwaukee General Hospital (MGH). As one of only two nurses left in the group by that time, I was supposed to oversee the experience of the other volunteers. The first time I put in an appearance at MGH was Friday night of the July 4th weekend. I got there before the change of shift, and the nurses going off duty oriented me to the unit. That was fortunate, because the night shift was composed of floats from other departments who had never worked ER before. In addition, July 1st is when new interns and residents begin their tenure at major teaching hospitals. On a holiday weekend, having arrived an hour before anyone else, I was nearly the most experienced person in the unit (except the physicians, who never know where anything is or how the system works).

If you are ever injured and end up in the emergency room (ER), try not to do it over the 4th of July holiday. There were motor vehicle accident victims, stabbing and shooting victims, and people with food poisoning from food left out in the heat, and I was the only person who knew where anything was. I stayed far beyond my assigned time and ended up in the operating room (OR) observing surgery on an elderly man that they thought had an appendicitis attack. My observation was arranged by a Marquette medical student who had been assigned to the ER that night and followed this particular patient up to surgery. I have always loved the OR, so I was glad to go along and observe. Unfortunately, the patient turned out to have a bowel cancer, and they just closed him up again.

The medical student took me back to the house where I was staying shortly before dawn, and we arranged for him to pick me up later for a trip to a local lake and concert. We dated a few times before I left for India. He was another person who tried to talk me out of going but wasn't successful.

We're on Our Way!

In July, we were on the way to New York to depart for India. Sylvia Bray and I stayed with Susan Krawiec's family in New Jersey. On our one free day in New York, Susan and her family took us for a ride on the Staten Island Ferry and we saw a bit of New York. A day or two later, we were on a plane to London.

We had a rather lengthy layover in London (somewhere in the neighborhood of eight hours or so), and Peace Corps arranged for us to be transported from Heathrow to London proper. I remember being amused by the wax paper consistency of toilet paper in the airport. We split into several small groups, and I can't remember exactly who I was with. I do know that Sam Rankin and John Lievore were part of the group, because I ended up changing the dressing on Sam's surgical incision in a side chapel in Westminster Abbey, with John standing guard. I don't know how we would ever have explained ourselves if anyone had seen Sam with his rear end hanging out.

At some point in our peregrinations, we encountered Randy Stoklas. We were all reluctant to try buying anything, although we did have some English money. Randy, therefore, was assigned to buy something from a vendor and see what kind of change he received. I have a picture of him standing by the street vendor's cart trying to understand how much money he should give the man. I seem to remember Randy finally opening up his hand with a bunch of coins in it and letting the vendor take what he pleased. We must have gathered back at the pickup spot before we were scheduled to be there because I have some very poor quality pictures of several of us sitting around on low walls just waiting.

The flight from London was long, and I remember we stopped at least twice. Once, I know, was in Tehran, and I think the other was Beirut. At one stop, probably Tehran, we were led from the plane to the airport waiting area with armed guards stationed everywhere. We didn't do any sight-seeing in either place, although I was able to buy silver charms for my charm bracelet in both airports. Somewhere in the next two years, I lost the silver filigree tea pot charm that I bought in Beirut but I still have charms from most of the other places I visited on the way to and from India.

On the last leg of our journey, we experienced the infamous disintegrating plane engine adventure. I wasn't close enough to look out the window and see the engine losing its parts, but I did see the stewardess lean over to look out the window and then pull down the shade before hurrying forward to inform the pilot. I'm glad Mike was able to get a picture of the engine from the plane window. Otherwise, people probably wouldn't believe us. I think we were all rather surprised when a U.S. representative from the embassy greeted us with the information that we made headlines. According to the Delhi papers, a bunch of American Peace Corps volunteers narrowly avoided death when their plane began to fall apart in midair.

The first few pictures I took in India embody the juxtaposition of contrasting cultures. The first two are of the façade and

fountain of the India International Center and the next is of my first cow, seen on the road immediately outside the Center entrance. India continued to be, for me, an ever changing and puzzling mixture of the old and the new—modern buildings and Coca Cola next to abject poverty, taxies and tongas (small horse-drawn carriages), cows in the streets and rats bigger than tomcats, forts and palaces, ancient looking fishing boats and modern airplanes.

In-country Training

After our official welcome in Delhi and whatever else we were subjected to on arrival (it all has blurred away), my half of the group made its way by train to Bombay. We were met with the traditional Peace Corps welcome—a brass band. I don't remember the name of the hotel where we stayed. It was a step down from the International Center, but still pretty ritzy, and you could even get clean ice in a coke. We were shipped from there to our training village on the coast outside of Bombay. I want to say that the name of the fishing village was Dehanu, but I could be wrong. That was where we got our first exposure to cow dung floors and thatched roofs, neither of which was as bad as I had thought it might be.

I don't remember much of our time there except practicing my Marathi on the inhabitants and being wrapped in a nine-yard sari (*nowari*) which promptly disintegrated around me in the middle of the village. I also remember a trip several of us made to a USAID staff compound just up the coast. The women in the enclave told us about their Indian dancing lessons and occasional shopping in the bazaar, but they spent most of their time inside the walls of the compound. They had everything they needed and really didn't need to interact with the host culture at all. I remember thinking how terrible it would be to come to a place like India and never experience any of it. They didn't seem to mind, though.

I think their attitude was similar to that of some U.S. diplomatic wives I encountered on one of my return flights home two years in the future. We were all congregated in the back of the plane waiting to use the restrooms and several of them were talking about how dirty they found Tel Aviv. I felt like saying that, after two years in India, I would have been comfortable eating off the streets in Tel Aviv. I guess it's all in one's perspective.

Back in Bombay, I was faced with the problem of not having a site mate. Originally, Sylvia Bray and I had planned to be together. I had known Margie Pope, one of the former volunteers, who was part of our in-country training staff, from both high school and USF. She had been two years ahead of me in both programs. There was a spot for a single volunteer in her former village. I promptly was slated to go there, being relatively fluent in Marathi and of a rather independent nature (how times had changed!). At the last moment, the village decided they didn't want another volunteer. Sylvia was already paired up with Kathy Kelleher, and only the girls shifted over from the other half of the group were left unpaired. Carolyn Jones and I decided that we could probably tolerate each other, so we were assigned together to a primary health care center in Vita, Sangli District, located pretty much in the center of the Deccan Plateau about 100 miles south of Poona.

Village Arrival

Vita was a bit off the beaten track. While everyone else was dispatched to their villages by train, Carolyn and I were loaded on a bus that was part of the State Transport system (ST or *ishty,* which is also the word for bus in Marathi). Our trip was supposed to be only about eight hours. It was the tail end of the monsoon season, however, and there were several small flooded rivers to cross that significantly extended the travel time. Finally, sometime after midnight, we reached a flooded river that was too deep to drive through.

We waited in the bus for a couple of hours until another bus pulled up on the far side. The two buses shone their headlights on the river to light the way as we waded from one bus to the other. We had to carry our belongings across with us. Fortunately, the conductor convinced one of our fellow passengers to carry across the rolled mattress I had bought in Bombay. Carolyn and I balanced the rest of the stuff on our heads to keep it dry. It was also fortunate that we did not have our trunks with us. Peace Corps Bombay had decided to send them out to us later with a PC jeep and driver. Why they didn't send us by jeep is beyond me. I supposed they wanted us to get "immersed" in the host country right away, and that's **exactly** what happened.

The river was chest deep on me, and there was a fast flowing current pushing us to the left (I wonder why I can remember that silly detail). Carolyn and I were holding on to each other with the hands that weren't keeping our suitcases on our heads, which turned out to be fortunate. About half way across I was swept off my feet and quickly headed down river. Carolyn's grip on my arm was enough to get me back on my feet. In the effort, though, I lost the Girl Scout canteen I had had since I went to camp at age ten. I suppose someone downriver was delighted to acquire a nice canteen when it finally made it to shore.

After we got into the replacement bus, we continued on our way to Vita. We arrived there about 5:00 am, nearly twelve hours after our expected arrival. We were soaked, bedraggled, and miserable, and there was no one at the bus station to meet us. Not surprisingly, the folks from the health center, which was on the other side of town, had given up and gone home for the night. In my halting Marathi (Carolyn wasn't much help because she had learned Hindi), I tried to explain that we needed someone to contact the health center staff and let them know we were there. The station master kept insisting that we couldn't possibly intend to end our journey there, after all this was a very small village called Vita (apparently nobody else in the village knew we were coming). Surely, we must be intending to go to the bus's terminus in Sangli, and we should get back on the bus before it left. The bus conductor was able to convince the station master that our tickets were, indeed, to Vita, and I finally talked him into sending a message to the *pratamic arogia kendra* (primary health center). Apparently, my accent was good enough that he understood that phrase and sent a runner with a message.

After a seemingly interminable wait, during which someone at least gave us some hot tea, the health center jeep arrived, and we were whisked away to the other side of town. We were installed in Dr. Mulla's house and fed omelets with a ton of *mirchi* (hot peppers), and then were allowed to sleep for a few hours. They woke us way too soon to go to a vasectomy camp in one of the outlying subcenter villages. Carolyn went with them, but either the river water I had ingested in my dunking or the peppers in the omelet did a job on my intestines. I could barely manage to make it from the bed to the latrine, never mind going to another village for a vasectomy camp.

I was left on my own all day, making my way periodically to the WC (toilet) for another episode of severe diarrhea. At a certain point, I was so weak from dehydration that I could only crawl there. By the time Carolyn and the rest of the health center staff returned, I was in bad shape. I knew I needed fluids, but could barely convey the word *pani* (water) when asked what I needed. I did finally manage to get the idea across and was given water. Of course, it had not been boiled, but, at that point who cared? In the interim, they had rounded up two old style metal hospital beds and installed them in the bungalow assigned to Carolyn and me. Gratefully, I crawled into the bed and passed out. It always seemed to me rather miraculous that I was pretty well recovered by the next day.

The next day, our fellow PHC staff took us shopping in the village for the household items we would need. We bought pots and pans, a kerosene stove, a set of stainless steel dishes for each of us with a *loti* (water carrier), cup, large plate, and two small dishes for *dahl* (a legume soup) and other soupy items. We had our names engraved on the *lotis*. We really didn't want to spend that much of our sparse cash for the stainless steel items, but our compatriots convinced us we needed these things. I still have my stainless steel set, although we sold or gave away the rest of the items when we left the village. We also bought a more common brass *loti* to be used for washing in the toilet (Carolyn had brought a trunk full of toilet paper, but we rarely used it. One of the indispensable items in our trunks, though, was a two-year supply of tampons).

I had bought a mattress in Bombay, and I think the health center came up with one for Carolyn. I know hers was a lot thicker than mine. They also gave us some wool blankets and mosquito netting. We had sheets and pillows, but I'm not sure where they came from. I know we brought towels from home. We bought some basic food items (rice and *dalda* (lard), potatoes, and onions) and hired one of the washer women from the PHC as a temporary cook. One of our more important purchases was a clay pot for storing and cooling our boiled water. It was amazing how cool the water could get just from evaporation on the outside of the pot. Once we were outfitted we got down to work in the health center.

Working in the Health Center

The next two years were an amazing mix of adventure and excruciating boredom. We engaged in all of the activities of the health center, even including (for me) delivering babies, educating people about nutrition, starting an immunization campaign,

developing a patient record system, sterilizing equipment, and dealing with diseases I had only heard of in nursing school. Each of these experiences was a challenge and a memorable moment for me.

My first delivery was a terrifying experience. There was a woman in labor in the health center while the rest of the health center staff, including the experienced midwives, were away at a scheduled activity in one of the subcenter villages. Carolyn went with them, leaving me alone in the center to deal with this laboring mother. I had brought my obstetrical (OB) nursing textbook to India with me, and throughout the ordeal, I was reading one page ahead of this woman's labor and talking to myself. "Okay, now she's moving into transition. It's a good thing she hasn't started trying to push yet because it's too early. At least I know how to say "pant" and "push" in Marathi, but what am I going to do if she needs an episiotomy?" When the baby's head actually started coming out of the birth canal, I could tell by feel that the cord was wrapped around his neck. Fortunately, it was loose enough so that, between contractions, I could get my fingers under the cord and slip it over the baby's head. All of us survived (without an episiotomy needed!), and holding that tiny newborn in my hands was one of the most moving experiences of my life. I have since used an expanded written version of that delivery to help graduating nursing students get over their fears that they won't be competent when they get into the real world of nursing practice.

I learned to do other things in relation to deliveries that I would never have thought of doing here in the states. For example, when women have been in labor for a long time, they frequently develop a calcium deficiency that leads to muscle cramps as well as ineffective uterine contractions. When I was an obstetrics (OB) student, we dealt with that using a slow intravenous (IV) drip to replace the lost calcium. However, In India we only had one IV set up, and we tended to reserve that for massive fluid replacement for patients with cholera. To deal with calcium replacement, we gave a liquid calcium solution using a huge 30cc syringe. Calcium is tricky stuff, though. It plays a role in adequate heart function, but too much administered too fast can cause difficulties. So we had to administer it slowly over a period of time. That meant you sat there with a needle stuck in the patient's vein for about an hour, slowly administering small increments of fluid with the syringe. It's a good thing I didn't have the minor arthritis problems I've developed since then. Maintaining that continuous, even, but minimal, pressure was hard on the muscles of the hand and arm.

The staff at the PHC also had a really creative way of keeping the newborns warm. Here in the U.S., we use heated isolets and cribs. We didn't have anything like that in the village. Newborns (who were almost always so tiny they would be considered low-birth-weight here) were placed in metal cradles that hung across the end of the mother's hospital bed (also metal with a very thin mattress pad). To keep the babies warm, we took rolls of cotton batting, cut strips to wrap around arms and legs, and tied them on with strips of cloth. We also put cotton over the head and kept it in place with frilly little baby bonnets. During the hot season such measures weren't really needed during the day, but we were high on the Deccan Plateau, where it cools off considerably at night (great for sleeping), and it can get into the upper 40s or 50s during the cold season. From these experiences, I learned to cope creatively with situations with what was available to me, a skill that has stood me in good stead ever since.

Creating a patient record system for the health center was another challenge. No records had been kept until we arrived. Unless someone specifically remembered a patient's prior visit, we never knew if they had been there before, what they had been seen for, or what was done for them. I decided we needed a written record system, so I created a basic form that could be filed alphabetically by name and pulled at the time of a subsequent visit. My command of written Marathi extended to writing my own name (which I can still do), and a knowledge of the alphabet. Working with the center staff, we created a form that the literate members of the staff could complete without much difficulty. Then with my knowledge of the alphabet, I was able to file the records so they could be found again.

Sterilizing the equipment that we used for deliveries and other procedures was another terror-fraught adventure. The health center had been equipped with basic equipment by UNICEF, but the staff were only using one piece of any kind of equipment and then sterilizing it by boiling it before a subsequent use. The staff knew the equipment was expensive and could not be replaced, so they would use one piece (e.g., one pair of scissors) until it was unusable and then get out another one. This was fine except when you had multiple patients for whom you needed the same piece of equipment. There wasn't always time to sterilize stuff in between. Besides, we had no way to sterilize non-metal supplies, like dressings and so on.

One of the unused pieces of UNICEF equipment was a steam-under-pressure autoclave intended for sterilizing both metal and nonmetal supplies. The PHC staff, however, didn't know how to use it. I had used a small autoclave working as an aide in my dad's medical practice and knew the basic principles of sterilization, but I had never seen anything like the monster we had at the health center. It was a hollow cylinder about 4 feet high, raised about a foot off the ground on metal legs and with a hatch-like lid at the top. You lowered the items to be sterilized into the inner cavity, sealed the hatch with huge screw-down bolts, then placed a kerosene stove beneath the autoclave, and pumped it up for all you were worth. Unlike most autoclaves encountered in the U.S., this one didn't have a safety valve. You had to be in constant attendance, watching the pressure gauge until it reached the appropriate level, maintaining the pressure level for at least 20 minutes, and then opening the manual release valve to let off the steam. The whole apparatus had to cool completely before you could open it without risking a severe scald from escaping steam. Then you had to let everything dry before you could store the metal stuff in covered, previously sterilized containers. The nonmetal supplies were wrapped in paper prior to sterilization, so they stayed sterile on a shelf, as long as they didn't get wet.

Every time I fired up that autoclave, I was convinced it was going to explode on me. I couldn't leave the room because I had to be sure that the pressure was maintained at the appropriate level and that it didn't get too high. I was trapped with a lethal bomb just waiting to go off. Before we left India, I made sure that the PHC staff knew how to use the monster. While we were there, they were perfectly happy to leave that duty to me. Who knows if they continued to use it when we left? Maybe they went back to boiling each piece of equipment.

While I deal with our experiences with ordinary afflictions such as tetanus, cholera, and typhoid elsewhere in this narrative, we also had to deal with Hansen's disease, better known as leprosy. As in most ancient cultures and still among many people in the U.S., the word leprosy conjured visions of horror in our village despite the fact that most forms are not highly contagious and it can now be effectively treated. The PHC had an itinerant leprosy control worker (whose actual title escapes me), who visited each center periodically to administer treatment to patients with diagnosed leprosy. At one point, Carolyn and I were concerned that the little girl that we nursed through typhoid might have leprosy. She had some areas of depigmentation on her face and arms, so we arranged to have her tested by the leprosy worker. Fortunately, he found that she only had a very mild vitiligo, a benign condition in which areas of the skin lose their pigmentation.

At another point, though, we encountered an elderly man who quite obviously had leprosy. He had already experienced a lot of cartilage deterioration and had the typical loss of parts of his nose and other disfiguring complications. One of the most famous leprosaria in the country was not more than 30 miles from us. We knew they would be able to help him with rehabilitation as well as reconstructive surgery but first we had to get him there. Bus conductors would not let him on the STs, and the local "taxi" driver would not take him in his car, even though Carolyn and I offered to pay the taxi rental (by this time we had accumulated a few rupees). Although we tried to convince the PHC staff of the minimal communicability of leprosy through casual contact, even the PHC doctor wouldn't authorize use of the health center's jeep until we agreed to pay to have the whole jeep washed down inside and out afterwards.

Some of our endeavors were less successful. One day, Carolyn and I decided we were tired of the dirty windows throughout the PHC. Out of boredom, we started washing them. This was work that was definitely not appropriate for *pukkah sah'bs*, but we sort of shamed the rest of the staff into helping us. Clean windows that you could actually see through didn't last long, though. The staff painted all the windows white to avoid having to wash them again. Oh, well! You win some, and you lose some.

Life on Display

One of the other major challenges I think all volunteers experienced was the sense of living in a fish bowl. We were of consummate interest to everyone in the village, and they had questions about every aspect of our lives. Although Peace Corps training had tried to prepare us for this, the lack of privacy was still mind-boggling. We were okay with people asking about really personal aspects of our lives, but we had difficulties dealing with always being on display. It got to the point that during the afternoon "siesta" time, we would practically barricade ourselves in our house with the padlock on the door to discourage a constant stream of visitors.

For Carolyn and me, the fishbowl phenomenon was intensified when four nursing students from the government college came to Vita to do their public health training. As a nurse, I was more or less responsible for their training. That was kind of neat, and I learned then that I loved teaching nursing. However, because we were also the only ones in the PHC compound who had room in our house, all four of them were foisted on us for two weeks. I ended up having to move out of my room into Carolyn's and leaving it and the front room for the students, while Maggie (our cook) slept in her usual spot in the kitchen. Needless to say, we were not as welcoming as we could have been.

There were some amusing aspects to being the village oddities, however. Periodically, one or more of the kids next door would peer over the wall of our back court to see what we were doing, and the kids from the government "college" across the road from the PHC would stop by frequently to "practice their English." Surprisingly, it was more often the boys than the girls who did so.

Village Hospitality

An invitation to a village wedding was always an interesting experience, and being *pukkah sah'bs*, we were treated as honored guests. That meant we were usually seated with the men during the ceremony rather than behind a screen with the rest of the women. I distinctly remember one wedding in which Carolyn and I were seated in the middle of a sea of men. All of the men were seated cross-legged on the floor but, because the villagers knew that Americans usually sit on chairs (although we had no such things in our own house), they had scrounged two rickety metal folding chairs. Carolyn and I sat perched on these chairs above the rest of the throng. Although I might be the first one to insist on a little respect, I have never had a desire to be enthroned. The experience was just a little uncomfortable.

77

Inviting the Americans to dinner was also something of a status symbol in the village. Some days we could hardly walk through the village without people stopping us to invite us in for tea or whatever. One of the times I remember best was when a young girl we knew accosted us in the market and asked us to come to her house so her mother could meet us. Her mother was deaf and spoke in basically unintelligible grunts. Her daughter, however, knew what she was trying to say, and so we spent an hour or so in "conversation" with the daughter as interpreter.

Dining out was also an experience because I loved Indian food and rarely refused seconds. Carolyn, though, experienced a lot of stomach problems due to the spicy food and would usually eat very little when we were invited to someone's house for dinner. Everyone was amazed that I, who was considerably smaller, ate so much more than Carolyn.

People in the village eventually got used to us bringing our own boiled water when we were invited to dine. I think they thought we were a little crazy and didn't believe anything about bacteria in the water. We finally convinced them that our bodies were used to different water and so we had to be careful. We also finally managed to get around the polite convention of refusing subsequent helpings until your hostess practically forces more food on you. Over the two years, people became accustomed to the fact that if we wanted more food, we would accept it, but when we said "no," we meant no.

Carolyn and I had been forewarned about everyone wanting you to come for a last meal before you left for the U.S. and home. We decided we would be smart and avoid the whole leave-taking hassle by not telling anyone we were leaving until shortly before our departure. Big mistake! We still got invited to everyone's house and found ourselves eating as many as five meals in a day just to accommodate everyone. As is the custom in my own very German family, you couldn't get away with eating just a little. I have never felt stuffed to the point of nausea before or since.

In most areas, however, the people in our village were amazingly accepting of our cultural differences, frequently

referring to them as "another crazy American habit." They did manage to talk us into putting coconut oil on our hair once (yuck! Never again!), but we finally convinced them that we were used to our hair feeling clean and dry rather than oily. Another thing they had difficulty accepting was our habit of going to the PHC well to draw our own water when our cook was busy. They would say, "But you have a servant for that." We probably never did convince them that in the U.S. most of us don't have servants and do all our own work. After all, all Americans are rich, aren't they? Judged by village standards, I guess we are.

It was a good thing that we had servants or we would never have gotten any work done in the PHC. It took Pandu, our first cook and Maggie, our second one, all day to prepare our meals. As soon as breakfast was over, they started working on lunch, and then on dinner. The same thing was true of washing clothes. It would have taken us all day (and a lot of wet splashing) to take our clothes down to the river, pound them clean on the rocks and then spread them on the ground and bushes to dry.

Foreign Visitors

We had been coached so carefully about the need to make sure we didn't interact inappropriately with members of the opposite sex. We were pretty careful in our interactions in the village. Nevertheless, I am sure the villagers thought we were typically "fast" American girls when we had a succession of visits from our male Peace Corps colleagues. Being one of the few groups of single women in country, I must admit we had lots of visitors. While no one ever said anything to us, I'm sure they wondered what was going on in our house when men came to spend a few days. Most of our visitors were welcome, but there were a few that we were glad to see leave. One was a particularly troublesome volunteer who had attached himself to me in Bombay to the extent that everyone else (especially Tom Trautman) teased me about his persistent attentions. He was really a nice guy but I just wasn't interested.

One day he showed up unannounced at our house and proceeded to make himself at home for several days. He seemed to think we weren't capable of doing anything without his assistance. He annoyed me even more when he tried to take over the repairs I was doing on one of the back screen doors. I threatened to hit him with my hammer if he didn't get out of my way and let me finish the work. My mom raised me to be independent and capable of minor repairs without depending on some guy.

I often wondered what the villagers thought about our male cook, Pandu, who slept in the small front room of our house. Perhaps because he had an obvious leg deformity and a limp or because he was a servant, he wasn't considered in the same category as our male visitors.

What's for Dinner?

In our house, we tended to eat a quasi-American diet. Both Pandu and Maggie had cooked for Americans before (Maggie for three other volunteers and Pandu for Miss Moose, a longtime resident in India and PC staffer when we arrived in Bombay), so each had a smattering of American recipes. They were sometimes a little different from what we would have eaten at home. For example, I never ate bread pudding until I was in India, and it has never tasted quite the same here at home.

There was very little protein available in the village. Once in a while, you could get tough and stringy goat meat, and periodically we would go by bus to Karad, two hours away, to buy beef. Because we had no refrigeration, however, we couldn't buy much meat and then had to boil it to try to keep it a little fresher. Our only real source of protein was eggs, and we soon became the major outlet for every egg laid in and around the village. It wasn't at all unusual for a tiny child to arrive on our doorstep with two or three eggs in hand and ask *undi pahije ca* (Do you want eggs)? If I remember correctly, we paid about 50 np per

81

egg (one rupee is 100 np), which was more cash income than some of the families saw in weeks.

It was also not unusual for us to eat 4-6 eggs a day. It got to the point that I developed a fat deposit on my cornea, an extremely annoying and irritating condition, but one that resolved itself when I cut back my egg consumption. I wonder if all those eggs have any bearing on my cholesterol levels now.

Carolyn and I did some cooking ourselves on occasion. My mother, God Bless her sweet generous soul, used to send us periodic care packages. Despite a very limited income, she sent everything she could think of in the way of nonperishable food items, from canned spam to Vienna sausages, to cake mix and cornbread muffin mix. In that age before freeze-dried foods, she even convinced the local Latter Day Saints organization (Mormons) to sell her cans of freeze-dried items that they ordinarily reserved for their own missionaries. We got cans of dried peaches, apples, and apricots, as well as green beans. Then she wrapped every single item in colored tissue paper, decorative wrapping paper, and tinfoil and put it in a plastic bag, so the food would keep better and we would have craft items available. To avoid taping and tearing the tissue paper, she cut bands of brown wrapping paper and put them around the wrapped items and then taped the brown paper. She also wrapped them in yards of the satin ribbon she used to make her famous bows on Christmas and birthday presents. It was always an event when we got a package and people in the village would come by to watch us unwrap it and see what we got. I have to admit, we weren't very generous in sharing our goodies but we did make an occasional pie or cake that we shared with others. Typically, we saved them until we had other volunteers visiting us, and then fixed a feast.

Baking those pies and cakes was an adventure in itself. We had an oven of sorts, which consisted of a metal box with a hinged door that had a glass window in the middle of it. The box sat on top of our usual kerosene stove and served as an oven that cooked <u>relatively</u> evenly. Similar to the autoclave, however, there was no temperature control, so you had to be careful to make sure your creation was well cooked but did not burn. We weren't about to let any of our bounty go to waste!

Otherwise, our diets were pretty blah. As I said earlier, we had occasional meat, lots of eggs, and were sometimes able to buy bread in the village. There was only enough buffalo milk available to flavor our tea (we rarely drank coffee). On our rare trips to Bombay, we would buy canned cheese and feast for a day or two. Neither of us really learned to cook dahl and the only other items readily available in the village bazaar were potatoes, onions, and plantains all year, and tomatoes for about 9 months of the year. However, the seasonal fruits, although not available for long, were wonderful. That was my first exposure to papaya, mango, jackfruit, and something we called "custard apples" that I have never seen before or since. During mango season, <u>everything</u> we ate had a mango base, with treats ranging from mango chutney to pureed mangos with *poori* (my mouth waters just thinking about that), to fresh ripe mangos by themselves. I was in heaven, and I love mangos (and papaya) to this day, although papaya is more difficult to come by even here in California. We can get Mexican papaya but that isn't quite as good.

Household Décor

Mom's tissue and wrapping paper and ribbon were used for a variety of things, such as wrapping presents when we spent Christmas at the Trautmans' in Bombay, making paper flowers to decorate our walls, and so on. When we left, we gave what was left over to some of the PHC staff.

I had some difficulty in adjusting to the stark plainness of the whitewashed walls of our house. Consequently, I exercised my creative talents and painted figures from Alice in Wonderland on some of them. The Cheshire cat grinned knowingly over the door leading to the courtyard and the latrine, and the Red Queen and White Rabbit graced the kitchen walls around the bath area. In the front entry I painted a representation of the Golden Gate Bridge with the inscription: "I left my heart in San Francisco."

Dealing with the Local Fauna

Village wild life was another area with which we learned to cope. On first arriving in the village, we arranged to have screens put on all the windows and over the drain from the bathing area to keep out the mosquitoes, the frogs, and the snakes that came in to get the frogs. We also had three screen doors built, one for the front door and one for each of the doors to the courtyard. One courtyard door led out of the kitchen and one from Carolyn's room. Just explaining to the village carpenter what a screen door was required an enormous amount of patience and a great deal of halting Marathi. Once he understood the concept, he couldn't understand why in the world we would want something like that. We finally just gave up trying to explain and said, "Just make them, and we will pay you." Then we had the difficulty of actually getting them finished and installed. Tomorrow became tomorrow and tomorrow and tomorrow. When they were finally completed, they were so flimsy, the mosquitoes could have knocked them down with little effort, hence my efforts with the hammer.

Screens and screen doors kept the snakes out of our house. Yet, we actually did see a cobra that had been captured beneath the house next door. Cobras were also common in the field beyond our house, and, although I would have loved to walk out to a giant banyan tree some distance from the house, I never did for fear of snakes. We did have several people come to the PHC in the last throes of reactions to cobra bites. Unfortunately, they waited until they had tried all the local remedies and came to us too late for any help.

The door and window screens weren't very effective, however, in keeping out mice and scorpions. More than once I woke up with a mouse perched on my shoulder when my blanket dragged just low enough off the side of the bed for the mouse to scamper up. One night we were both reading in Carolyn's room when we spied a little visitor. There was a window between Carolyn's room and the front entry on which we kept the shutters closed. We were using the window ledge as a book shelf for some of the books from the book locker (the original cardboard

shelving had long since deteriorated after passing through the hands of several generations of volunteers). A rather foolish mouse ran out on the edge of one of the books and couldn't figure out how to get down or turn around to get away. Carolyn picked up her industrial strength rubber zoris and clapped the mouse between them, killing it deader than a doornail. She got hysterical and started screaming and she made me pick up the stupid dead mouse and get rid of it.

Another less than welcome visitor was one of the small scorpions that got into the kitchen. Maggie, our cook, was stung by it and we really didn't know what to do. We ended up putting a band around her leg to prevent the poison from spreading (not quite tight enough to be a tourniquet) and then just had to wait it out. She was in quite a bit of pain for a couple of days, but at least she didn't die.

We also had a few unwelcome encounters with bedbugs, not in our own house, but when we traveled. When we were getting ready to come home, we went to Miraj and spent the night at Maggie's son's house. In the middle of the night, I woke up covered with bites all up and down my legs. The itching was so fierce I couldn't sleep, and I spent the rest of the night in an old fashioned canvas back lawn chair with my feet immersed in a bucket of cold water. I was probably contaminating the family's drinking water supply for the day but, at that point, I didn't care.

Drought in the Village

Water got to be something of a problem in our second year in the village. Because of a protracted drought, many of the wells in the area went dry, including the one in the PHC compound. At one point, the villagers tried blasting with dynamite to deepen the well, but all they managed to do was blow rocks from the wall of the well all over the compound. It was a wonder no one was killed by falling debris. Until the monsoons came again, the district government brought water into the village in tanks mounted on the back of bullock carts. Every other day each household was allotted one 5-gallon bucket of water that was supposed to suffice for cooking, drinking (after we boiled it at our house), bathing, and washing. Needless to say, we minimized our bathing, hair washing, etc. Our first priority was water for drinking and cooking.

Dressing the Part

Earlier I mentioned that the people in the village were remarkably accepting of our strange ways. Although we tried not to violate too many taboos, there were some things we just had to do our own way. For example, we started out wearing white saris like the rest of the female PHC staff, but they were way too cumbersome to work in effectively. So, eventually we shifted to white dresses (even though only little girls wore dresses in our village). People in the village had enough knowledge of America to know that nurses wear white uniforms, so our dresses were acceptable as nurses' uniforms.

We didn't wear dresses when we traveled, and most of the time we didn't wear saris either. Punjabi dress with pants and tunic always seemed safer and also allowed us to clamber up into the luggage racks on those 3rd class unreserved train trips.

Getting Around

Traveling was always an adventure. Since our village was two hours by bus from any train station, much of our travel was on the good old ST buses. When we went to visit the closest other volunteers in Karad, we went by bus. If we were lucky, the bus driver would make an unscheduled stop outside the guys' house. Otherwise, we had to go all the way into Karad on the bus and then a take a tonga back several miles to their place.

On one such trip, I was on my way to Bombay to represent I-44A in the monthly meeting of volunteers. One of the guys in Karad was representing his group, so we were going to meet and go in to the city by train from Karad. Either the bus driver was behind in his schedule that day (although when did the buses ever stay on schedule?) or he was just being uncooperative. At any rate, he refused to let me out by their house. I hired a tonga for the ride back in the dark and didn't notice that the tonga driver was driving illegally without a light. Just after we crossed a bridge over a fairly large stream or small river, a truck coming from the opposite direction hit the tonga. It was a good thing we were already across the bridge or I would have been doused again, if not worse. I remember turning end-over-end as I went flying through the air and thinking to myself, "Oh rats, I'm going to die in India and Mom will never forgive me." I hit the pavement and the next thing I knew I was surrounded by what seemed to be a large crowd of people. The truck driver that hit us had stopped but the tonga *wallah* had run away. Several other cars on the road had also stopped. Fortunately, one of the drivers spoke good English because I was in no shape to explain anything in Marathi. I was able to explain to him where I wanted to go and he delivered me to the house. Then he explained what had happened to Bob, Fred, and Sig because I was pretty incoherent. The most painful part of it all, though, was the PC doc poking and prodding at my badly bruised leg to make sure it wasn't broken.

Most of the rest of my travels were considerably more fun, although not deficient in a certain amount of drama. On the one long leave that I took while in country, I went south to Bangalore, Mysore, and Madras. Several of us (some folks from I-41, I-47 or 48, and me) had rented a car and driver to take us to Bangalore. We had a flat tire out in the middle of nowhere. Of course, the car didn't have a spare, so we sat by the roadside while the driver hiked somewhere to get another tire. Fortunately, it wasn't during either monsoon or the hot season, so our wait was relatively comfortable.

In Bangalore, we made sure to frequent a little place known to most volunteers in the southern half of India as one of the few places in the country where you could get fresh pasteurized milk. Though we were only there for a couple of days, I think each of us tried to drink enough cold milk to make up for what we missed during the remainder of our in-country tenure. From Bangalore, we went to Mysore for the Diwali festivities. During Diwali, *pukkah sah'bs* make their ritual *pujah* (obeisance) to the Maharaja. Had we been there earlier, we could have registered as foreign visitors and participated in the ceremony. As it was, we could only watch from the grounds of his extensive palace.

The crowds were huge and when we entered the palace grounds, the men were separated from the women. The men stood around the perimeter of the central field and the women were all seated cross-legged and knee-to-knee on the ground in the center. Like most crowds, when word spread of the Maharaja's approach on his elephant, everyone stood up to see better. The security force (all big Sikhs), was having none of that, and they threatened the crowd with their billy clubs to get them to sit down. When they stood up, all the women had surged forward and there wasn't enough room for everyone to sit back down. I must have been slower to respond than the rest of the

crowd because suddenly I was standing, surrounded by all these women seated on the ground around me. There was literally only enough room for my feet, and there was no way I could sit down without sitting on someone. Suddenly there was a huge man in a military uniform bearing down on me. I had visions of being arrested for not obeying the order to sit down. All he did, though, was reach over the crowd, grasp me by my elbows, lift me over the heads of the seated women, and deposit me on the edge of the crowd.

After the ceremony, we met up with the others in our party at the gates to the palace enclosure. The crowds were horrific and I tend to get panicky when I am tightly enclosed. I was trying to hold onto the strap of my *pishwi* (shoulder bag) and my camera and still hold onto the shirttail of one of the other volunteers so I didn't get lost or trampled. Suddenly I was again faced by a very large Sikh who seemed at least two feet taller than me. We had all heard tales of the aggressiveness of Sikh men toward foreign women and I thought I was in for it. Boy was I surprised when he whipped out a camera, took a picture of me, and then forced his way back through the crowd!

From there we went to Madras and visited Mahabalipuram, the city of temples beside the sea. It was fascinating. We were approached on our arrival by a young boy of about twelve who offered to be our guide. He was amazingly knowledgeable (unless he was making it all up) and spoke passable English, so we had a wonderful tour of the place.

During my two years in India, I also saw Ellora and Ajunta along with any number of forts. While I liked all of it, I think I was most impressed by the forts. They all seemed to be such symbols of strength that faded as one conqueror succeeded another—probably a lesson there that strength isn't everything! One of the most dispiriting things, though, was at Daulatabad Fort, where it was obvious that a significant historical site was being used as a latrine. Little had been done to preserve many of these sites. Although they have survived for centuries, how much longer will they continue without more careful maintenance? It would be a pity if they are lost to subsequent generations.

A Taste of Home

I also went up to the hill station where the missionaries typically spent the hot season and where their children went to boarding school (Kodaikanal, spelling questionable). The missionaries in Sangli and at the Miraj Mission Hospital were a godsend for us. We could always get a respite from the fishbowl of the village when we went to visit them. Bob and Nancy Ramer had met and married in India and raised their four children there. Bob was an engineer and taught in a vocational program in Sangli. Nancy was a nurse who supervised a clinic and taught the public health nursing component of the nursing program at the government college and the mission hospital. Both were always welcoming. Nancy was from Scotland, and

Carolyn and I both loved the daily ritual of three o'clock tea. We could speak English there and be understood in the context of our own Western culture. Their house was a refuge from the daily stresses and frustrations of life as the village oddities. Their oldest daughter, Lynn, has since become a nurse, and all four kids were actively involved in a variety of humanitarian activities. Their parents were great role models for them as well as for Carolyn and me.

Over the years, after each furlough in the U.S., the Ramers and other missionaries had managed to accumulate many of the amenities of a U.S. household such as washing machines and regular furniture. Visiting them was like being home and helped alleviate some of the homesickness we experienced on occasion. I will have to say, however, that I wasn't as often affected by homesickness as some of my fellow volunteers. Even as a child, I was always eager to go somewhere new and different (a trait somewhat at odds with my shyness around strangers, but go figure)! Even now, wherever I am is home for as long as I am there, whether it's a hotel room in Japan, a house in an Indian village, or a school dormitory in Taipei.

Interaction with other Peace Corps volunteers (PCVs) was another release from the frequent boredom and frustration of life in the village and the routine work at the PHC. As I said earlier, we visited the volunteers stationed in Karad fairly regularly. We also saw PCVs from other groups who were stationed in Sangli, Miraj, and Kolhapur, all of which were relatively easily accessible by bus. Once in a while, we also made trips to Poona to visit some of the volunteers there. One time, Carolyn and I arrived in Poona to welcome some newly arrived volunteers and got a rather frosty welcome. For once, we had traveled in saris, and they thought we were missionaries come to proselytize.

We had surprisingly little interaction, however, with the members of our own group. That was probably a function of the way we were spread out around the entire state. Lynne Graham was the closest to us and we saw her on occasion. Kathy Kelleher visited our village after Sylvia got married, and I stopped by Mary Welch's site on my way to and from Bombay a couple

91

of times. Everyone else was in places that were too inaccessible from our villages, so we either saw them in Bombay or, as with most of them, not at all.

More Getting Around

A few of the guys from the other half of the group (44B) came to our village or we arranged to meet them on vacations. That didn't work out too well on occasion. Mike Simonds and I had arranged to meet in Bombay for a short vacation, but his leave pay didn't come through in time and he had no way of notifying me (no cell phones in those days). I went on into Bombay and was mildly aggravated that he never showed up. I spent my time with a nice guy from a Canadian organization similar to PC (except they were only in-country for a few months). We had a great time running around Bombay, so I didn't miss Mike too much. When I got back to my village, there was a letter explaining his absence, and I eventually forgave him.

That trip was back in the days when PC Bombay had arranged for special rates for volunteers coming to the city to stay at the Woods Hostel. We more often referred to it as the "Woods Hole." Right across from the Gateway of India and the wharves, it had as many rats in residence as it did guests. The rats were as big as the bobcats in the hills outside my house here in San Diego, and I was definitely not fond of them. We stayed in open dormitories and had to be careful to guard our belongings waking or sleeping. We also made sure we didn't bring anything up into the dorm area that would attract the rats. We were eternally grateful when Tom and Joan Trautman joined the PC Bombay staff and opened their home to visiting volunteers, particularly the women.

Another really interesting trip was made in the company of a businessman from Karad who had arranged for the Rotary club to fund the start of our immunization campaign. He had invited both Carolyn and I to go with him on a business trip to some tool and dye company in the south with which he was thinking of doing business. Carolyn managed to find someplace else to go at the time, so I was on my own. I wasn't particularly comfortable going by myself with this gentleman just because appearances might be misinterpreted, but it all worked out. When we got to our destination, we stayed with the family of the owner of the company he had gone to visit. I got dragged on a tour around a factory that made no sense to me; I was bored but polite. Then at a dinner for us and several of the company employees, I was asked to sing an American song to entertain the group. I was embarrassed but I managed to remember most of the words to "The Sound of Music" and performed creditably at least. Then the "young people" were turned loose to amuse themselves, and I found myself out drinking and dancing with several young Indians and a German fellow who was interning with the company. It was a weird weekend, but kind of fun. I had, fortunately, gotten over most of my fear of strangers by that time, but I was still a bit uncomfortable out on my own in a foreign place.

Adapting to Life in the Village

In between adventures, dealing with the boredom of village life was a particular challenge. Carolyn and I had the good fortune to inherit one of the Peace Corps "book lockers" from a group of departing volunteers. Whoever conceived of those book lockers as a way of keeping volunteers sane had a great idea and very eclectic literary tastes. As someone who has read throughout my life, I can say those books kept me grounded in sanity. As women, we were basically confined to our house after dark. Women didn't go out and about the village at night, so there we were with little to do beyond read. I remember that Carolyn had one issue of a U.S. news magazine that she probably read a hundred times. Sometimes our evening reading was done by electric lighting. When the electricity went out, which was often, there were always the kerosene lanterns that we inherited (purchased, actually) from some departing volunteers. We also bought a ceiling fan from them, but that was less reliable than the lanterns.

We also spent a lot of time philosophizing, verbally with each other, and in writing to PCVs stationed throughout Maharashtra and those in Rajasthan. We wrote about love and India, our daily experiences and our frustrations, and the meaning of life. Somewhere I still have the half of the correspondence I received; I will have to look at those letters someday.

One of the books in the book locker was the *Harad Experiment* avidly read by most of the volunteers. We spent quite a bit of time discussing the concepts of free love and male/female interactions. Thinking back, the naiveté of those discussions amuses me.

As someone breaking out of my traditionalist shell, I decided I needed to find out how other people saw me. So I did what was, for me, a very daring thing. On one trip to Bombay, I met several of the volunteers from the infamous I-40 group. One of their group members was hospitalized in Breach Candy Hospital, so I tagged along with them for visiting hours. When I got back to my village, I wrote a letter asking for his candid view of me on first acquaintance. I think I really caught him off-guard but he responded in a way that seemed to be both honest and favorable, giving another boost to my self-confidence.

I think, as a whole, our half of the group fared better than the guys up north in terms of longevity. I know we lost a fair number of people who didn't return for the second summer of training and a few more who didn't go to India with us or went with other groups (e.g., Susan Krawiec, who ended up joining her husband Hank's group already in country). We also gained Carolyn Jones, Cheryl Taub, and Don and Robin Schatzberg when they got shifted from agriculture to health. We lost Sam and Kathy for health reasons and lost Sylvia to the north when she and Jerry got married. I can't remember losing anyone else once we got in-country (that's not to say we didn't lose others, because my memory has a few holes in it these days). From what I remember of letters we received from the northern group in the first few months in India, I think we adapted better than they did, even though we were more isolated from each other. On the other hand, perhaps that isolation contributed to our adaptation.

I know we adapted better to Indian food because I remember letters from Mike and Bill and George about living for days at a time on peanut butter sandwiches (we didn't even have access to peanut butter in our village!). Maybe their proximity to Udaipur made a difference, too. Most of us were out in the sticks, where it might take us all day to reach civilization. Consequently, we made the best of being stuck in the village. It may also have had something to do with the fact that most of us were single women and other people, both villagers and others we encountered, like the missionaries, watched out for us more carefully. Although I know a couple of us had bad experiences, for the most part we were watched over and well cared for. As the only single American women around, we also were courted by a lot of the other volunteers in Maharashtra, so we felt valued and welcomed.

Regrets

I guess I have two "failure" stories to share, even though, on the whole, I think we accomplished something worthwhile in India. One of them I've learned to live with and to value and I use it in teaching my students. The other still bothers me 40 years later, and I still cry whenever I talk or think about it. In fact, I have tears in my eyes as I write.

In all my four years as a nursing student, I only saw one patient die, and she wasn't even my patient. I had a couple of patients that were terminal, but they didn't die "on my shift" so to speak, and I was at least able to bring them some comfort in their last days and weeks. The issue in India was the knowledge that something could have been done and the lady didn't need to die. Modern US medicine could have easily saved her and even the Indian system had the capability but didn't exercise it.

We had three outstanding midwives attached to our PHC but we also had a number of untrained traditional midwives in the village and surrounding area. Most of them had no concept of asepsis (keeping things clean), didn't wash their hands, and used any old knife to cut the umbilical cord. As a result, the incidence of cord tetanus in both mothers and babies was high.

Chances are they are still high, although I have not checked the data recently.

One day, a family brought in a young woman who had delivered at home, attended by a village midwife. By the time she got to us she was already exhibiting symptoms of an advanced stage of tetanus. As a student, my medical-surgical textbook still had pictures of the classic feature of tetanus, the "rictus of death." As the disease progresses, muscles go into continuous spasm and the facial muscles contract so the patient exhibits a hideous grin that exposes all their teeth. This is accompanied by muscle contractions that severely bow the patient's back, almost like an acrobat doing a back bend. It is extremely painful and there is no way to relieve the pain except for narcotics and even they are not terribly effective at the end.

For some reason I was deputized to sit with this woman while she died. It took hours and she was conscious and in excruciating pain the entire time. We didn't have access to any kind of pain medication, much less narcotics. The most frustrating part of this (for me) was that the mission hospital was two hours away. They had a supply of tetanus antitoxin. It might not have saved her but, then again, it might have.

When I asked why we didn't just transport her to the hospital, I was given the very pragmatic answer. The health center jeep was gone and transportation by means of the local taxi (a fabulous old Chevy touring car) would have cost the family every penny they had. They made the decision to save their resources to meet the survival needs of the remaining family members.

I was alone with her when she died. Not even her family stayed, and I can kind of understand why. I have never been able to put that experience behind me. I know there was nothing I could have done to change the outcome and yet my feelings range from grief, guilt, anger, to frustration. It shouldn't have been that way!

That was when the cultural differences between the U.S. and India smacked me in the face. Up to that point, cultural differences, though often frustrating, were part of the adventure.

Here in the US, we have serious health care access problems and disparities in health outcomes across groups. Nevertheless, most of us do not face the Faustian choice of choosing death for one family member to let others survive.

In my subsequent career, I have frequently had difficulty finding a source of care for some clients. It has often taken hours for me and my community health nurse colleagues to find a provider who will care for an indigent patient. However, I have never had to let someone die for want of care. As I recall, the infant in this case survived the delivery, but probably died soon after.

What we would consider a terrible waste of two lives was common in India. Maybe that was why Carolyn (Jones) and I jumped on the idea of providing immunizations (including tetanus) in Vita and the subcenter villages. Besides, this gave us a much NEEDED activity to occupy our time.

My second failure story isn't precisely a failure but we sure could have done a much better job than we did. Oddly enough, it relates to the immunization campaign we started. I was fresh out of nursing school and Carolyn wasn't even a nurse yet. In those days, nursing school didn't teach you anything about program development or evaluation.

Although I recall some warm fuzzy stuff about community organizing (or whatever they called it back then) in our PC training, nobody ever exposed us to the principles of planning. Yet, there we were trying to plan and implement an ambitious undertaking—immunizing the kids in the village against diphtheria, tetanus, pertussis, and polio. We didn't have a clue what we were doing.

We did some things right, mostly by accident. But we also did a lot of things wrong. For example, we decided we could just go into the school and give the immunizations. After all, we had a captive audience, right? (It was literally "captive" since we snuck around the walls, nipped into the school yard, and barred those huge gates to keep the kids from running away). It seemed like a good plan to us. After all, what kid wants a shot if they can avoid it? Besides, this is India. Who needs parental consent?

97

We know best. We'll just give these kids the shots they need to prevent future sickness and even death.

What didn't occur to us was the need to educate people about the typical side effects of DPT injections such as mild fever and sore arms. Not surprisingly, all the parents panicked and complained to the medical officer who forbade us from going back into the school for subsequent doses. From then on, we had to stick to giving immunizations only to those kids whose parents requested them.

We did have one thing going for us. Kusum was one of the 4th class *peuns* (servants) at the PHC. When her oldest daughter, essentially adopted by Carolyn and I, developed typhoid, we took her into our house and nursed her through it. Fortunately for us, she survived with no after affects, and Kusum became our "apostle of change." Given her low social status, her influence was limited, but she was known to most of the uneducated mothers in the village. Many of her conversations began with "Mayri *Moushi* (aunt) and Keroleen *Moushi* say....you should get the shots and drops for your children. And you should eat eggs, etc." Primarily because of Kusum, we ended up immunizing a good number of children in the village.

Another screw up was keeping too much control of the whole program. We were the only ones who gave the immunizations (and I was the only one to give DPT injections, since I was the nurse). After all, we controlled the vaccine supply and the syringes. That meant even if someone wanted their child to be immunized, it was not going to happen unless we were there. It also meant we would get lots of interruptions during our afternoon siestas.

Only when we were almost ready to go home did we realize we needed to do something fast if we wanted the program to continue. We had to scurry around, taking one of the PHC staff into Bombay to show him where we purchased the vaccine. We had kept that duty to ourselves because it gave us a legitimate reason to get out of the village and into the city every six weeks. If I recall correctly, we used to fight over whose turn it was to go get more vaccine.

We also had to arrange for a continuing supply of used syringes and needles from PC Bombay (although PC used supposedly disposable equipment for all the nasty shots they gave volunteers, both syringes and needles could be boiled and reused until they just fell apart). I now realize that we should have involved our local PHC staff from the beginning. I think we just needed the psychological ownership of something we could claim as an accomplishment during our two years in the village.

We also put no thought into the evaluation of the program. We just assumed that we would immunize kids and they would be free of disease. We never even kept track of the number of immunizations we gave, although we knew how many doses of vaccines we purchased. We wasted very few, so we probably immunized several hundred kids.

The immunization program, despite our ineptitude and lack of expertise, was really rather successful. The last letter I got from someone in the village (about three years after we got home) indicated that the program was still up and running. Of course, India is one of the few nations in the world (six remaining, last time I looked) that still has endemic wild polio virus outbreaks. I can only hope our kids were just a bit better protected than kids elsewhere.

Lessons Learned

In addition to reducing the burden of childhood disease in our village at least a little bit, the immunization program taught me a lot about program planning. I didn't realize that until I was in my community health nursing master's program and used the project as a case study for my program planning class. Now I teach program planning and evaluation to both undergraduate and doctoral students. The other night, I used the immunization project as an example of how NOT to plan a program. I think the students learned as much as from my description of what worked and what didn't and the consequences of violating basic principles of planning as they would have from reading about a "perfect" program.

After class, one of the students told me she enjoyed hearing about our experiences, and that the story really brought home the principles I was trying to convey. Maybe we don't think we accomplished much in India, but we learned some lessons that have allowed us to accomplish a lot since. Without those experiences, we might still be floundering around without purpose or direction, much like we did then.

After two simultaneously long and yet short years, we left our village and left India. I really only fleetingly considered extending my term (for about thirty minutes), but I think I left a part of me there and brought a part of India home with me. Throughout my life, I have had a compulsion to bring order out of chaos, to the point that when I was an associate dean, one of my faculty members complained that I was too organized and expected everyone else to be organized as well. I think part of what we accomplished in India was an effort to do just that, provide a little order, even it if was just in coping with a polio epidemic.

On the artistic side, I have had a life-long ambition to create the most beautiful something that has ever been seen. I haven't a clue what that something might be, but I keep working at it. One embroidery project that I started in 1982 might approach that level if I ever finish it. It has been close to completion for several years, but I always set it aside in favor of something else, so it's never done. Maybe I haven't finished it because I am afraid I will be disappointed that it doesn't measure up to my expectations.

I have accomplished a number of goals since I returned from India and some of them are rather significant, particularly in my professional career. And yet, I feel I am still creating. I think we all were engaged in creation while we were in India. I was creating relationships with people in my village, other volunteers, and people from around the world. I think we were also creating an image of America that I hope has influenced the people we encountered there. Most of all, I was creating, or maybe discovering, myself as someone who is competent, who can be successful, and who can accomplish something with next to nothing. I'm much more tolerant of my own foibles and those of others than I was before my experiences in India. I am still engaged in that creative endeavor and, like my embroidery, this journey to myself is not finished yet.

CHAPTER 4

From the Tobacco Farms in North Carolina to a Small Village in India

Haywood Turrentine

I grew up the fifth of seven children born to James B. and Jessie (Rhodes) Turrentine on a rural farm in Durham County, North Carolina. We did not have running water or indoor plumbing. Neither did we own the land, nor the mules used to cultivate the land, nor the seeds for planting crops, nor the fertilizers used to raise those crops. We were truly tenant farmers and essentially survived on a fourth of everything we raised. We were poor by all reasonable standards.

One thing that we did have in abundance was the undeniable love of two wonderful, God-fearing parents. My father completed the fourth grade and then had to drop out to work on his uncle's farm. His uncle raised him from the age of two after his mother died. My mother completed high school, graduating with honors, and received a scholarship to attend college at a school in another state. Her parents were not interested in her leaving the state to attend college, so she stayed at home and eventually married my father.

Of the seven children in my family, the oldest three were female, then my oldest brother and then me. The females were the key to production on that farm. However, when they graduated from high school, they had had enough of the farm. My oldest sister went away to school and became a licensed Registered Nurse. When the next sister graduated from high school, my parents already had one child in school and could not afford to send another. As a result, my sister Shirley joined the United States Air Force as the first black female from our town to do so. She completed her tour of duty and settled in Detroit, Michigan, as far away from the farm as she could get. The next sister in line, Alma, went on to college and spent one year, later re-enrolling in a nursing curriculum to become a licensed Practical Nurse.

These moves took three members of the workforce away from the farm and the owner of the farm decided that it was better if my father also moved from his farm. We spent the next few years moving from one house to the next until my father finally purchased a piece of land and built his own place. This move impacted my life more than any other single event up to that time. By moving off the farm, my brothers and I were able to participate in athletics in high school. No doubt, being able to participate in sports was key to my maintaining any interest in school whatsoever, although I am not sure I would have been allowed to drop out of school even if I had decided to. My parents were intent on us getting our education; however, I was not. I went to class and did just enough to remain eligible to play sports the next year.

Now, you need to understand that I attended a very small high school. My graduating class consisted of seventeen students. In fact, I was so ashamed of the size of my school that I used to lie and tell people I went to a small private school. Most of the graduates went on to college or the military. My high school housed grades 1-12 and was so small that we could not even field a football team. We excelled in basketball and did fairly well in baseball. I played both baseball and basketball. In fact, I was named co-captain of the basketball team my junior and senior years. In my senior year, we won the state championship for the first time, losing only one game. I had scholarship offers, but the principal withheld them from me because he thought it highly unlikely I could make it at the college level. Instead, the guidance counselor suggested that I become a male nurse or a stock clerk. I have never figured out how those two professions meet in terms of skills required to be successful. Good old Mrs. Hooker, the counselor, said my vocabulary was not sufficient to make it in college. I, on the other hand, knew something that none of these people in the educational world were aware of. I could get passing grades, even though they were "C"s, with the minimal effort I put into studying.

I never took my books home and subsequently, never did much studying. Oh, I took books from the school building each day, but they were not mine. I would carry the books of the young lady with whom I was trying to gain favor. So, yes, I did take books to the bus, but they were not books that made it to my house. Think about it for a moment; if I never studied and I made passing grades, I must not have been totally illiterate. One could, however, conclude that I was making unwise choices. So, my grades were never a reflection of what I knew or my innate talents. Instead, they were a reflection of my priorities: girls and sports. I did pretty well in both areas. Long story short, I graduated and was at a crossroads as to what I would do next.

I knew I did not wish to go into the military and I knew I did not want to work at Duke Hospital for the rest of my life as an orderly or some technician in a lab. Quite frankly, I was not overly interested in going to work at this time. I knew I had to do something because you did not stay at the Turrentine household and do nothing. After taking inventory of the choices available to me, I decided that I would go to college. I knew there would be plenty of girls there and I could continue my efforts in that regard. At dinner one evening, my mother asked me what my plans were. Without hesitation, I told her that I planned on going to North Carolina College (NCC) at Durham. After she got over her choking, she said "son, you have not exactly set the world on fire academically and given those facts, are you sure that is what you want to do"? I told her that I was sure and that I knew I could do anything I set my mind to do. I told her that I knew I had not done as well as my other sisters and brother in school. I told her that I had not wasted my time studying like they did, that I enjoyed my time in high school. I told her that I was ready to move forward now because I had already had my fun.

My mother, forever the supporter of us, said "if that is your decision, we will provide you with a place to stay and some type of transportation," but that I would have to pay my own way. She said they did not have any money to contribute. I said that was fine by me. I worked and saved my money and went to NCC. I did not do too well on my placement exams and ended up having to take remedial math, remedial English and remedial reading, all non-credit courses. I paid a dear price for having fun in high school and not taking my studies seriously. I had to take a lot of preparatory courses in order to make it in college. Because I had to take so many non-credit courses, I did not have the proper number of credit hours at the end of my first two years in college. I could not go to summer school because I had to work to get tuition money for the next year. I had to work during the school year so I could buy books and eat. There were many days that I did not eat, because I had a choice of buying gas to get to class or eating.

I guess you can say that I had matured because I chose gas over food. I heard President Kennedy speak about this new idea he was suggesting for young people to get involved in and make an important contribution. I thought that I might be interested in doing that some day. Sometime during my junior year, a Peace Corps recruiter came to my campus. I went to the meeting and completed the application. Did I ask to be placed in India? No. I am not even sure I knew where India was, so I know I did not list India. However, when they came back and said I had been selected to attend a different type of training, I jumped at the opportunity. I suspect that my growing up on the farm and having to work my way through school contributed mightily to my decision to give it my best. The money did not hurt either because I had to cover my tuition my senior year.

I went to training at the University of Wisconsin in Milwaukee and met some of the most incredible people I have ever known. Some of those same people have been very influential in helping me become the person I am today, both staff as well as volunteers. What a tremendous experience sitting in training sessions with others from Yale, Cal Berkley, Clark, UCLA, San Diego State and the list could go on. Those were experiences that I cherish, even until this very day. It taught me that I could compete with the best of the best regardless of where they had studied as undergraduates. I matriculated from a historically black college and was able to contribute as well as those from larger, more prestigious schools. The training was some of the best I have ever experienced. The staff did a good job trying to prepare us for life on the ground in India.

Although they did a good job, I was not totally prepared for what I encountered when I arrived there. Before we arrived, we had to endure a plane ride that was longer than any I had ever experienced. It seemed that every couple of hours, we would enter another time zone and would be offered another meal. We finally arrived in New Delhi on an airplane that lost an engine during flight when most of us were asleep. Looking out the window and seeing part of the wing missing caused me some rather anxious moments. But the wonderful crew landed without incident, and we were finally ready to meet the people we had come to help. It was hot, hotter than I had been able to imagine. Everyone spoke so fast that I could not understand anything the people were saying. Keep in mind that this was in New Delhi, not a small village.

I had taken approximately 300 hours of language prior to arriving in India. You will recall that I stated earlier that when we were selected for Peace Corps training, it was to be a new type of training. We were recruited during our junior year in college and went to training during the summer between our junior and senior years. Again, that was a wonderful experience and I learned an awful lot about India and a host of other things. Yes, we had long Hindi language classes. At the end of training, we were given tapes and books for us to further study our Hindi. For some reason, I resorted back to a habit I developed during high school. I did not study by listening to the tapes weekly, as instructed. As a result, I was not where I should have been when I reached India. When we landed in India, I realized that I had squandered the opportunity to study my language and be better prepared for the challenges that lay ahead.

I did not have an awful lot of time for studying Hindi because I had to take an extra heavy load to have the required number of credit hours for graduation. I needed 124 credit hours to meet my graduation requirements. In order to get that number of credit hours, I had to take 23 credits the first semester and 24 credits the second semester. The maximum number of semester credit hours one could take, without special permission from the Dean, was 21. The recommended number was 18 credit hours. The Dean could grant permission to take a heavier course load under extreme circumstances. My circumstances were extreme. I had to graduate because I was scheduled to leave for some additional Peace Corps training at the University of Wisconsin in Madison and then ship out to India. I simply had to graduate on time without the benefit of summer school.

The Chairman of the History Department recommended that I petition the Dean to allow me to take the additional credits. I had made the Dean's List the last two semesters of my junior year. I petitioned the Dean and when I met with him, he was not immediately prepared to grant such a course load. He asked me why he should consider my request. I went all the way back to my high school days of playing around and not doing very well in class. I told him that I thought I was immature in high school and that I had made some poor choices. As a result, I ended up taking a number of courses that did not count toward graduation. I pointed out that I had matured and had done well in college. I told him that I had made the Dean's List the last two semesters and, if granted the extra course load, I would not disappoint him. Finally, I told him about my schedule going forward for final training and subsequent Peace Corps assignment. I pointed out that I had a schedule to meet and I intended to meet that schedule, with or without my degree.

I told the Dean that I was the first in my family to attend a 4-year college and graduate with a bachelor's degree. I impressed upon him how important that degree was to me. He looked at my transcript and concluded that there was a good chance that I could handle the extra course load, and he signed off on my petition. I am eternally grateful to the Dean of Students for granting my request. I was going to India and if I did not have my degree, so be it. I knew that if I did not get my degree, that I might not ever return and complete my studies. I needed 124 credits to graduate and I ended up with 124.5 credit hours, cutting it close. I had my degree on time without attending summer school. Who would have predicted that considering my high school record?

When I arrived in New Delhi International Airport and exited the plane, all the things they drilled us on in training came rushing back to my mind. I even wished I had spent a little more time listening to my Hindi tapes. We checked into the hotel and were supposed to get some rest before going to dinner. I went to sleep and slept through dinner. That presented a minor problem because I was going to have to wait a long time before the next meal, scheduled for the following morning. There were no snack machines in the hotel, and the only thing we would have to eat was whatever snacks we either carried onto the plane or received during flight. I survived the first day and cannot, for the life of me, remember anything about the next couple of days in India. At some point, we boarded one of India's infamous trains for a long ride from New Delhi to Udaipur, Rajasthan where we would undergo some in-country training. The train stations were an adventure in and of themselves.

We had our bags and the *chokidars* (porters) were grabbing our bags to place them on the train in hopes of a tip. We were not sure what they were going to do with our bags. One should keep in mind that in America, the people there to help you with your bags, the bellhops, are dressed in uniforms. Those in India were not dressed in any uniform and one was left to wonder who was wrestling for my bag and whether I would ever see my bag again. So, what did we do? We fought to hold onto our own bags. After a long while, we were safely onboard the train headed to no man's land, or so it seemed. As we looked out the windows of the train, we saw some unbelievable animals. The bullocks had horns that were majestic. The camels were plentiful. There were donkeys all over the place. Then, there were the water buffaloes. They looked just like the African cape buffaloes I had seen on television, and those guys were mean. Naturally, I was afraid of the water buffalo and the bullocks.

The train seemed to stop at every station along the way, which made the trip seem like it was taking forever. The seats were not cushioned like we were accustomed to when we travel in America. The benches were wooden and rather tough on one's backside. My butt was numb by the time we arrived in Udaipur. Everything smelled strange, and we had to get accustomed to that, among a host of other things. The food was different, and we had to get used to that. You were instructed not to drink the water unless it was boiled or we used quinine tablets. In that extreme heat, we wanted water in the worst kind of way. We were issued canteens and told to keep them with us at all times. One look at the sources of water, and you would swear not to drink any water for the next two years. I am not sure what we thought we would use to remain hydrated.

When we went to the bathroom, we were surprised to find that there was no toilet paper. There was a water pot to be used to clean oneself. That was strange, and I did not know exactly how to use it and not spill it all over my pants. Now, I had plenty of experience using old Sears catalogs or corn cobs, but never water. Yes, I ended up with more water on my pants than I did on my backside until I learned the art of doing it. Once I learned, it was not a bad experience. Did I tell you that the latrines were not outfitted with a stool? We had to squat, a technique that also demanded a bit of practice. So, that was something I had to get accustomed to before I could relax and relieve myself. There were a ton of things I had to learn, and no amount of training you might get stateside could prepare you for what you would experience once you arrived in-country. If you were not open-minded, you would have a very difficult time making it in India. In fact, I do not think it would be possible to make it without that flexibility.

I was able to draw on my many experiences on that tenant farm, time and time again, during my stay in India. Had I grown up in the city, I am not sure I would have made it in India. Many of my experiences provided me with a foundation upon which to build the needed stamina. For example, I was accustomed to being out in the hot sun and having to endure intense heat. I was accustomed to having to get by on less, and that was certainly the case in India. It seemed that all clocks had been thrown away, and time did not hold a very prominent place in the lives of the host country nationals we encountered. If you were to ask when the person you were scheduled to see would be available, the answer was always the same...*Kabe, kabe*... translated meant in a little while or that it/he was "just now coming." That little while could extend to a half a day. No one seemed to be in a hurry to do anything.

When I went to the local bank to open a checking account, it took me the better part of a day to get it done. What was I going to do? It was not as if I could go to another bank that wanted my business and find someone who would be glad to help me. The local buses and the trains were always running behind schedule. It was almost better if we would take off our watches and go with the flow. In so doing, it would lessen one's frustration. No running water, electricity only for a couple or three hours a day was the norm. If you think that was bad, all we needed to do was wait until we reached our assigned villages where there was no electricity at all, at least for many of us. I never realized how bright a Coleman lantern could be until I arrived in my village.

As a black man in India, I was someone that the locals loved to look at and refer to as the African. They did not know that any American was anything other than a white person. Once I learned the language and could communicate my thoughts, they thought I was from southern India. The Indians from places like Kerala were extremely dark-skinned. It was bittersweet because I was not thought of as the ugly American, yet I was thought of as a little lower than the Indians as an African or an Indian from Kerala or Madras. I will never forget the time that Bill Whitesell and a couple of other Peace Corps Volunteers were on a third-class train going to Bombay. Bill spoke Hindi better than anyone else in the entire group, along with David Dell. It was hot, and we were tired of the long train ride. We were sitting there minding our own business when one of the locals turned to me and commenced with some rather disparaging words to describe the whites on the train. He said the white blank blanks did not understand what the Indian was saying. Bill responded in kind in Hindi and scared the crap out of the guy.

He was being obnoxious and asking all kinds of questions to which no one responded. I guess he thought no one, other than me, knew what he was saying. It was a bit disconcerting to be constantly confronted by some wise ass asking "what is your name?" Then, if you would befriend a local, you were really in for a surprise. The young Indian males had a habit of holding hands whenever they were out in public. I do not need to tell you how that was viewed by us westerners. That was one custom that I never got used to, nor did I accept it. No, in America, men simply did not go around holding each other's hands. We would hold hands with our female friends, but that was as far as it was going. As a result and not wanting to offend them, I developed a habit of keeping my hands in my pockets when out in public. These guys would even hold hands when riding their bicycles down the road. I am not at all sure that they were gay, but I know that that is how I viewed men holding hands.

I never did get used to having the young kids constantly peeking in my windows when I was home or when I was on a bus or train. Actually, I grew tired of having eyes on me constantly. I got to the point that I would throw water on them when they would come to my house back in the village. On the trains, I resorted to more drastic measures. The train widows were open except for the bars across the openings. I would tire of them staring at me whenever we arrived at another station stop, so I started smashing them in the face when they came to my window. I am not proud of what I did. You could hold it in and become even more frustrated or you could let it out and maintain some semblance of sanity. I chose to release mine and not let it build up to the point that I was no longer in control of my emotions. Survival is a bitch!

Back to the training we received once we arrived in Udaipur. We were housed at a youth hostel that was connected to the local university. By this time, it was decided that we would concentrate on the use of hybrid seeds and chemical fertilizers to increase crop yields, rather than poultry, for which we were trained. We needed to know when to fertilize and how to irrigate to successfully raise crops. Water was always an issue for the farmers in Rajasthan. One must keep in mind that we had to be successful in pushing this hybrid seed revolution because, should a farmer agree to plant these seeds, he would have to have access to sufficient water or run the risk of losing his entire crop. The local wheat did not require as much water as did the hybrid wheat. It often involved a political decision as to whether our experimental farm was going to get the water needed to irrigate those plots.

Our training at the local university was designed to acquaint us with the local power brokers who could assure that our crops got the amount of water needed to flourish. The local Block Development Officer (BDO) was the key player in this political

system. In all too many instances, he was not on our side. He operated using fear and intimidation to get the farmers to go along with the program. He was not convinced that we knew what we were doing or that they needed our services. The decision to bring us in was made at a level much higher than him. He was simply told that we would be coming, and he had to make sure that we had adequate housing in our assigned villages.

My particular BDO was a real character. He tolerated us, but was not overly enthused to have us meddling in his affairs. It took me the better part of a year to figure out what motivated him to cooperate. He came to me one day asking for a favor. He had gotten his hands on a Sears catalog and wanted to know if I could get my "rich" family or friends in the states to get some items and send them to him. I contacted my sister and had her order the items from the catalog and send them to me. When I received the shipment, I contacted the BDO to let him know that his things had arrived. He wanted me to come to his office and bring the package. After he received that package, I was one of his favorite people and he stayed off my case the remainder of my stay in that small village of Thur. Moreover, my farmer always got the water he needed to irrigate his crops.

Before we broke training camp and shipped out to our respective villages, we were sent to a village for two weeks to get us accustomed to village life. Steve McKenzie, David Bauer or maybe it was Bob Proffit, and I were assigned to a small village. Boy, was that an experience! The first night there we got settled in our little living quarters. As fate would have it, we needed to go to the bathroom to relieve ourselves. There was one problem. There was no latrine, so we had to go in the open. That was an experience we had heard about, but had not experienced. We waited until dark before we attempted to answer nature's call. We wandered over to the back of the courtyard and settled in to do our business. Midway through the process, we heard these familiar snorts of a bullock. Then he charged, and there we were with our pants down around our ankles. We did not have much time to react so we grabbed our pants and our toilet tissues and ran like hell to the room just ahead of this charging bull. That was a close call, or as I refer to it, experience number one.

We were issued a small Coleman stove for cooking. That was not a major problem because I had learned how to cook before I graduated from high school. The problem came when we had to try to find some food to purchase in that small village. They ate, for the most part, some *dahl* (legumes) and *rotie* (a flat bread). We knew we would not be able to find any meat, but had hoped we would be able to find some fruit and vegetables. We ended up having to go into Udaipur to buy food. One day, and I am a bit fuzzy about the facts, we were out in the village and Steve did not go because he had a stomachache. Unfortunately for him, the last person out of the room closed the door and put the latch on from the outside. Steve was unable to get out in order to relieve himself. When the roommates returned, he was not feeling too well, as you might imagine. David really freaked out and said he was not sure he was going to be able to complete this experience. In fact, he did not complete the two weeks and decided he needed to return to the states.

The rest of us completed our two weeks and returned to the youth hostel to finish the remainder of our training. Upon the completion of training, we were assigned a village as our permanent site. I was sent to a small village about 15 miles from Udaipur, named Thur. My bicycle and I became very good friends. I would jump on that bike anytime I got fed up with village life and head to the city, Udaipur. There I could get ice cold cokes and orange Fanta. After the bike ride into the city, that was usually my first stop where I would rehydrate. Next to the soda stand was a nice restaurant called Berry's. There we could get a decent fried or scrambled egg and toast. We could also get real good Indian food. All the fellows would come to that location whenever they left their village and ventured into the city. Berry's restaurant was our meeting place. We spent a lot of our monthly allowance in Berry's so I am sure he liked seeing us come. He was a wonderful man who spoke good English and made us feel at home.

Some of the fellows could not come into the city and return to their village the same day, but had to stay overnight. Usually an overnight stay would turn into a couple of nights stay. Now, Steve had an impossible situation. It took him two days to get from his village to the city and the same amount of time going back to his village. It got real bad for Steve, and he eventually decided to give up and go home. Bob Profit was one of my closest friends, and he, too, ended up leaving early. He fell in love about the time we were to ship out to India and simply got homesick. He left early and returned to the states anticipating getting married. I do not know whatever happened to him. Had it not been for the fact that I could jump on my bike and get to the city at a moment's notice, I might not have found the resolve to stick it out. I often found myself staying in my room, days at a time, without as much as venturing to the post office to retrieve my mail. The post office was next door to my house!

The postmaster was a Moslem and a real sweetheart of a man. He would notice that I had not come out of my room and would bring me my mail or would send one of the young kids by with a cup of tea. When I would get up the nerve to venture outside the walls of my house, he would ask me to come and talk to him. He was extremely good for my mental health. We would often sit and talk for hours at a time. He was not political in any of these conversations. He was the one who told me of the assassinations of Martin Luther King, Jr. and Bobby Kennedy. I am not sure where he got his news, but he seemed to always be on top of things. I only had a citizens band radio where I could pick up Voice of America sometimes and BBC. Once a month, I would venture into the city and buy a copy of *Newsweek* or *Time* and, if I was really lucky, I would be able to find a copy of the *International Herald Tribune*. That is how I was able to keep up with what was going on in the western world.

The train stations did have an amazing list of bestseller books and I spent a small fortune there. I read more during my two years in India than I had read in my entire life. We developed the habit of passing books among our group. We would have rather stimulating discussions of the books we were reading over a cold Golden Eagle beer or some local booze. I learned to play bridge and chess during those stays in Udaipur. This was real heady stuff. I think most of us started our writing careers during our stay in India. We were spending less and less time in our respective villages. In fact, we were spending so much time in Udaipur that we found and subsequently rented a nice house so we would not have to stay at the hotel when we were in town. It seemed like every time we came to town, we would find another volunteer already at the house. If memory serves me correctly, I think Tom McDermott took up residence in that house. Somehow, Bill O'Connor (the regional PC director) got wind of what we had done and moved quickly to put an end to our little adventure. He forced us to shut the house down and return to our villages or run the risk of being terminated. Back to our villages we went.

My village was not an altogether bad situation for me because the schoolteachers at the elementary school lived in the village and would come over every night. They did a wonderful job of helping me learn Hindi. I also improved my ability to speak Hindi by going to the Indian movies. They liked to come by and listen to my radio. We did a lot of things together, and, as a matter of fact, they would be disappointed when I went into the city and did not return. When I could not muster up the courage to go out and visit some of the farmers, I would go over to the elementary school. Initially, I was able to secure some soy meal and start a school lunch program for the kids. That went over quite well. This gave me an excuse to visit the school daily, if I was in my village. I started a vegetable garden program at the school. We grew some really nice vegetables, and when it was time to harvest them, we would prepare lunch and feed the children. For some of the children, that was the best meal they received.

Remember, we were there on an assignment to introduce the farmers to the "hybrid seed" revolution. I reasoned that I was making a significant contribution because I was teaching the young kids how to plant and grow vegetables for consumption. At least their families would be able to eat. Also, I was teaching the future farmers how to sustain their families, or at least I convinced myself that was what I was doing. I felt that I needed

some tangible accomplishment to justify my stay in that village. I was receiving a tremendous education, from being in India, but what was I contributing to them?

I contacted a school in Colorado that raised money to construct schools abroad. I wrote a proposal and got funds to build an elementary school. Up to that point, the school in my village was a one-room school. I got my friend, the BDO, to come to the village and solicit a commitment for labor and skilled-craftsmen to build the school. He agreed, and I paid for the materials and supplies and completed the construction of the school. This was a big deal and made my stay in India seem like it was worthwhile and that I had made a contribution. I wish I could say as much for the hybrid seed deal. I am not so sure anyone planted the hybrid, high yield seeds or used chemical fertilizers after I

left the village. However, I do know that they planted another vegetable garden and continued the school lunch program.

At some point, Peace Corps decided to establish an advisory committee for the Tunisia Region. I was selected/elected as the Peace Corps representative by my group. We met on a fairly regular basis in New Delhi and I was able to fly up for the meetings. I enjoyed those meetings immensely. I got a chance to experience things in New Delhi that broadened my perspective beyond imagination. I was able to go to some Embassy functions. I met a couple of the Marines on duty as guards at the Embassy. A particular African-American marine from Pittsburgh, PA befriended me and would take me to the commissary and buy me booze. I would bring the booze back and would make it available to the guys in my group. They thoroughly enjoyed having a nice Canadian Club or a Johnny Walker.

One interesting story concerning those gatherings involved a volunteer named Roger W., a member of a later group stationed in Udaipur. Roger claimed to be a connoisseur of good liquor, among other things, and was a bit obnoxious about his 'skills.' One day, we decided to set him up. We took an empty Johnny Walker Black and filled it with an Indian whisky, Ambassador.

When we gathered at our "house" in Udaipur one weekend, we brought out the Johnny Walker Black bottle, the one filled with the local booze.

Roger, true to form, took one swig of his drink and declared that he was a connoisseur and that this was exquisite, that it was too good to be called a mere liquor, that it should be called a liqueur. We could hardly contain ourselves and finally someone told him how full of shit we thought he was and that the liqueur he had proclaimed was nothing but an Indian whiskey. He had a lovely wife, and to this day I still wonder how he scored her. Perhaps, it was his propensity for verbosity that swept her off her feet. However, we had a wonderful laugh at his expense. I still laugh, forty years later, every time I think of that incident.

Another interesting thing happened to me in Bombay when a group of us from Rajasthan visited some of our fellow volunteers from Maharashtra. We were at this restaurant where they had a band playing. The band had a person singing with them. The singer was dressed in a two-piece bathing suit. We all thought the singer was a woman. The singer came over to our table and tried to get me to come and dance with her. I protested that I was with a friend and would not be dancing. They insisted that I go on and dance. I went on and later discovered that this singer was not a female, but a male. The joke was on me and everyone had a big laugh on me.

There are so many wonderful experiences that I could share from my stay in India such as the many nights we spent at the Charter House drowning our sorrows with a cold beer, to a trip to Nanital and Schimla. We went to Agra once and saw the Taj Mahal during a full-moon—truly an experience to behold. I want to go back to India and take my wife so we can experience it together. When and if we do that, we will not repeat some of the things I did when we were there.

One of our stateside Hindi instructors was from Agra, and we visited his home for dinner. While the food and hospitality were excellent, something about that trip was not good for Don Nordin and me. We left Agra and returned to New Delhi where we were scheduled for some new training. I developed a fever and a headache. Don and I became so sick that the Peace Corps doctor had us admitted to the hospital, which was quite an experience. The nurse came in and took my temperature and when she read the thermometer, she dropped the tray and ran from the room. A short time later, a bunch of doctors and others came into the room and started working on me. I later learned that my temperature was 104 degrees. They started taking blood on a regular basis. Dr. Grossman was overseeing our treatment, but the locals were drawing the blood. I think they used the needles over and over again and they were dull. I ended up with a large scab on my arm where these needles were doing a job on my arm. They were sending my blood back to the States for testing. To make a long story short, I was in the hospital for a week before I was well enough to be dismissed. I never did find out what made me sick or what I was diagnosed with. I was glad to get out of that hospital and return to my village, the same village that I left every chance I could to go to the city. But, after a week in that hospital, the village was not bad.

The religious holidays and festivals were colorful and different. The weddings were interesting events. We were invited by one of our language instructors, Amar, to accompany her family to Punjab to attend her brother's wedding. He was an officer in the Indian military and had a splendid wedding ceremony. We had a ball and spent some wonderful times with Amar, her sisters Muna and Batchu, and their mom over on Radio Colony. They were the most wonderful family I met in all my time in India. They were all university educated, and I have often wondered what happened to each of them. I trust God that their lives continued to be enriched according to His glory. Bill Whitesell, Tom Corbett, and Michael Simonds and I would visit that family anytime we were in Delhi.

All of my experiences served to enrich me, and I only hope I did some small amount of good for the wonderful people of India. I do not remember very much about the debriefing sessions we had when we came to New Delhi to prepare for our return trip home. What I do remember very vividly is the intense heat while there for our final days. It was 120 degrees, so hot that we had to roll up the widows during cab rides, even though they were not air-conditioned. Don Nordin and I decided to travel together on our return trip. We had interesting experiences in Istanbul when we came in contact with some local entrepreneurs trying to market a couple of the local women. We were staying at the Istanbul Hilton, which was more than a step up from what we had experienced the past two years. We escaped that situation without any major harm. We went to a number of places that bear no long or lasting memory for me.

We did, however, go a few places that do hold a lasting memory for me. We had fun in Athens and were able to see some incredible sites. Once again, Don and I found ourselves in a sticky situation when we went to a local bar to have a cold beer. We had no sooner ordered our drinks when two young women came over and asked if they could join us. We said yes and the waitress came over and asked if we wanted to buy them a drink. We told the waitress that they could have what we were drinking. We had been in India for the past two years, but we were not stupid. The ladies spoke to the waitress in Greek and off she went to get their drinks. When the waitress returned, she did not have beers, but something else. It did not concern me because I was only going to pay for what I ordered. When she brought us our bill, the bill was something unbelievable. We inquired why the bill was so much. Long story short, she told us that the ladies had ordered champagne. We asked her what we ordered, and she said we agreed to buy them a drink. We said that we told her to give them what we were drinking. We refused to pay the exorbitant amount she was asking. She went and got the owner or bouncer. It did not matter to me who she brought over.

We told him what our instructions were to the waitress and that we were only going to pay for what we ordered. He said we would have to pay the amount on the check. I told Don that we were going to pay for what we ordered and no more. I then told him that we were going to leave after paying for what we ordered and to stand back-to-back with me and I would get us out of that bar. I was confident that I could handle anything in front of us, and all I needed was for him to make sure no one came in from behind.

The owner/bouncer said we could not leave before paying the entire bill. I told him that we had paid for everything we had ordered and if he expected to get any more, he had better get it from those who ordered it. I told him that we were leaving and if need be we would do it over his trampled body if he got in the way.

Now, you must remember that I had just spent two years in India where the sun had further darkened my skin and the constant bike rides had honed my body to appear well equipped to handle any light work I might need to perform. I guess this guy felt that it would not be in his best interest to take us on. Out of the dark he said, ok, ok, just pay the amount of the ticket and we could take the girls back to our hotel for our pleasure. We weren't having any part of that and let him know of our lack of interest in his proposal. He finally stepped aside, and we left. We ate some really good food, but stayed clear of the women and that particular bar. We did not spend too much more time in Athens. We proceeded to go to Rome, where we managed to stay away from the local entrepreneurs, if they existed.

While we were engaged in those highly intellectual discussions back at our house in Udaipur, our conversations invariably shifted to where we were going to do our graduate studies. Until that time, I had not given much thought to graduate school. But because we were all competitive, I also applied to graduate school. Dr. Theodore Speighner, chairman of the geography department at NCC, was a strong advocate for graduate studies. I wrote him and told him that I wanted to go to graduate school. He sent me applications to Kansas State, Clark, Marquette, Michigan, and the University of Cincinnati (UC). I was accepted at Clark, Kansas State, and Cincinnati. Kansas State offered a fellowship paying me $2400 and Cincinnati offered me a fellowship that was paying $2800 plus a tuition remission of fees. I was good enough at math to know that $2800 was more than $2400, so I accepted the fellowship to do my graduate studies at the University of Cincinnati. I was able to boast of being accepted to do my graduate work at UC.

It turned out to be the best decision I ever made because that is where I met a young lady who would later become my wife and the mother of my son. But before that was possible, I had to overcome a couple of major hurdles. Cincinnati required their graduate students to undertake a personal interview as a requirement for acceptance. I was half a world away and unable to do a personal interview. Dr. Speighner had sent a couple of other students to Cincinnati to study geography. He contacted Dr. Howard Stafford, Chair of the department at Cincinnati and made arrangements for one of our fellow students to do the interview in my absence. Phillip Kithcart did the interview for me and I was accepted. He remains one of my very best friends today. Not only did he do the interview for me, he contacted my mom and told her that when I returned home from India that he would have housing and transportation available for me. When I went to Cincinnati, he picked me up at the airport and gave me a place to stay until I could draw my first check and find a place to live. He let me use all of his books and gave me copies of all his statistics papers. I did not know anything about statistics, yet all graduate students had to take a stats course. Had it not been for his largess, I do not know whether I would have been able to pass that course.

I needed to get some wheels, and my father made arrangements for me to buy a brand spanking new Chevrolet Chevelle Super Sport. While I was in India, I had $75 per month taken from my money and sent to my baby brother who was in college at NCC. He subsequently graduated and took a job with the Social Security Administration. He agreed to make the payments on my car while I attended graduate school. My car was new, and he was driving a used car. That is indicative of how my family rallied behind each other to augment what our parents tried to do to usher us through school and onto a better way of life. My brother and I are inseparable to this day. I went on to complete my graduate studies and ultimately earned a masters degree. Keep in mind that this is from a person who barely made it through high school, and had it not been for the fact that my father bought land and built a house, I might well have not finished high school. The line between success and failure is truly a thin one.

Back to my return trip home! Don and I split up somewhere in Europe and I came on home. I landed at Logan in Boston and I called my oldest sister, the registered nurse, in Washington, DC and told her that I would be arriving at Dulles. She told me to come on over to her house once I arrived. Dulles seemed like it was in another state; actually it was, in Virginia. In any event, I cashed in some travelers checks and caught a taxi to her house. She greeted me and immediately asked what I wanted to eat. She had just taken a pan of homemade biscuits out of the oven. I looked at those pretty, brown biscuits and asked her if she had any peanut butter and milk. She put a gallon of cold milk and a jar of peanut butter on the table and that was my first meal back in the states. I had not had a cold glass of milk in so long that I finished off that gallon of milk as well as that pan of biscuits. That was like heaven to me. I stayed with her for a couple days, and my mom insisted that I come on home.

I flew home to Durham for a wonderful reunion with my family. It was a bit strange, but I quickly adjusted to being home. I called my girlfriend and told her I was home. She agreed to come by and pick me up. I was getting excited (in more ways than one). After all two years was a long time. I could not wait for her to arrive, yet it seemed like it took a week for her to get there. She finally arrived and we went for a ride to get reacquainted. After we rode around for awhile, I was getting a bit anxious and ready to move forward. Perhaps sensing my mood she said there was something she needed to tell me. I eagerly said fine, what is it? She proceeded to tell me that about three weeks earlier she had met a young man, and they had decided to get married. That was the furthest thing from my mind. I thought she was going to tell me that she was on her period or something. After I picked myself up from the floor, I asked if it was what she really wanted to do and she said yes. I was left with nothing to do except accept our fate. It was not as difficult for me as it might have been had I planned to stay in Durham and work or go to graduate school. Since I was going away again, I was able to get over the shock. I left early for Cincinnati in an effort to put this behind me and close that chapter of my life.

I told my mom about the situation and said I was going to get on out to Cincinnati to get myself ready for school. She asked if I was going to be ok and I said sure, I'll be ok. She asked me if I was mad at the young lady and I told her that I was not angry, just disappointed. I could not be angry with her because she had no way of letting me know she had fallen in love with someone else because I was traveling through Europe when it happened. She and I remain friends to this day, and I respect her for the choice she made. She had not lied to me or led me on knowing that she was going in another direction. I was a bit detached when I went to Cincinnati and did not let anyone get too close to me. I dated, but did not get too involved. I guess I did not know if I could trust women.

I entered graduate school because the other guys were going to graduate school. I was duly influenced by the other volunteers that I served with in India. I had no one else to influence me because I had already gone further in school than anyone else in my family. Why did I choose geography? Because I had better grades in geography and "Doc" was actively involved in help-ing his majors and minors get into graduate school. I minored in geography, and must have made an impression on him because when I contacted him about my desire to go to graduate school, he did not hesitate in telling me where to apply and made sure I had the applications necessary to do so. Other than "Doc", I owe my decision to go to graduate school to my association with the wonderful people I served with as Peace Corps volunteers in Udaipur, Rajasthan. I am eternally gratefully to all of you for inspiring me to reach a little higher.

It was that decision to attend graduate school in Cincinnati that brought Lelani and me together. I had dated, but nothing serious. Then one December, we were invited to a party by some young ladies who had attended many of the parties we held. On this particular night, one of the young ladies pressed her room-mate to go with her to a party. This roommate turned out to be Lelani Butler. Sharon told her that there were a group of really interesting guys in graduate school at UC who would be at the party. Lelani was not really that keen on going and meeting anyone because she had just broken off a relationship with a former classmate. Somehow, Sharon prevailed on her, and she agreed to attend the party. When I saw her, I was impressed. She was pretty and could dance really well. All the guys kept dancing with her all night, and I was having a difficult time getting to talk to this pretty young lady. I would dance with her and at the completion of a song, would resume my conversation with her. Before we could get very far in our conversation, someone else would approach her for another dance. Finally, I decided that if I expected to get an uninterrupted conversation with this young lady, I was going to have to isolate her from the others.

I took her in the bedroom of the one-bedroom apartment and locked the door so we could talk. She was really interested in what I had to say about my experience in India. I asked her for her number, and she was so sure that I would not call her that she actually gave me her real phone number. She later told me that she never gave her real phone number to guys she was just meeting. We exchanged numbers, and she said she never expected to hear from me again. She could not imagine some- one with my experiences taking the time to call her and show any real interest. After I got her digits, I unlocked the door to the bedroom and we returned to the party and dancing. At the end of the party, I walked her to her car and asked her if it would be okay if I called her. She told me that she would be away from her home for a few days having a medical procedure, but that she would be home by a certain date. On that date, I did not call her. I waited until the next day and called her. I did not want to appear too eager.

She was quite surprised to receive a call from me. I asked if I could come over and she said yes. We started dating from that point and continued to do so until I took a job in Washington, DC. We saw each other every day and truly cared for each other. I stopped dating anyone other than Lelani and was totally into her. She even typed my MA thesis, and we spent an awful lot of time together. I later took a job in Washington, DC, and she just knew that would be the end of our relationship. I told her that that was nonsense, that I wanted to marry her. She had to go back to complete her graduate studies, and I had to go to DC. I told her that when she completed her studies I wanted her to come to DC to be with me. She completed her studies and came to DC, and we were together. She did not have a job, but we figured we could solve that problem. She was able to get jobs, but not very good paying ones. Finally, she was able to land a job with the National Association of Broadcasters.

I was working for the Laborers' International Union of North America in their education and training program. We provided health and safety training for the members of the union. I was traveling continuously throughout the United States. Lelani called me one day and asked me to have lunch with her, and I did. She was a bit uneasy, and I sensed something was eating at her. I asked what was on her mind. She told me that she thought we should start seeing other people. I did not ask why, but told her that I needed some time to think about it. I thought about it for maybe fifteen or twenty minutes and decided that that would not work. I knew her well enough to know that she did not operate well in a relationship with multiple partners. I called her and asked her to join me for lunch.

During lunch, I told her that I had given her proposal some thought and that I was not in agreement. I told her that it meant either we were going to move our relationship forward, or she was going to drop me because I knew she was not going to be able to juggle more than one man in her life. She asked what I intended to do. I told her that we should take a weekend trip and take inventory of our lives. She agreed under one condition. I asked what that condition was and she said if we agreed not to discuss our relationship. Naturally, I agreed. We went to King's Dominion, an amusement park in Doswell, VA and had a marvelous time. We realized that although we had been together for more than seven years that was the first time we had ever stayed in a hotel together. We did not mention our relationship all weekend and had a wonderful time.

I secured tickets to go to New York to see *The Whiz*. We took the train up and attended the play and went shopping. We called David Dell, another member of 44B, and had him come to the hotel and have dinner with us. We had a great time that weekend and took the train back to DC. That Monday morning, I went shopping and bought her an engagement ring and an airplane ticket. Armed with those two items, I called her and asked her to join me for lunch. At lunch, I told her that I had given her proposal careful consideration and that I rejected it out of hand. She appeared puzzled at my insistence that we would not agree to start seeing other people. She asked me what I intended to do to prevent it from happening and I gave her the ring and told her that we were going to get married. I then handed her an airline ticket and told her to go home to Kentucky and tell her mom the good news. This happened the week before the 4th of July. She looked at me and asked when. I told her that it would be either her birthday or mine. Her birthday was August 17th, and she said that was too soon. I said fine, then it will be on my birthday. My birthday is September 15th and we were married on that Saturday, September 16, 1978.

Marrying Lelani was the best decision I have ever made in life. She went home and announced to her parents that we were getting married, and her mother laughed in her face because she had concluded that Lelani would never get married. I called my parents and told them that we were getting married. They were excited because they loved Lelani. A week or so later, I called home and my mother asked me who was going to be my best man. I told her I did not know, but I probably would ask my brother. She asked me if I had considered asking my father, that he had expressed an interest in serving as my best man. That thrilled me more than anyone could possibly know. My father was a very special person in my life and I could not imagine anyone as lucky as I was to have my father be the best man in my wedding. Lelani also loved my father, who treated her as another daughter. My father had a stroke the next day and never left the hospital. He passed away, and I must say that I had a very heavy heart at my wedding. On his death-bed, he asked me to wear his wedding band and to always take care of Lelani. I was proud to wear his wedding band and to pledge that I would always love and take care of her. I sat Lelani down and told her that I was

129

going to marry once and that I would always be married. I told her that if she was not committed to doing the same, now was the time to back out and call it off. She said she was cool with that and here we are, 33 years later, more in love than ever. We have one son who is the joy of our lives. She is the most outstanding mother any child could ever want. Our son adores her and he, in turn, means the world to both of us. Lelani embodies the spirit of through thick and thin, 'til death do us part.

I think Peace Corps helped me to realize that commitment and responsibilities are personal attributes that, if followed, will sustain you during tough times. Living in that village I learned that I did not have to have all the answers all the time, but I had to always seek answers to every situation. That mindset has served me well in more ways than I care to remember. I learned that I could not pass the buck, that I had to accept the responsibility for my life circumstances. I learned that when I made a commitment to someone, I no longer had an option of backing out. We have taught our son the same thing. I remember us telling him that if he studied hard and made good grades, we would send him to the school of his choice for undergraduate studies. We were put to the test when he graduated from high school. He was a high school All-American in track and I kind of wanted him to run in college. However, he had been running since he was seven years old and was tired. He was an outstanding high school student also, becoming president of the Student Government Association in his senior year.

He announced that he wanted to attend the University of North Carolina at Chapel Hill. He did get an early decision award at Carolina but they were not giving full scholarships. He received full scholarship offers from four other schools. I remember very vividly one night after we attended a particular university recruitment activity and they gave him a full scholarship offer on the spot. He turned to me and said "Dad my life has just become real complicated". I asked him what he meant by that. He said he knew we did not have the money to send him to school and although he had a full scholarship offer from this university, he wanted to attend Carolina. I explained to him that his life did not become more complicated, it just became easy. He asked me how I reached that conclusion. I told him that now that he had that offer in hand, he could use it to bargain with Carolina. He still seemed puzzled because he really wanted to go to Carolina, and he knew they were only offering a partial scholarship and a loan. We would be required to pay the remainder.

I sat him down and told him that we made him a commitment early on and we were going to keep our commitment to him because he had done his part. He had done well in school and was an outstanding, all around student. The agreement was that if he held up his end of the agreement, he could go to the school of his choice. Long story short, he went to Carolina and received an outstanding education. A couple of his teammates/classmates went to different schools and ran track. James refused to run, even at Carolina, but he was able to do internships and upon graduation, he had job offers. He graduated on the 15th of May 2005 and started a job with the William Wrigley Company on the 17th. He also had an offer from the Phillip Morris Company. His teammates were not able to get jobs because they did not have any experience; they had to train and run during summers. We had a responsibility to keep our commitment to our son. This is a lesson that he carries with him until this day. I am his hero; he looks to me as his role model.

I took that same approach to my work life. If I gave you my word, that was all I had, and I was not going to allow anyone or anything to cause me to go back on my word. I wrote my MA thesis on urban transportation, and I have never worked a day in transportation. My first job was at the University of Cincinnati in the Education Development Program as a counselor. One of the staff people told me one day that the thing that separated me from the other black males on the university faculty and staff was that I knew who I was and where I wanted to go. I am not entirely sure that I knew all that, but I am sure I gave that impression. I guess she was right because I did know who I was and where I was going. I did not always know how I was going to get there. I think I made a difference in a lot of young people's lives while at UC.

At the Laborers International Union, I traveled and experienced things I never imagined possible. Perhaps the highlight of my tenure with the Laborers was being nominated by the General President to serve on the National Environmental Justice Advisory Council (NEJAC) for the United States EPA. We were constantly involved in cases involving industries' misuse or violation of the Clean Water and Clean Air Acts. The NEJAC held hearings around the country and took testimony from various stakeholder groups concerning permits and their disparate impacts on communities of color. I was on one of the subcommittees that developed a model plan for public participation in permitting. That plan was accepted by the EPA, and promulgated to all Federal agencies. That was a major accomplishment, in which I take a great deal of pride.

After serving on the Council for two years, I was voted in as the Chair of the NEJAC. I was in the position where I provided EPA Administrator Carol Browner advice on matters involving environmental justice. I was the first black person to serve as Chair of NEJAC. The work we did there was the most important work I was involved with in my entire professional work life. Nothing I studied formally ever prepared me for this very important work. However, the same reasons that attracted me to the Peace Corps were no doubt the qualities that motivated me to take up the causes we accepted at NEJAC. It seems almost prophetic that I would get involved in the area known as environmental justice. After all, the environmental justice movement is rooted in the transport and illegal disposal of toxic waste along roadways in North Carolina, my home state. In 1978, oil-laced PCB was dumped along roadways in fourteen of the state's counties. When those same roads were cleaned up in 1982, the state needed a disposal site for the contaminated soil. State officials decide on Warren County, NC, a predominantly poor, African American community as the dump site.

In 1990, Bob Bullard published his book *Dumping In Dixie: Race, Class and Environmental Quality* in which he asserted

that all communities are not created, nor are they treated, equally. If a community is poor, inner city, or inhabited by people of color, chances are it will receive less protection than an affluent, suburban, white community. What started out as a community-based grassroots struggle against toxins, facility location, and transport of waste, blossomed into a national environmental justice movement. We concluded that environmental justice is achieved when communities of color and low-income communities are not singled out for the siting and permitting of waste and other pollution generating and emitting facilities instead of communities inhabited by non-minorities and more affluent people. The work that we undertook has been written about widely and is available for anyone interested in learning more about this very important work.

Life is filled with choices. We all make numerous choices daily and must realize that all choices have consequences. As a result, we should weigh all our decisions and choices because they will invariably affect countless numbers of people we do not know and may never know. Our actions, undoubtedly, will out-live us; so be careful what you do. In that same respect, I can imagine that an awful lot of what we did in India is having an impact on the lives of untold numbers of Indians today. We may well never see them or get to know them, but our actions, thoughts, and decisions during our tenure probably still affect life in India today. To the extent that impact is positive, our tenure will have been worthwhile. That is the nature of the legacy we left behind as Peace Corps volunteers.

CHAPTER 5

A Nomad Returns

Tom McDermott

My problem in writing lies in not knowing where or how a story begins—or ends. I have the same problem with history. After all, what is history, if not a set of interweaving stories—none having a beginning, and none having an end? I have a choice here, so let me start in 1989. Let's call it a moment "in the middle"—at age 43.

Nairobi—1989—Age 43

I opened my eyes. I guessed it was mid-afternoon by the way the sun was coming in the windows. Above me hung a neatly tied white mosquito net—around me, white sheets. On both sides of me there stretched a row of identical beds with identical mosquito nets and identical white sheets—a hospital ward. What hospital? Where? How did I get here? All of these questions were beyond me for the moment. In time I learned that I was in Nairobi, medevaced there with typhoid. Slowly I started to remember—falling sick in Mogadishu, my wife caring for me through the fevers, the Russian doctor, the injections, and being told that I had missed my own farewell party. Isn't missing your own farewell something like missing your own funeral?

My idle mind wandered, reflecting on the Somalis, thinking how tough they are as people, not easy to like or even to get to know. However, once you get to know them, and they to know you, they are extraordinarily warm and open people. I liked them, liked their sense of independence, even their pride and confounded arrogance. Nomads, I thought—like me, people with no fixed address. Loners, like me—people with no alliances beyond their clan.

Somalis were not the first nomads I had come to know. I had worked with others in western Sudan, eastern Bangladesh, Indonesia, and India. What defined them was not so much their constant movements as it was their stability. Those who don't know them often imagine that nomads move aimlessly. The truth is that nomads move in circles, returning every few years to where they have stayed before. Okay, not exactly circles. Nomadic lives are more like spirals, circles never quite closed, each separated in time. They return to more or less the same place, but it can never be quite the same, as both the nomad and the place have changed.

I finally had time to think—something I had so little of in Somalia, and now, suddenly, so much of it. The past year had been enough adventure for a lifetime, to say the least—the outbreak of a brutal civil war, an army massacre of civilians in the north, secret police searching for members of my staff, other staff shot up and then dragged by camel liter across the desert to refugee camps in Ethiopia, Russian agents and American agents. Yes, enough adventures for a lifetime. I tried to put it all in the context of my times in other war zones, but could not. During those times, I was only a witness to the aftermath—the return of refugees, the attempts to rebuild and restart. This time, I was not only a witness, but an unwilling participant in the beginning of a war that would drag on for many, many years. It was a feeling akin to watching a car begin to slide down an icy hill, knowing where the passengers would end up, yet also knowing that there was no way to help them stop before they hit the bottom.

How I loved being there in the thick of things at this critical moment—the rush, the adrenalin, being in the midst of a crisis that few in the world knew or cared about. I felt needed, able to do a job others could not or would not attempt.

The transfer orders had come as a shock. Didn't they understand that I was needed here at this critical moment? The voice on the phone had told me what they always say in these situations: yes, yes, you are doing an important job, but now we need you somewhere else. Of course, then came the obvious argument; Somalia is no place for a family. They knew I couldn't argue on that one.

Somewhere in that long chain of assignments after India—Indonesia, Bangladesh, Nigeria, and Thailand; back for second tours in Bangladesh and Indonesia, Boston for a master's degree.—Somewhere along that long trail I had found myself in Sudan where, by some miracle, I met and married Viviane. The next assignment was Saudi Arabia where, by a second miracle, our son, Dan, was born. I was still a nomad, but now one with company on the journey. And yes, like it or not, it was time to fold the tent and move on.

Why India? I had promised myself never to work there again. For one thing, I knew the reputation—the Indian Government and the United Nations—two giant bureaucracies met in one huge country to produce....what? Big mission, big bureaucracy, big problems! I liked small offices where I was in charge and where I could be forgotten by headquarters. I liked small governments, however loathsome—ones I could get to know and who could come to know me. This would never happen in India.

I had been back for brief visits, to Delhi at the beginning of the war with Pakistan in 1971 and to Calcutta, while working in Bangladesh in 1973. I never went to the village, never to Bhuder, to Kherwara, or even to Udaipur. This time I knew that I would have to go back and close the nomad's circle.

I thought back to my first "transfer orders" to India in 1966. I opened my mail box in the student center one day and found a letter. "Congratulations," it read, I had been selected to join an advanced training course that summer for Peace Corps volunteers going to India the following year. I joked later to my friends that on the application I had said that I would serve anywhere in Africa or Asia, but had forgotten that India was part of Asia. This was not true, of course, but the fact was that I had wanted to go to Africa or to the Far East. India held no special charm for me. Moreover, the group was to work on poultry—

poultry! I had hoped to teach in a school. What did I know then, or even now, about chickens?

A year later the objective of the group had morphed into the introduction of high-yielding varieties of wheat and corn to village farmers. Corn farming! That had given my grandparents, who had grown up on farms, a good laugh. This kid didn't know which end of the hoe went in the ground. And that was true. What could I, a spoiled kid from the suburbs, teach a farmer about farming?

The afternoon turned to evening and the sun began to fade. I closed my eyes and thought of that young man who 22 years ago had arrived in the village of Bhuder. He was me, but a different me. What in the world was he doing there? Had he done anything useful? Years from now, would I look back on these times in Somalia and ask myself the same question? Did we ever really change things? Perhaps we were just voyeurs, watching dramas in languages we would never understand? Were we nomads, coming, looking, then moving on? Sleep came again—not an easy sleep, but a deep one.

Bhuder—1967—Age 21

Two young men stand by the side of a truck, helping unload all their worldly goods—for each a bicycle, rope bed, lantern, primus stove, suitcase, a trunk of books and some basic foodstuffs. It is mid-afternoon in Kherwara and there is no one around. The local government offices (the *Panchayat Samiti* or, more often, just called "the Block") stand empty, looking desolate—perhaps abandoned. Had someone made a mistake and delivered them to the wrong town? Even the town looks dead and perhaps abandoned. The truck drives off, back to Udaipur.

They wait on a bench. Hours pass, and soon they have exhausted the water in their canteens. Finally the Block Development Officer (BDO) and a few of his staff arrive. The officials seem perplexed. Yes, they knew some foreigners would be coming, but not today, or anytime soon. Now what do we do with you? The weariness on the faces of the two young foreigners must be convincing, because eventually, hospitality overcomes inertia, and they are given food and a room where they can sleep for the night.

The next morning they separate. Bicycles, beds and other possessions are loaded on two jeeps. One is to head north and west, the other south and east, far from each other and from others in their group. The two young men say goodbye and good luck. The BDO, young and affable, accompanies one of them to a village called "Bhuder", 20 kilometers to the north and west.

The jeep rolls along the highway for 15 kilometers and then turns off on what begins as a dirt road, but soon becomes just a path over the hills. The jeep follows the track, though at times the young man wonders how. Finally, they top a steep pass, and there below—at least according to the BDO—lies Bhuder. As they draw closer, he sees that the village is just a collection of a few houses and a shop. Overnight, officialdom must have kicked into motion as the BDO announces that he had arranged for the young man to stay in a room over the village's one small shop.

The shopkeeper and his son are there to show him the room. The room is just that—a room just big enough for the rope bed and a small table and chair. In the front of the room one can see an open space and a square hole through which pokes a rickety ladder. There is a trap door, which the landlord explains via the BDO must be closed and bolted at night.

He learns that his new landlords are Jains, and that they live nearby. In time he will learn that the Jains are themselves foreigners here, separated from the big Jain community at the temples in Rikhabdev—five kilometers to the east. In addition to the shop where the landlord sells dahl, potatoes, onions, and salt, his real business turns out to be lending (or more accurately, collecting) money. The young man learns in time that the Jains regard him with a degree of fear—fear that he will be a source of pollution to their ritual purity. The BDO may have pressured them into renting out a room over their shop, but they want to be no closer.

As he unpacks, people crowd in to watch as each of his possessions is unpacked—as though he is an itinerant magician, pulling odd-looking goods from a bottomless trunk. He decides it is better to leave most things packed, aside from his radio and the book he is reading. The radio is a thing of true wonder—not because it is a radio—but because of its size, its dials and long antenna. This is confirmation for the villages that the CIA has now arrived, that they and their village are truly "on the map."

Someone brings up a pot of dark green liquid. He first assumes it is some kind of spinach soup. He learns it is not soup, but water from the village "tank" or pond, where everyone goes to bathe; it is the only source of drinking water for the village. He decides that he is not thirsty for the moment. He inquires through the BDO about the availability of a latrine." No", says the BDO, "but they will build a good one for you—we will give them the latest design." That evening someone shows him the field near the village pond where everyone goes to squat—women to the left of the field, men to the right.

The BDO apologizes that he must leave now. He has to get back to the Block. He promises to come back regularly and to send his staff, but both the young man and he know that this is unlikely. With a last dubious look at the young man, the BDO and his driver start their jeep and head back to Kherwara.

The community is made up almost entirely of tribal people, the Bhils (bow-men)—long known to the Rajput rulers of the area for their skill with bow and arrow—invaluable in hunting and in times of war. Nothing in his training has prepared him for this. "How in the world am I going to communicate?" he asks himself. Their language is Vagari, though most also speak bits of Gujarati and Hindi. Unlike Hindu or Muslim farmers who live in a village and go out to their fields, Bhil families live far apart from their neighbors, each with a house next to its own plot of land. They farm for part of the year, and spend the rest moving, partly hunting in the hills, and tending small plots where water can be found. Religiously, they are neither Hindu, nor Jain, but animists. Their "temple" holds no image of the gods, and serves more as a meeting house than temple. The Bhils have retained a deep belief in spirits and magic, even more so than the village-bound Hindus.

The first afternoon and evening pass quickly. The young man is busy setting up the bed and mosquito net, boiling water, sorting out his things. No time now for loneliness—that will come later. Presently, he is just overwhelmed by the novelty of everything. He sleeps well that night.

The next morning a boy arrives, sent by the landlord. He is a Bhil, and so considered by the landlord to be equally impure to the foreigner—someone without caste, an eater of meat, and purveyor of who knows what other horrors. The young man puts the boy to work filtering and boiling water. The boy has never used a primus stove before and so the process takes forever. Eventually, the boy goes off and returns with a chicken for dinner. It is soon clear that the boy has never killed or plucked a chicken. The boy may be a tribal, but the process of killing a chicken is clearly alarming. Thereafter, the young man vows to "go veg" and live as the village does, on dahl, onions, and *makhi ke chapati* (corn flat bread).

A few days later teachers from a school somewhere further to the west pass by on their way to Rikhabdev. Hearing that a foreigner is now in Bhuder, they stop to chat. He learns from them the area's basic cycle of life. "The Jains are village money lenders. The tribals are nomadic farmers and hunters. The Jains steal from the tribals throughout the year. Once every year or so, the tribals get fed up and return to steal back their money from the Jains. That is why your house has that trap door. Be sure you close and bolt it every night."

Each day the young man forces himself to go out to look for farmers. He finds a few, even manages some brief conversations about corn and wheat, but wonders what he can offer. No one here can afford to buy seeds, let alone insecticides or fertilizer. The plots are small and mostly rain-fed. Many are far away, up in the hills. There are only a few small open wells, and they lack the Persian-wheels with which farmers elsewhere irrigate their fields. There is not a single tube well in the village for agriculture or for drinking water.

One morning, the young man asks the boy to go to the market at Rikhabdev to buy vegetables and rice. He asks the boy

what fruits might be available. The boy looks blank. "Fruits," says the young man in his badly accented Hindi. "You know, fruits, like apples, bananas, pears?" "Ah yes," says the boy. "They have fruits in the market." "How much should I buy?" "Oh, buy 5 kilos of apples," says the young man. The boy looks shocked, and repeats, "Five kilos!" "Yes, five kilos." The boy goes, alternately riding and pushing the bicycle across the hills to Rikhabdev. The young man wanders off to visit the one or two farmers with whom he has managed at least a few words about their crops.

The day is hot, and all day long the young man dreams of those apples. He can almost taste them now—ripe and juicy. In the evening, he sits on the patio and watches intently the place on the hill where the path back from Rikhabdev crosses through the rocks. Finally, he spots the boy, struggling as he pushes the bike over the pass, an enormous bag on the back of the bike. Soon, he hears animated discussion below, and several people are working alternatively to push and to pull the burlap sack through the trap door. "There you are, sahib, five kilos." The young man learns that while the Hindi word *saib* may mean apple, the word *saiv* refers instead to that hot spicy form of corn meal fried with chilies and onions—a mix many Indians like to eat while they sip tea. Of course, five kilos of this precursor of cheetos takes up a lot more space than would five kilos of apples. Moreover, the young man can't stand the stuff. So, he tells the boy to give it all to the village. That night, he falls asleep, dreaming of apples and saying repeatedly to himself, "saib not saiv".

One night some of the younger farmers invite him to join them at the temple. It is a feast night, when they will consult the gods about the harvest. They sit, pray, chant and chat around a fire for an hour or so. A bottle of *mowua* (local liquor) is passed around. Whether it is due to the fire, the smoke, the chanting, the alcohol, or the gods, the young man feels strangely comfortable—for the first time a part of the community, although he clearly has no clue about what is going on around him. He cannot even figure out who is the priest, or even if there is a priest, since the men alternately take lead roles in chanting. Suddenly, one man rises, and, just as suddenly, falls into the center of the circle, babbling, as if in a epileptic fit. The others hold him down to keep him from rolling into the fire. He is growling in a strange new voice, deep and haunting in tone. And, just as suddenly, it is all over. The man is helped to his feet. Everyone gets up to leave. On the way back to the shop, someone explains that the gods have spoken through the man who had the fit. The young man, however, understands so little of the language that he still has no idea what the gods might have predicted. Were the predictions good or bad? Perhaps it doesn't matter. The important thing is that everyone seems satisfied. The young man sleeps well that night.

Another night the teachers come by, again on their way to Rikhabdev. There is a circus in town. Would the young man like to join them? No hesitation. "Yes, of course." The plaza near the three great temples is surrounded by buildings, three stories high, each small apartment has a balcony looking on to the plaza. The light of torches and pressure lamps flickers, casting weird shadows like some psychedelic disco. The plaza is the setting of a 17th century opera, a stage ringed by rows of boxes. A huge crowd gathers. The teachers, with the young man in tow, rent one of the small apartments above, from which they can watch the proceedings. The performances go on all night—jugglers, acrobats, poets, and musicians. The young man and the teachers sleep, wake, and sleep again like all those around them. The acts go on, the music fades and rises. Sometime in the morning, they sip tea and then start back, pushing their bikes along the dusty road to Bhuder. The teachers will continue well beyond.

The pass above the village begins to take on special meaning to the young man. Having pushed his bike up one side of the hill, he pauses each time to sit there and rest on a rock. In the evenings a young herder often sits near the pass with his goats. There is little either can say beyond the usual greeting of "Ram, Ram". In place of words the boy has his flute. The young man listens to the flute and looks down on Bhuder, on the shop, the temple, and the haze of smoke from charcoal fires. The haze catches the last light of the sun and the village glows. Magic!

The young man looks forward to the nights, which seem enchanted. He wants more of the temple, the circus and the flute. However, the days are something else. Day by day, he grows wearier—weary physically, but weary also of the place, of his inability to communicate, of the isolation, of the treks to the field to defecate, of the constant boiling and filtering of water. "What am I DOING here?" he asks himself. Each morning he reminds himself that he is here not just TO BE but TO DO—to do something, anything. By afternoon, the urge TO DO has subsided into a torpor of heat.

No one comes from the Block—no BDO, and more importantly, no agriculture officer. "Well, no surprise there," he thinks to himself.

After a week or so, he rides his bike to Rikhabdev and takes the bus back to the block offices at Kherwara. Neither the BDO nor the block agriculture officer can be found. A few days later, back in Bhuder, he learns that the Block Agriculture Officer has come to the village, but has not bothered to visit him.

He has promised himself not to go back to Udaipur for at least a month. He knows that he must settle in and settle down, get used to the place and the people. Instead of staying all day in the village, he begins to travel farther and farther into the hills on his bike. He tells himself that he is out finding the farmers and their hidden plots. The reality, however, is that all he finds are more isolated houses, more tiny fields, but he has no means to open conversations, nothing to tell these farmers, and nothing to offer them.

He finds himself one day in Rikhabdev, intending just to buy provisions. He decides instead to break his vow, and take the bus to Udaipur. In Udaipur, he has a meal, and chooses to take the night train to Jaipur. He tells himself that the trip is only to recharge his batteries. When he arrives at the station in Jaipur, he does not get off. He decides instead to take the train on to Delhi. He tells himself that he will ask for a change of village. The train is pulling into Delhi, and he is no longer kidding himself about the purpose of this trip. He will not ask for a change of village. He is finished. He wants to go home. He wants a real job and a real life—anything other than Bhuder.

At the Peace Corps office, he asks to see the Country Director. The Director does not ask why the young man is not in his village but greets the young man as though he were expected, almost as if to ask "What took you so long?". The Director waves off all attempts to talk, and instead invites the young man to come home for dinner and to stay the night. The young man tries again to explain why he has come. "Tomorrow," says the Director. "Come home now, and we can talk tomorrow." The young man suddenly encounters real food, a real family, and a real bed. The next morning is Saturday, and the young man again tries to broach the subject at breakfast. The Director explains that the family has a busy day ahead. "Let's leave it for Monday," he says. Saturday and Sunday pass. By Monday, the young man has little left to say. He feels small and embarrassed for having given up so quickly. The Director has clearly played out this act many times with other volunteers. He knows the value of a good bed and home-cooked meals.

The Monday morning meeting comes down simply to saying that settling into the village is tougher than the young man had imagined. He just thanks the Director for his hospitality and heads back to the train station. Two days later, the young man finds himself back in Bhuder and nothing has changed.

Kherwara—1968—Age 22

Four months have passed. The young man's visits to the Block at Kherwara have become more frequent, and more frustrating. The officials there seem friendly, but totally unable to help. They have no loans to offer farmers, no incentives, no educational materials, and no idea of how to influence local farmers. They have no idea what they are to do, let alone what a young foreigner might do to help.

On one of these trips, the young man meets an elderly English woman in the market. She explains that she manages the old Protestant mission station on the hill above Kherwara. Over a cup of tea, he learns that she came to Kherwara as a young lady some 43 years earlier. Both the woman and the mission station have long-since ceased to serve any overtly religious role. As an alternative, she raises cattle and water buffalo, which she then sells to farmers in the area as breeding stock.

The woman explains that the mission is also the occasional home to an English doctor. The doctor is almost always "out", working in the villages. His wife and children are in the South, at Ooty, where the children go to school for most of the year.

Eventually, the young man meets the doctor, a middle-aged English man, quiet and a bit withdrawn; however, the doctor has a passion. He has dedicated himself to the eradication of guinea worm. The worm is a scourge of the area, particularly for those farmers whose infected legs become paralyzed, leaving them unable to tend their fields. The doctor spends weeks running "camps" out in the surrounding villages, removing the worms from infected legs, educating villagers on how to avoid infection, and—when he can find the funds—installing hand pumps and bathing platforms that allow villagers to draw water without stepping into the water where they may infect others.

The young man accompanies the doctor on several rounds of the villages. He admires the doctor's dedication and skills. Here at last is someone who knows what he wants to do and how to do it. The young man knows well that here again he has little to offer. He is no doctor, no water expert, and cannot even speak the local language.

The young man senses that, in the old woman and the doctor, he has found people with whom he can talk and learn. At least, they have figured out the TO DO of their lives.

Fed up with life in Bhuder and with inactivity, the young man at last makes a decision. He moves out of Bhuder and takes a room in Kherwara. Once again, he finds himself in a room over a shop, this time on the main street of the town. Here there are shops with plenty to buy, a tea stall, running water, and, glory of glories, even a latrine attached to his room. Of course, it is not a flush latrine, just a hole in the floor with a basket below, cleaned out every few days by a sweeper, but still a big improvement over the nightly stroll to the fields. He even finds a cook—a real cook. A cook in the apartment plus food in the market equal real meals again.

For a few days he is happy. He finds everything he could want, shops, buses, the Block, the mission station, and even a post office. One thing he does not find, however, is farmers. Of course, there are farmers who go out to fields around the edges of the town, but he finds it even harder to connect with them than he did with the Bhils in Bhuder. The language is now Hindi, so in theory communication should be easier, but in fact it remains difficult. As with the farmers of Bhuder, he has nothing to offer. Moreover, he finds no welcome in the temple, no teachers to accompany to the circus. The doctor is busy removing guinea worms in the villages. The old English woman is busy with her water buffalo. The officials in the Block are busy with their papers.

He hates to admit it, but he regrets having moved out of Bhuder. Eventually, he stops asking himself silly questions, like: "What am I doing here?" or "What am I going TO DO TODAY?" It is enough just to be and to survive.

Kherwara and Bhuder—Late 1989—Age 43

I opened my eyes. It was late morning. The jolting from potholes in the road had finally bounced me out of a deep sleep. We were about to cross the "border" between Gujarat and Rajasthan on National Highway 8. I tried to remember whether the road had that lofty title back then? I had known it only as "the road from Ahmedabad".

This time I was not riding the bus. I was in a car—my own car—a big new Toyota. I had paid for a driver from the Delhi office to come with me to Bombay to drive the car back because I did not yet have my Indian driver's license.

We passed over a hill and, suddenly, there was Kherwara. It was not the Kherwara I remembered, of course. That Kherwara was a village. This Kherwara was a town. Where once there was our only tea stall there now stood a row of many. There was even a proper bus station. Up on the hill a building of the old mission station still remained but had since been converted into a girls' college.

I got out, stretched and began to walk up the main street. Everything looked different, smaller than I remembered, but also impossibly crowded and dirty. I could not even find the building where I had once lived or the shop that was once below it. Perhaps it had been rebuilt. I did not want to try out my very rusty Hindi by asking what happened to the shopkeeper or, more important, to my former cook. The crowd overwhelmed me, and I felt suddenly tired. I quickly returned to the car.

I saw no point in wasting time, trying to reconnect. After all, Kherwara was a place I had never really connected with back then when I had the chance.

I got back in the car and we drove on to Rikhavdev. The kilometers went by quickly—too quickly for my thoughts to form properly. What did I want to say in Bhuder, a place I had run away from so quickly? And why was I so drawn back to Bhuder, where I spent such a short time, and not to Kherwara, a place where I lived much longer?

We asked directions at Rikhavdev. I was surprised when people in the market told us that we could easily drive to Bhuder in a normal car. I remembered how hard it used to be by jeep. We bought water and some snack food and then turned onto the road to Bhuder. The car crossed the hills quickly on a road that was now mostly paved.

Bhuder was now a village, no longer just a collection of a few houses and a shop. Near the shop above which I used to live there was a collection of jeeps. A tent had been erected next to the shop.

It was election season and the *Sarpanch* (head of the *panchayat* or local government) was running for re-election. The appearance of a new sedan signaled the arrival of someone important, so soon the *Sarpanch's* staff members were pulling me out of the car to meet the *Sarpanch*. In good English, the Sarpanch asked my connection with the village. I explained that I had briefly lived there as a Peace Corps volunteer, working on agriculture. "Ah", said the *Sarpanch*, and immediately launched into his speech, saying how he and the Congress Party had brought prosperity to the farmers of the area by bringing "foreign experts like this to the village". My cheeks turned red.

I sat bewildered and wondering what I had gotten myself into. I could not have been more embarrassed—sitting here letting the panchayat politicians pretend that my couple of months here had any impact at all on agricultural production. What was I to say? Thankfully, it was soon over and the *Sarpanch* and his crew moved on to the next village.

People started coming up to me and saying that they remembered me. How could this possibly be? I remembered no one. People who now looked old must have been children when I was there. Collective memory and myth must have kept alive the story of "their" CIA agent. We sat, chatted and drank tea in front of the shop above which I had lived.

Bits of my Hindi came back, but language did not seem important. Evening was coming on and more people gathered. Someone recalled my "saiv" vs. "saib" story, making everyone laugh. "We ate saiv for months after that," someone added.

I asked about the boy who previously cooked for me." Sorry," they said, "he is not here." "Where is he then," I asked. "Oh, he is working overseas." "Really?" I asked. "Yes, he owns a big restaurant in Kuwait. You taught him to cook very well." Red cheeks again—twice in a day to be credited with achievements with which I had nothing to do. I kept trying to imagine this boy who could not kill a chicken, now running a big restaurant in Kuwait. Really?

"Would you like to meet his wife?" someone asked. Nothing could have surprised me more than to be introduced to a wife— at least, here in rural Rajasthan. "She runs the ICDS center (Integrated Child Development Services—a nation-wide program which provides health and day care for mothers of young children). Off we went to the ICDS center. She greeted me as though a member of the family, remembered her husband's stories about me, showed me around the center—full that day of mothers and children waiting for the visit of a doctor.

The village now had electricity, hand pumps, an ICDS center, and even a visiting doctor. No doubt, it was a very different Bhuder from the one I had known. I looked at faces and realized that despite their claims of "remembering" me, few people had been here "back then". Most were the sort of village Hindu farmers one found everywhere in Rajasthan. Everyone spoke Hindi now. I guessed that most of the Bhils had been pushed out, further into the hills, as "regular' farmers had pushed in to the area to take advantage of the irrigation water now available from a new dam up in the hills.

Sunset was approaching and we needed to get back on the road to Udaipur. We said our goodbyes and I promised to come back soon (though perhaps they knew this was like the promise to return I had made so many years before).

At the top of the pass out of the village, a young goat herder sat on a rock beside the road. We stopped and I got out to

150

look back down at Bhuder. A different Bhuder—yet I still felt strangely at peace. I had come—however briefly—home. The boy played his flute. The smoke of charcoal fires rose above the houses—the haze lighted with the last rays of the sun.

Udaipur—1969 —Age 23

The past year-and-a-half had been a difficult period for the young man. Four months in Bhuder, nine months in Kherwara, and now nearly six months in Udaipur. Yet, at last, he had begun to "find himself".

His trips to the villages with the doctor in Kherwara had built his interest in issues related to water. Water, after all, along with earth, sun, and air, was one of those essential elements of life and of agriculture. Water for the fields was almost entirely dependent on rain, and rain was in the hands of the gods. There were no dependable lakes, rivers or canals to irrigate the fields. The water available in "tanks" (ponds) and wells was often infected with guinea worms and various intestinal pests. Well water would disappear each dry season, as water tables dropped below the shallow layers of rock that limited how deep villagers could dig.

When the doctor could no longer find funds from donors at home, he would use his own funds (and often his own hands) to build safer platforms for drawing water from village wells. Missionary doctors, however, did not earn much and it was clear that one-man efforts like these would always be limited in scope.

The young man began to visit the university in Udaipur where he got to know the dean of the agriculture engineering college. Over cups of tea the dean helped the young man put together a project proposal. The college needed opportunities for their students to learn some of the practical issues facing farmers. They also had some equipment for well-deepening. If the young man could find a tractor, air compressor, and someone trained in dynamiting, the students could visit villages and help farmers to deepen their wells.

The young man discovered a non-governmental organization (NGO) in New Delhi that specialized in agricultural development. He visited the NGO and was surprised to find them open to the idea of providing equipment. They would loan him a tractor and air compressor so long as he would provide monthly reports. Moreover, they put the young man in touch with a sister organization in Ajmer where he could be trained.

A VSO (British volunteer) in Ajmer took charge of his training. The young man had not imagined in the beginning that he, himself, would have to handle dynamite. Now, however, he understood that this would be the only way to get the project going. He had to apply for a license "to buy, store and handle" explosives. The VSO was a good teacher—patient and careful. The young man appreciated the "careful" part of the description.

The next challenge was to bring the equipment to Udai-pur. The young man realized that he had no money to pay a driver and, moreover, even if he did have the money, he could not trust someone to drive all the way to Udaipur. Sensing an adventure, the young man mounted himself on the tractor, tied his bag on to the back of the seat, and set out on the road to Udaipur.

Tractors move slowly and Indian truck drivers are not patient men. Nevertheless, the sight of a foreigner driving a trac-tor, pulling an air compressor behind it down a major highway, caused plenty of people to slow down—just for a look, perhaps a gentle or not-so-gentle jibe, and then a smile and shake of the head. If a man drives a truck long enough in India, he sees everything—even a *sahib* on a tractor.

The tractor was still only half way along the route when evening came. The young man found a truck stop which offered rooms. He was exhausted. After a quick meal, he went to the tiny cabin which served as a room. He slept immediately. Later in the evening, he discovered the larger purpose of the rooms. Indeed, the proprietor had been surprised when he said he needed a room for the whole night. Usually, truck drivers rent these rooms only by the hour. Ah yes—on either side of him, in stereo, the rhythmic bumps and grinds, the wails of feigned passion, went on all night.

It was not a restful night to say the least. In the morning he ate his *chapatti* (unleavened flat bread), drank his tea, and left for Udaipur. It was night again when he arrived.

He lived in a small house in a residential area of Udaipur. The other room in the house was rented by a young sociologist from Kerala. Together they shared a kitchen, bath, and the salary of a boy who cooked and cleaned. This was a long step up from both Bhuder and Kherwara. He had a kerosene powered fridge, electric lights, running water, and, of course, a city outside his door.

The work began quickly. The "team" however quickly came to mean only him and two part-time students. The young man eventually learned that the two 'students' were actually being paid by the dean. The dean had not been able to coax real students into doing this kind of manual work.

The list of villages to be visited grew, and at each village, requests came to move on to yet another village. Farmers would bid with each other to offer meals and a bed—anything to keep the team in the village one more day. The nights were magic. The farmers' wives offered good food. The kids would gather around to gape with wonder at the foreigners—as the rest of the "team" were as foreign to them as the American. Stories would be told that the foreigner could not understand, but it didn't matter, sleep would come easily.

It was easy to understand the reluctance of the students of agriculture engineering—this was hard, dirty work. One had to go down to the bottom of the well with a jack-hammer, drill out shot holes in the rock, insert dynamite, fuse and packing, and get back to the surface with the ignition wires, take cover, and blow it. Usually, the process paid off fairly quickly. Water would begin to seep in through the cracks in the rocks. Other times, the rock would be piled up, and the farmer would have to return to digging. At least now the digging was a bit easier, because the top layers of rock had been shattered.

One day the volunteer found himself down a well, as one of the students drilled the shot holes. As the rock and dust settled, they saw thin fuses emerge from the rock all around them. He knew that it was not uncommon. A farmer would hire some local *wala* (entrepreneur) to place dynamite in the well. The fuses would fail and the work would be abandoned for a while. It was not unusual but it would have been nice of the farmer to tell them that they were about to enter a well full of live charges.

Though none of this should have been a surprise to him by this point, the young man came out of the well furious and looking for someone to throttle. One person in the crowd provided him with the needed spark by calling him a "white monkey". For the first time in India, the young man really was ready to strangle someone. Fortunately, probably more fortunate for the young man than for the heckler, another Peace Corps volunteer was there that day, separated them, and calmed him down. "Come on now, just another day," he said.

Maybe, it was just time to go home.

Udaipur—Late 1989 Age 43

I opened my eyes. The house was still there, on a quiet back street of town. The sociologist from Kerala who formerly lived there had moved on and a young teacher in the university now lived there with his family. Udaipur had changed, but not as much as I had thought it would. The favorite restaurant, cinema,

and some of the hotels were the same. Now, however, there were more tourists, more shops and more people.

There was little now to hold him in Udaipur. Udaipur had been a stopping off place, like Kherwara. It held none of the magic of Bhuder. No one here would claim to remember him, introduce him to the wife of his cook or recall his dumb mistakes.

One more circle closed, time now to move on to the next. It was time to go home—this time to his family in Delhi.

A few notes about the Bhils

The Bhils once ruled much of southern Rajasthan and northern Gujarat. Some ethnologists argue that the Bhils originated in north and central India, and were gradually pushed into the hill country of Rajasthan and Madhya Pradesh as Aryan tribes moved south into India from central Asia. They are generally seen as one of the non-Aryan or aboriginal peoples of India. Many centuries after the Aryans arrived, the Bhils were again defeated by Mewar Rajput invaders in 1398. Surprisingly, the Bhils formed an important bond with their new rulers.

When the Mughals conquered most of north and central India, the emperor Akbar pushed into Rajasthan. The Bhils supported the Mewar ruler, Maharana Pratap Singh, during his epic, but ultimately futile battles against Akbar's forces. It was said that when the Mewars lost the crucial battle of Haldighati, it was thanks to the archery skills of the Bhils that the Mughals, not the Mewars, suffered the most casualties. The Bhils then took Pratap Singh into hiding in the hills for years to follow. As a result of their loyalty to Pratap Singh, each new Maharana of Udaipur to this day is anointed by a Bhil, who with a newly pricked finger smears blood on the maharana's forehead. On the seal of the Maharana of Udaipur, a Bhil stands next to the Maharana.

Knowing all this, the British had little difficulty in understanding the importance of the Bhils to the regional stability. British officers noted the fighting skills of the Bhils and moved quickly to establish "the Bhil Corps". British doctors and missionaries followed. The doctors were intrigued by the unique

155

approaches Bhils took to disease and healing. As they were neither Hindus nor Muslims, missionaries looked on the Bhils as comparatively easy candidates for conversion to Christianity.

The first senior British official to come to Kherwara was probably James Tod, who arrived in 1818 at age 30 as the newly appointed Political Agent for Mewar. One year earlier the Bhils had revolted against the Mewars over land issues. It was the first of a series of Bhil revolts linked to land issues, primarily whether communal land belonged to the state or to the tribe, and was sparked largely because of British concepts of private land ownership being introduced into Mewar thinking. Later revolts against the British focused more on the issue of military conscription.

Tod noted that the Bhils called themselves *Bhumiputra* (sons of the earth) or *Vanaputra* (sons of the forest). He saw in the Bhils the possibility of an independent fighting force, free of the complicated Hindu bars of caste. Tod only regretted that the Mewar rulers already held the loyalty of the Bhils, writing,

> Had the wild tribes been under the sole influence of British power, nothing would have been so simple as effectually, not only to control, but to conciliate and improve them; for it is a mortifying truth, that the more remote from civilization, the more tractable and easy to manage, more especially the Bhil.

The British established their first "permanent" base in Kherwara in 1840. Kherwara became the headquarters for the newly formed Mewar Bhil Corps. During the great mutiny of 1857 the Bhils showed themselves loyal to the British. A rebel group from the Bengal Lancers passed through Kherwara and tried to convince the Bhils to join the revolt. The Bhil leaders politely declined. When the rebels marched on to Dungarpur, the Bhils followed, and killed every member of the group.

British doctors came and went in Kherwara, but few took much interest in the Bhils until Thomas Hendley arrived in 1871. Like those before him, Hendley's job was mainly to deal with the small contingent of British troops and families stationed in Kherwara. Hendley, however, was caught up in the scientific racism of his time, and, therefore, was anxious to catalog the ways in which Bhil anthropometrics differed from those of their Hindu neighbors. While busy with his measuring tape, Hendley compiled the first extensive look at Bhil approaches to disease and healing. He found the Bhils largely free from some of the ailments affecting other parts of Rajasthan. He noted that cholera, for example, was rare and venereal diseases were almost totally absent. On the other hand, guinea worm and malaria were common (see below about Ronald Ross). Hendley noted that the Bhils had developed an array of herbal medicines and treatments unknown elsewhere in Rajasthan. They even had their own system of smallpox inoculation. The one common element with Hindus of the region was the widespread use of burns and cauterization to drive out evil spirits.

Central to the Bhil approach to disease was the role of the *dakran* (women with both medical and magic powers) who Hendley and other British officials called "witches". These women had the power to both curse enemies with illness and to protect their own families. Every family needed to have a powerful *dakran* among their members to ward off the evil wished on them by enemies. Most Bhil men to this day wear a blue string on their right arm, sometimes attaching an amulet, to ward off the powers of enemy *dakran*.

When a person became gravely ill, the family would seek a *bopra* (a spirit talker) to identify the guilty *dakran*. If the *dakran* could be caught, she might confess and then be exiled from the area. However, according to the British Commandant in Kherwara in 1851 about 100 such cases happened each year, with one in ten cases leading to execution of the "witch". The British Resident in Udaipur reported that in 1842 a number of "witches" were executed in Udaipur City as part of the celebrations for the accession of Maharana Sarup Singh. During the 1850's, the British forced the Maharana to outlaw the killing of "witches". The belief in the power of the Bhil *dakran*, however, persisted among both Bhils and Rajputs. Well-reputed *dakran* were often asked to travel great distances from Kherwara to help families deal with diseases that seemed unresponsive to other treatments.

The *bopra*, like the *dakran*, also had (and still has) great healing powers. Families would seek a bopra to offer sacrifices at the graves of family ancestors. Bopras generally lived in the hills, much like Hindu hermits and sadhus. They practiced what was called *jantra-mantra*, a type of spell with magic powers. Like other workers in the Bhil country, the currency with which the *bopra* was paid was usually liquor. Liquor was prized for its ability to take people "to another world".

Hendley's accounts of Bhil herbal medicine and magic caught the attention of many other British doctors working in India. The approaches of the Bhils had similarities, yet also stark contrast with the ayurvedic traditions throughout much of India. This also flew straight in the face of the "modern scientific medicine" brought by the British. The more the British pushed into other tribal areas of India, the more they encountered customs similar to those of the Bhils. The result was that many other doctors, and later sociologists and anthropologists came to study the Bhils.

The missionaries came first, however. Like other non-Hindu tribal peoples, the Bhils were seen by Christian missionaries as easy targets for conversion. The missionaries were wrong. Generations of frustrated missionaries came and went, with few Christian converts to show for their efforts.

Reverend Charles Stewart Thompson arrived in Udaipur in 1880. He was sent by the Church Missionary Society (CMS) in England to head a new mission station in Kherwara. The wife of a British officer in Kherwara had raised the needed funds. Thompson spent his first year in Udaipur learning Hindi. The following year he moved to Kherwara.

Thompson, unfortunately, arrived in Kherwara at a bad time. A British doctor had just left town after having admitted to paying Bhils to come to him for medical treatment. The doctor had then proceeded to carry out surgeries on his patients without their consent. The Bhils were already suspicious of English medicine, and the story of forcible surgery led to complete rejection. Thompson had hoped to use his knowledge of medicine as a way to meet those he hoped would become future converts. No Bhil, however, would give Thompson even the time of day.

Thompson's second misfortune lay in arriving at the start of the latest in a string of Bhil revolts. As with earlier uprisings, this one was, in theory, against the Mewars and not against the British. However, the uprising had much to do with British attempts to survey lands and conduct a census. A basic Bhil belief was that whatever a man could count would be reduced, and hence their houses, cattle, lands, and ultimately the Bhils themselves would be reduced through any counting. The Bhils understood that the census and land survey formed the basis for new taxes. The taxes, in turn, were being imposed to pay for the British invasion of Afghanistan that year. The Bhils quickly understood that the British were seeking not just taxes, but men of fighting age who could be conscripted and sent to Kabul.

A further cause for concern was the outlawing of trade in the *sowar* liquor, made from a local flower and important in Bhil ceremonies. A Hindu trader had been granted a monopoly on the sale of liquors imported from elsewhere in India, none of which met the ritual needs of the Bhils. When the government tried to seize local liquor, the Bhils went to arms.

It took many years for Thompson to overcome the distrust of the Bhils and even then, he managed to find only a few converts. The Bhils believed in their own spirits who lived deep in the hills and forests. They respected, but had never adopted the beliefs of Hindus, Jains, and Muslims. They were ready to respect the British god but were not about to adopt him.

Thompson eventually came into his own during the droughts and famines that struck the region. He became a voice for the Bhils within the British establishment, demanding relief and government aid. Ultimately, he died trying to deliver such aid during a famine and cholera outbreak in 1900.

And then there was Kherwara's most famous scientist.

Kherwara—1897—Ronald Ross Age 40

In 1897 Dr. Ronald Ross of the Indian Medical Service was working hard in a hospital in Secunderabad (later to become a city in Andra Pradesh). By day Ross worked as a hospital physician. By night he worked as a researcher on the great mystery disease of the 1800s—malaria.

Dr. Ross was by no means a star in the Indian Medical Service. Born in India in 1857 (the year of the Great Mutiny), Ross had been pressured into a medical career by his father, a Scottish officer in the British Army. What Ronald really wanted to be was a writer. Perhaps as a result, he graduated near the bottom of his medical school class and then flunked the entrance exam to the Indian Medical Service. On a second try, he barely passed the exam and was assigned to low-grade posts around Madras.

Like other physicians of his time, Ross had come up with various theories about the manner in which malaria was transmitted. His own theory was that malaria was a form of bowel fever. However, on a trip to London in 1894 he met Dr. Patrick Manson, who had researched malaria in China. Manson showed Ross for the first time the malaria parasite in infected blood. Manson also put forth the idea that mosquitoes might be the means of carrying the malaria parasite. Ross returned to India, determined to prove the theory. To do so, he needed to discover the entire life cycle of the parasite. He worked feverishly on collecting mosquitoes and blood samples from infected patients.

His superiors in Bangalore, however, did not welcome or approve of the time Ross spent on such "idle speculation." One superior ordered him to stop collecting mosquito larvae and dumping out stagnant water collecting around the hospital, on the grounds that he was interfering with the natural order of life. Perhaps Ross did not recognize how strong this opposition to his disruption of the natural order was or perhaps he did not care.

Ross made his first great discovery in 1897. He found indications of malaria in the stomach wall of a mosquito. He would later find the parasite itself in the insect's saliva. It was his eureka moment. He believed that within weeks he would now be able to unravel the rest of the life cycle of the parasite.

The transfer orders came as a shock, especially since they arrived one day after he had written to Manson and others in London announcing his discovery. He was first called to Bombay and then handed orders to proceed to the village of Kherwara, "somewhere in the deserts of Rajasthan." "Where in the world will I find mosquitoes in the desert?", he asked himself.

Arriving in Kherwara, Ross found himself heading the dispensary of a small British Army post. He called Kherwara "the filthiest town I have seen in India." He settled into a deep depression, calling Kherwara his "Devil's Island".

It was early winter and no one had seen a case of malaria in months, but Ross decided that he could not afford to waste time. Since there were no human cases of malaria to investigate, he decided instead to research Kherwara's pigeon population. He immediately found malaria among the birds and set about experimenting with transmission of the disease to various types of mosquitoes, flies and lice.

After five unhappy months in Kherwara, in 1898 Ross was rescued by his friends in London. He was transferred again, this time to Calcutta. He found the time and the facilities in Calcutta that he needed to complete his research. As much as he resented the interruption of his work by the Kherwara assignment, Ross later looked back on it as a critical moment in his research. It was here that he came to sort out the interaction of the malaria parasite with birds.

Four years later, in 1902, Ronald Ross was awarded the Nobel Prize for Medicine for his work on the malaria parasite.

—◈—

And a final mention for my personal hero of Kherwara:

Kherwara—1967—Dr. Arthur Banks—Age Unknown but perhaps late 30's.

Dr. Banks worked tirelessly on behalf of the Bhils in the fight against guinea worm. He rarely saw his home or his bed. He nearly lost his family over the time spent apart from them. My greatest regret in leaving India was to lose track of this great man.

CHAPTER 6

The Pilgrim's Deconversion

William Whitesell

I pushed through the crowd, desperate to reach the dark man in flowing white robes before he left the hall.

"Swami, Swami," I cried, "Why? Why do we have to go through the intellectual phase before attaining self-realization?"

Swami Chinmayananda turned, gazed deeply for a moment into my eyes, and placed a gentle hand on my wrist. "Just as the plant must flower," he whispered, "before the fruit appears."

Then he was gone. That summer, I became a Hindu. If I had been wealthy, I would have left right away to seek self-realization in India. However, I was a scholarship student, the first of my family to attend college, a role model for six younger siblings. In the fall, I returned for my junior year at Yale. To get to India, I signed up for early admission in the Peace Corps.

Training began the next summer in Milwaukee. We were to become "agents of change." We had social activists in our midst, burning with righteous causes. Civil rights, the anti-war movement—What was I to make of all that? I wanted to become one with God. But I was reading Siddhartha, who chose life in the world rather than the path of a monk. And I became good friends with the Program Director's wife—there were hints of romance. It was a confusing time.

During my last year at college, I lost interest in my regular course work. I had been a business major, but that seemed pretty meaningless to me now. I did, however, continue to study Hindi with an Indian tutor.

Finally, the next summer came and I arrived in the pictur-esque Indian city of Udaipur as a Peace Corps volunteer. Was I an agent of change? Well, *I* was changing, sleeping under a mosquito net, squatting over holes in the floor, wiping my butt with water, and drinking paregoric and gin when I had the runs.

On a two-hour train ride to the villages where my buddy, Mike, and I would live for the next two years, I wrote a list of questions to ask the local leaders. What were the needs of the people, the key institutions and power structure of the village, and the resources we could bring to bear for change? No one met us at the train station. We overpaid to have our luggage brought to a shuttered, single-room government building. Some kids were playing soccer nearby. Having learned that you could often reach the adults through the children, I dashed off to show them Americans also knew how to play soccer. By the end of the afternoon, I was sick with sun-stroke. From that moment on, survival became the main goal. I never did ask those questions about the power structure.

After a few days, I bicycled two miles along a dusty, dirt road from Fatehnager, where Mike lived, to the more remote village of Sunwar, where I would stay. I passed a couple of wooden carts pulled by huge, black water buffalo and, more rarely, a pedestrian. The women wore colorful but faded saris, usually pulling them over their heads to cover their long hair. The village men wore fluffy, white dhotis that looked like big, loose diapers.

As I came into my village, a group of kids playing at the side of the road pointed at me and shouted, "Ghora, ghora, ghora!!" or "White, white, white!!"

I learned that I was going to live in a castle. At the main gate was huge wooden door open on both sides. A faded painting of a hunting scene was barely discernible on the door, a relic of centuries gone by. The inner courtyard was 30 square meters of bone-dry dust, with no greenery in sight. The resident Rajput ruler sat at a desk in a small room to the left of the gate. He had been the ruler and the owner of most of the land in the village before India gained its independence and implemented land

reform. Now, he seemed to be merely maintaining a pretense of his former importance.

The Rajput rented me a suite of rooms at the back of the courtyard. I had a living room, a bedroom, and a large wash-room with a hole in the floor that emptied beyond the castle wall. Toward the back was a small veranda with an enclosed 5-meter square of dirt that was all my own. I once tried to grow a corn plant back there, but it died. I had no electricity, no running water, no screens on the windows, and no toilet.

To relieve myself, I had to cross the main courtyard, walk up a set of stone steps to the second floor, and then turn a few corners to a small room with a hole in the floor between two stone footpads. There was no door to close. I looked down through the hole in the floor and realized that the room was perched beyond the edge of the lower wall of the castle. Directly below was a farmer's field. I was definitely going to create fertilizer here. The village began just beyond the edge of the field. If I used toilet paper, the winds would end up carrying it floating through the village. I had to remember to carry a flask of water with me up to this room.

Water was delivered to me in large earthen jugs twice a week. The woman who carried these jugs on her head was old and lame but she had a job in keeping with her caste. The water, of course, had to be boiled before I could drink it.

I also had a cook. He had been a traveling salesman who peddled various trinkets to surrounding villages on a rented bike. He lived in a single rented room with his wife and six children. After becoming my cook, he bought a small wooden cabinet and set it up as a tiny shop on a street corner in the vil-lage. He was beginning to move up in the world.

The Peace Corps had given me a tiny bit of training in poultry and farming. The Rajput eventually gave me another room at the side of the courtyard where I kept 30 chickens. The Rajput col-lected eggs for rent and Mike and I ate most of the rest of the eggs. I tried to sell eggs to the villagers. but my eggs were not to their liking. My eggs were twice the size of the local eggs, because I fed my chickens properly with nutritious feed that I bought in Udaipur. My eggs, though, lacked the pungent flavor of the local variety. My chickens didn't run free eating bugs and scraps from the ground, and, as the villagers complained, I had no rooster.

I kept my chickens in production for the full two years of my Peace Corps service. As my time in India drew to a close, I asked the Rajput if he wanted to continue the poultry project on his own. He declined. Mike and I then ate a few chickens. I couldn't sell any in the local market because of the stigma of their tasteless eggs. I decided to take the chickens to Udaipur and sell them there. I discovered that the train would not accept live cargo. With some assistance, I lifted the basket full of chickens up onto the top of a bus. The bus driver then asked me to pay a full fare for each chicken.

"What? They're all in a covered basket on the roof. I'm not putting each chicken on a seat by itself inside the bus!"

"That doesn't matter," the bus driver replied. "They each pay a full fare because each one has life in it!"

The glories of Eastern spirituality escaped me at that moment. After a strenuous argument, I managed to pay a half fare for each chicken.

My adventures in giving agricultural advice were no less daunting. I rode my bicycle alongside an Indian extension worker who began each day by popping into his mouth some snuff-like material from a small covered bowl in his living room. I wondered why he always seemed to be in a better mood than I was, but less talkative. Eventually, I learned that his "snuff box" was filled with fried marijuana mixed with sugar. He never offered me any.

I sometimes carried sacks of fertilizer on my bike and lent them to farmers. A few of them paid me back. One came to visit me after the season and complained that the fertilizer had ruined his crop. He had no irrigation and the rains had failed, so the fertilizer just sucked the remaining moisture out of the soil, leaving the crops withered and parched.

Once I sent away for some films on improved agricultural practices. The district agricultural officer drove me in his jeep to several villages to show the films. He asked me to say a few words in Hindi before we began the agricultural films. Prior to that, however, he showed a more popular historical movie. After watching clips about the massacre of Indians by the British at Amritsar, I was a little queasy as I got up to speak, the only white guy in a sea of Indians.

At one village, we stopped at a house where a man was dying of typhoid. We tried to convince his family to take him to the hospital. They decided instead that they would put their trust in prayers to God.

After I had read through the big box of books that the Peace Corps provided, I was usually bored sitting in my rooms in the castle in Sunwar. I often rode my bike the two miles to Mike's village. Fatehnager was a growing little town, with train and bus stations, and numerous shops. As I arrived in town, local merchants would frequently insist that I stop, come into their shops, and sit beside them. They weren't so much trying to make sales, but rather to relieve their own boredom with conversation. As I entered their shops, they would reach out and grab my hand. They held onto me through the whole interview process. Complete strangers would ask me the most confidential questions.

"How old are you? Are you married? When will you get married? How much money do you make? How much do you send home to your parents every month?"

When I explained that my parents didn't need my money, their esteem for me plunged. How could I convey the idea that a share of my $55/month salary would be useless in America?

Mike lived in a large single room apartment in the center of town. He had electricity but no running water. He also had a chamber pot in a tiny room just outside his apartment, a convenience of urban living. The chamber pot was emptied every day by a "sweeper," the lowest caste allowed to live in the village, one step above an untouchable.

After a year, the advantages of town life became so attractive to me that I got permission to move from Sunwar to Fatehnager. I took a ground floor apartment not far from where Mike lived. Once, I was woken in the night by a rat running along the side of my rope bed. I was grateful that the mosquito net had provided some protection. In the morning, I noticed gnaw marks in the grease my cook had left in the flat cooking plate he used.

I put out some rat poison, but then ended up smelling the dead rat hidden somewhere in the walls of my apartment for many weeks afterward.

Eventually, I developed a better system for coping with the rats. I kept a flashlight and two sticks beside my bed. When a rat woke me up by running across my bed, I would turn on the flashlight, and walk over to turn on the room light. With one stick, I would flush the rat from behind the bookcase where it could always be found at such times. As it dashed out, I killed it with the other stick.

Once, a very large rat eluded me. I kept chasing it through my kitchen, living room, and front veranda, whacking away with my stick, but missing it every time. By the time we reached the front of the apartment, the dogs had been alerted. Stray dogs ruled the streets of Fatehnager after dark. I had a screen around my veranda and the dogs were gathered there, barking and snarl-

ing at the chance. The rat was climbing on the inside of that screen and I was smashing away with my killer baton. Suddenly, the rat dashed to one side of the veranda, found a hole at the top the screen, jumped down into the street and, before the dogs could snatch it, dashed into a masonry hole and thereby escaping into the adjacent apartment. One might learn a lot about survival from that rat.

Toward the end of my stay in India, I once again met Swami Chinmayananda, who had converted me to Hindu philosophy four years earlier. He was giving a talk in Bombay (now Mumbai), not far from where he had an ashram. After having lived for almost two years in rural India, the Swami seemed so westernized to me. He had lost his exotic allure. And I had lost my aspiration for spiritual realization. I had come to accept my identity as an individual. In India, I had learned that I was an American. Being a spark of the divine didn't seem so meaningful any more. I now wanted to make the trains run on time. I was heading back to business school in the States.

CHAPTER 7

Letters from India

Katherine Kelleher Sohn

From June 1967 until May 1969, I resided in India as an American Peace Corps Volunteer after two summers of training stateside in Milwaukee, Wisconsin and two additional months of in-country training. Assigned to the Primary Health Center in Risod, Maharashtra, India, I spent many hours writing home. Fortunately, my mother, Teresa Kelleher, kept those letters, which have helped me construct a portrait of my life those many years ago.

November 11, 1967

Dear Mother, Dad, and family,

Our Public Health Office, Dr. Hore, invited Sylvia and me to a week-long celebration of Diwali [the festival of lights] with his extended family last week in a nearby village. His brother, whom we called Uncle Farmer Hore, hosted a picnic under one of the huge Banyan trees that grow all over India. He grows grapes, jowar (a type of wheat), oranges, lemons, and limes. He knows about modern methods of farming and a lot about American crops. He said to us, "You write your mother and father and tell them to fly over here and come to Arjangoan and bring all American good stuffs and champagne, and we will have a big feast under this tree." Now how can you resist such an invitation? Our favorite character was Grandpa Hore who at 101 years old sits in his white turban and healthy wrinkled face, takes evening walks, and still practices ayurvedic medicine. His face lit up whenever we greeted him or when he delighted in the antics of the children with their fire crackers.

We stayed up until one o'clock one night with all of the Hore family from college age up asking questions about America, and we were able to correct some of their stereotypes as they enlightened us about our impressions of India. Their main questions were whether American women are equal to men in everything and what love marriages are like. They were curious about divorce, but also about the position of Blacks which we equated to their untouchables, about whether we believed in God, and what our feelings were about the afterlife.

Ironically, while I was there, I broke out in hives from head to toe, a reaction perhaps to a very spicy mutton served for the festival meal. Five of Grandpa Hore's sons and one daughter who are doctors of all kinds treated me, so I don't know whether it was Western or homeopathic or ayurvedic medicine that stopped the itching.

It was great hearing about the Christmas tape which you are making for me. How I long to be with you at this time and how difficult it will be for both of us, I am sure you realize. But can you see how close it's bringing us? I've never felt closer to home than when I receive news about details you may feel are tedious, and Christmas time will bring us even closer. Hugs and kisses, Kathy

This letter recounts our trip to Arjangoan, Maharashtra, the home place of our Public Health Officer, Dr. Hore, soon after our arrival in Risod. Our group, India 44-A, had come to India after graduating from our respective colleges and finishing our training in Milwaukee, Wisconsin. Upon saying our goodbyes to our families, we departed JFK airport on July 27, 1967 for a long, long trip to New Delhi and eventually Bombay (Mumbai). After two months in Palghar and Umroli near the Indian Ocean, we were sworn in on September 27 and then were on to Akola, our district town where we registered before finally ending up in Risod. Our trip with Dr. Hore's family introduced us to educated Indians and taught us more about their culture.

September 13, 1967
Dear Mother and Daddy,
Sylvia and I took a walk to the salt fields the other day. It's the only place to be alone, and it's beautiful. Any people that go by ignore you which we found unusual. We were both frustrated because the language teacher was completely overlooking our needs in Marathi class. The one great thing about Sylvia is that she senses my feelings, and I sense hers so we talk it out. We both agreed that at our final site, we would not set ourselves up as entertainment for the village. She knows when to make a joke—after we talked seriously about our site and decided to talk to the instructor about what we needed, we started laughing at the situation. So Syl and I come out with how we feel and laugh about it which eases the tension. The other day she told the visiting women that I was in the market for a husband, and they got a huge kick out of it.

Last Friday we took a tonga ride into town. You might have thought that it was the 18th century riding along in a horse drawn carriage and the mountains on one side and the beautiful palm trees against the blue sky and little Mirawis herding the goats and cattle to heaven knows where and the click of the horse and the peace of the morning and you're in a sari. Until a bus comes by, you'd swear you were back in time.

Keep smiling and keep up the letters because they are my sunshine. Much love Kathy

Sylvia Bray was my roommate until she transferred in March 1968 to Rajasthan upon marrying another Peace Corps volunteer, Jerry Weiss, who was in our brother project, India 44B. She was two years older than I was, enjoyed living, was honest, and had an engaging sense of humor. I particularly liked her take charge sense of confidence and her worldliness, especially when contrasted with my sheltered background. I remember now that her dad painted and that I met her sister who lived near Milwaukee.

What led people like me and Sylvia to this village of Risod at the end of the paved road, this place where dirt paths were worn by bullock carts, cattle, and water buffalo? What led me

and my fellow volunteers to choose a life with no running water (our water was delivered by the *pani walla* in huge adobe urns carried on either side of his body), where cooking took place on kerosene stoves, where sleep was found on aluminum beds with sleeping bags and mosquito netting? And what about going to the latrine with a loti (container) of water and no toilet paper? Whatever possessed us to think we could survive hot seasons and monsoons? Who could have anticipated the language barriers despite all of the training ahead of time? What were we thinking; or were we thinking?

   To answer these questions for myself, I had to examine my formative years, growing up as the oldest of eight, the daughter of Leo and Teresa Berry Kelleher. We were Catholics in North

Carolina among Protestants and a few Jewish folks, and where fundamentalists condemned Catholicism as a cult. Some locals asserted that Catholics were not Christian because they called priests "Father"; the Bible says only God can be addressed as Father. We were always outsiders, but we had a marvelous pastor, Monsignor Dolan who, even before Vatican II, made changes in his church by celebrating the Mass in English so that our Protestant friends who came with us to church would understand the liturgy.

In addition to my Catholic education where I heard daily about serving the poor, the Berry family (my mother's side) had its own mantra of serving others. Mother had three sisters who were nuns and one brother who was a priest. Mother and Daddy with other Black parents sponsored an integrated dance for my senior prom in a local hotel since our Catholic bishop, afraid of riots, forbade dances on school property. My mother regularly protested against Republican policies that victimized the poor.

While she was a feminist before her time, my mother had rigid expectations of southern women. Before I went to college, Mother, so afraid I would embarrass her with my awkward, gawky behavior, sent me to Mrs. Ainsworth's Charm School where I learned to walk, talk, and smile correctly. I laughed when another volunteer recently said he thought I was a proper Southern lady; how pleased my mother would have been to hear that!

My sheltered life continued under the protection of the Daughters of Charity at St. Joseph College. I was never sure what I wanted to do after college, so I majored in English because my aunt, Sister Margaret Ann Berry, taught the subject and thought it would be a good background for any field I might pursue. Unsure of my future and wanting to do some service, I thought at first of becoming a nun until I met red-headed Nick Lucker my freshman year. Then when President John Kennedy invited us to a life of service and began the Peace Corps, I heeded the call. Joining the Peace Corps was far less of a commitment than joining the convent. Because of Aunt Margaret's interest in India (in the mid-sixties she obtained Ford

174

and Fulbright grants to study in India), and my uncle's (Father Thomas Berry) stories about Indian people and their religions, Hinduism and Buddhism, I knew that India was the place I wanted to go. Therefore, I was most happy to be notified that was where I would be going. And, though I was deeply in love with Brian Morley, my college sweetheart, he promptly moved to the second spot on my list. I knew I could always get married but would probably never again get the chance to go to India. Brian said he would wait two years for me; how fortunate for me that he did not!

Upon my acceptance, I traveled to Milwaukee, Wisconsin, for the Advanced Training Program, a concept that Peace Corps thought would turn out better prepared volunteers for the host countries. They reasoned that volunteers could spend the summer in language and cultural training after their junior year of college and return for their senior year with the idea of continuing language or area studies independently or in regular courses. Though I have sweet memories of our training over that first summer, I still remember a session with the Peace Corps psychologist who remarked that I was not participating in small group discussions. How could I? I was meeting people I could never imagine—hippies from San Francisco, in-your-face New Yorkers, Wyoming cowboys—fine people with totally different values and worldviews than my own. I wanted to hear what they had to say and was reluctant to reveal my own naiveté and ignorance. This summer was excellent preparation for India because it was so culturally different from my North Carolina upbringing.

When I came back to campus after our first training summer, I recall questioning my moral theology teacher, Monsignor Kline, about the church's position on birth control in the face of massive poverty. I had been taken by a family planning presentation by Helene Moos, a family planning worker in India, who spent the summer with our group. Perhaps because I did not worship him as did my other classmates or perhaps because my questions made him uncomfortable, the only response I received for my questions beyond a grimace was a D on my grade report.

However, I was opening up my mind. I remember being upset about the vasectomies and tubal ligations which would take place in the primary health centers in Maharashtra where we would be working. I understood the point of birth control as a way to help alleviate poverty, but I had difficulty with sterilization. In early August, in our training village outside of Bombay (Mumbai), I recall witnessing a vasectomy performed in pretty rustic operating conditions. Although the primitive anesthesia overpowered me, I walked out of the operating room also because I was wrestling with emotions and conscience. The Indian government encouraged men and women to consider the surgery after they had two or three children. The program promoter, the doctor, and the patient all received governmental incentives. Though my evolution was gradual, I opened my mind after I witnessed a woman in our village die from a poisoned placenta, another woman losing her baby in delivery, and numerous cases of malnutrition in outlying villages. Eventually, I became enraged with a church that ignored the human condition, and I quickly lost my self-righteous attitude about the morality of birth control.

August 30, 1968

Dear family,

*I am disappointed with the Pope's [Paul] encyclical [On the Progression of Peoples]. His decision may have been based solidly on theological opinion and traditional teaching, but it lacked the humanity a man of God needs in the world today. He seems to ignore the fact of the population increase and insufficient food supply (which is a very **real** problem) and the recommendations of a 56 member commission that Pope John had set up—it isn't right and just. I would like to take the Pope through the streets of Bombay where little beggars search the trash of richer people for food. You see, Catholics in the US will make their own decisions regarding birth control, but Indian Catholics are unusually devout, and they can't afford to listen to the Pope when their country has so many starving people.*

Love, Kathy

India also challenged me physically. We witnessed the birth of animals in our front yard as this poem records, and monkeys regularly invaded our kitchen where they absconded with our potatoes and bananas, and I fantasized in a journal entry that "people will see them dying around my house, those despicable creatures." In a letter home, I reported the mouse found in my sleeping bag and others which Sylvia and I chased out of our house. At the same time, I became friends with a lizard in my new apartment because he ate the mosquitoes and I, as a consequence, no longer needed a mosquito net.

The sunshine
Dried out the rain
While
In papal like irrelevancy
Strings of Bach's violins play
As another ass is born
In the midst of hell.

For Christmas of 1967, I sent a homemade card to people back home with the photo of Sylvia and me in front of the only elephant we ever saw in India.

The sun fades
And impressions of one million
Within a moment of time—
The richness of the softness,
The stillness of shadows
Speaking softly
Under stars and lanterns
And the turban nodding to his bullocks—
The music of the wooden bump
And oxen bells lightly into
     the popple of the wheat grinder—
Static cinema, a life beyond—
Laugh at snow sleds in Kashmir.

The adolescent poetry above was written after a few days in the village and tries to convey its incredible peace; the sounds refer to the first visit we took on a bullock cart to an outlying village with our lady health visitor. Seeing an Indian movie in our village, we could not believe the laughter when the audience saw snow sleds.

October 25, 1967

Dear all,

Would you believe that it's gotten cold enough to have a blanket on top of our sleeping bag? Guess what we have? Chickens! We got them today in Washim, the next largest town and the site of the Church of the Nazarene mission hospital. We paid twelve rupees each for two layers, but we figured it was worth it for the money we would save on eggs which we have been buying from the Muslim children. We're really excited about being real farmers. The villagers are looking for a coop for us to house them in. People are so nice.

We went to see a garden on the outskirts of town and it's absolutely beautiful. It has zillions of trellises and millions of gorgeous multicolored flowers from which the owner of the garden had the gardener pick a bouquet for us. We went with our Marathi tutor, Sri Krishna Deshmuck, a retired teacher and delightful human being. There are trees there with huge trunks the kind you'd like to climb and many winding paths.

The tutor's lessons aren't good as far as enriching our Marathi, but he does so many things for us and says, "You are my daughters and anything I can do for you, I do with pleasure." He's so afraid that we're going to be cheated by the shopkeepers that he buys us things and we pay him back.

He came in the other day for a lesson and Syl and I were drinking Kool-Aid. When we asked him if he'd like some, he told us he wouldn't take it because we might have something alcoholic in it. We were not offended at his distrust because he said it in such a natural way. When we asked him again about having some because we did not drink alcoholic beverages, he took some of the Kool Aid powder home with him. He told us that he's never touched flesh, or eggs, or alcohol in his life. And I guess that's why he's so healthy and perky for 65.

Love Kathy

Those chickens provided us with a great India story. Before Sylvia married Jerry Weiss, we had an adventure on our cook's day off. Bored with our vegetarian meals and hungry for fried chicken, we decided to kill one of these chickens, the one that was not producing very many eggs. Although Jerry's group had poultry training, we had none. Sylvia recalled that her grandmother used to wring the chicken's neck, so she took on that duty (she says that I kept grimacing and saying, "Ooh, Sylvia, ooh!). My chore was to pluck the feathers as the chicken looked at me with one pleading eye. Sylvia cut the chicken into pieces as we pumped up the kerosene stove and heated the peanut oil. We set the table with a tablecloth, played a Simon and Garfunkel tape, and sat down to eat. I don't recall who took the first bite, but we chewed and chewed and realized quickly that it was inedible. Before we could cry after all that work and no fried chicken, we had to bury the feathers and debris so that Bainabai, our cook, would not suspect that we had slaughtered the chicken and actually eaten the meat since she was Hindu, and we were careful to respect local customs. Later when I was married, I received a book with instructions on how to kill a chicken and finally understood our mistakes: we had neglected to drain the blood, we should have dipped the chicken in hot boiling water to loosen the feathers, and we should never have started with a diseased chicken.

After Sylvia moved to Jerry's village, I was alone and missed her companionship. I continued my center work, attending deliveries, teaching some English at the high school, working with the Balik Mandel (women's groups), preparing posters for publicity, creating kitchen gardens, and working on nutrition programs. My biggest project was enlisting the help of the Rotary Club in the district town to cosponsor a triple antigen vaccination program for diphtheria, tetanus, and whooping cough for children in the village. I remember the huge ceremony on the grounds of the Primary Health Center and the crowd of children who came. I count this among my achievements since it is difficult to measure the effectiveness of anyone's presence in India.

October 14, 1968
Dear Folks,
Everything for the Triple Antigen Campaign program turned out so nicely—the turnout was just marvelous. Dr. Ghate, the Akola Rotary Club president, didn't expect the crowd that came and neither did I—he only brought out enough vaccine for 500 children and 600 showed up—so we had to turn about 100 away and told them to come another day. The job couldn't have been done without everyone working together. What makes me feel good is that the Primary Health Center Staff did most of the work, and so it showed that once given the incentive, the staff work hard and that they'll carry on the work. Dr. Jain, our District Health Officer as well as the Block Development Officer, was extremely pleased. Because they have seen the town reacting like this in such a big turn out, they are really anxious to get the eye camp out here and after that polio vaccine. I feel just a little bit of pride that I got the Rotary Club to come out and just real happy that the town reacted as it did. But it's neat having work to do and I've been utterly exhausted lately, that really satisfying exhaustion where I can say, I did something worthwhile today.
Love Kathy

After the hot season, the monsoons came, and though the rains could create havoc, they provided relief from the stultifying heat. I recall a bus on my way back to the village getting stuck in the mud for a long time, so that at some point, I had to urinate behind a bush which really wasn't all that hidden. There were times like this that my height and blond hair were liabilities. I recorded the following poem in my journal.

Merlin said to learn
And I smiled (well I cried)
Standing in rich velvet green grass
And feeling the tickle of tender new trees
That rain had enlivened.
To hear the uncanny sound of baby buffalo—
All is fertile, young, growing and innocent
Even in the knowledge of what happened before

On those nights when sterile trees would not waiver
And grass died
And the sky stiffened the brain in its sultry manner
And the only thing to do was die
Or hope for the single sway of a branch and breathe.

The end of my time in India is a blur and the date of the last letter that my mother saved is April 4. From the time Sylvia had left for Rajasthan, I had requested a transfer. There was talk in one of my letters of assigning me to the village where Mary Jo Dummer and Carolyn Jones lived (other volunteers in our group) so that I could work with them until the end of our time in India. What I recall is that there was some glitch, the nature of which I do not remember, so I was sent home early, missing the termination conference and the travel through Europe which I was planning to do with friends. Early termination also resulted in an earlier than usual reunion with my family.

March 19, 1969

Dear Folks,

I was just in Bombay for a week. Our director, Tom Trout-man, called me in and wanted to know if I'd like to terminate early, that he was worried about me. He came in February to visit our sites and said mine is the worst of any in our group. Last July, when I asked for a transfer, Tom was not our director or else he would have immediately done so. They've had three cases in the last three years of volunteers who've had nervous breakdowns because they were unhappy in their sites. And so he wanted to avoid that. I said that I would think about it, but think I will persist because it's only two months till the termination conference.

I am tired tonight and thinking that it's been a good two years, that I've grown in so many ways only to find out that there is always room for self-improvement—being alone and living with one's faults is not easy and so I have a slight inferiority complex— I can get unbelievably tense at times—this is due to the pressure of suppressed emotions, those times when you really want to blow up at the doctor or shopkeeper cheating you or a drunk Indian man who last week grabbed me. I got on the bus and he followed me

and kept trying to say something to me. I asked a man from Risod to help me, and he had the man arrested. I can't take this place when I am treated as a cinema attraction.

Love Kathy

The letters from the summer of 1968 until April 1969 portray a tremendous support network of other Peace Corps volunteers, doctors and missionaries, Peace Corps staff, and letters from home. I spent a brief time at the Presbyterian hospital in Poona where they could not figure out why I could not even keep down a cup of tea. I recall our one year left in India celebration in Udaipur at the Lake Palace Hotel—how nice it was to be with American guys who weren't grabbing at your body parts (without permission). Other memories of Sylvia and Jerry's wedding in Bombay at the cathedral and all of us dressed up so nicely, of trips to Goa and Bangalore, of Peace Corps conferences where we could be ourselves again—all of these added up to the growth experience that was India.

Epilogue

In May 1969, I came back to a different world: Robert Kennedy and Martin Luther King had been assassinated, and

Nixon elected to office. I returned to Greensboro anxious to see my family but irritated by the youngest in the family. I worked in rural community organizations for the Office of Economic Opportunity but had problems as a white female supervising a more experienced African American community worker with six children. I was soon enrolled in graduate school in student personnel in higher education which led to my job as a career counselor at Howard Community College in Columbia, Maryland where I worked with women returning to college. I worked briefly for the American Lung Association, but in between met my husband Mark and got married in 1973.

After he finished his doctorate in education, Mark began applying for jobs, and we eventually settled in Pikeville, Kentucky. By then, we had been married a year-and-a-half. Located in the 300 million year old Appalachian Mountains, Pikeville is actually a lot smaller than Risod (6000 as opposed to 20,000) though Risod was located at the end of the developed road and reachable only by bus, 2.5 hours from the district town.

My first nine months in central Appalachia were far worse than my adjustment to living in India. I expected India to be different; I did not expect any town in America to be so different from the places I had grown up and gone to college.

I was so homesick I could die. Isolated in these steep and narrow mountains so unlike the Smokies near to where I grew up, two or more hours from an airport, living on the mountain top where the college was located, a coal tipple at the bottom of the hill which often blocked our car access into town when 144 rail cars would come through, I thought I had come to the end of the world. No one came to visit, and with no job, I cleaned the coal dust from our bookshelves and furniture, waxed the kitchen floor, and flew into a rage when Mark walked across the street from his Dean of Students' job to our centrally located home on campus and did not notice my efforts. Anyone who knows me will understand that this behavior was unlike me. For sheer survival, I began interviewing for information, a technique I learned from Richard Irish, a headhunter in Washington, DC before I moved to Pikeville. This included making contacts with leaders in Pikeville and Pike County to learn as much as I could about the community and the job market before I went job hunting. Because of the economic downturn in the coal industry on which everything in the region is based, I learned that the job market was closed to me. I worked with a college art teacher who had set up a part-time community education program which she thought I might expand since she did not have the time. With support from the college, external foundations, and eventually federal funding, I designed and directed the Center for Continuing Education, which offered the only noncredit courses offered in Pikeville and Pike County at the time.

As we learned later, the reason people didn't approach us with the traditional banana bread welcome to town was that they were watching and waiting to see how we would respond to the area. They wondered if, like other outsiders before us, we would make unflattering comparisons of Pikeville to the city we had left. Outsiders—missionaries, politicians, federal and state programs of "uplift"—had come to the region for years, and, although not all that they did was harmful, they conveyed a general feeling that the people of the region could not solve their own problems. In consequence, they generally created ill feelings and, sometimes, learned helplessness.

Sensitive to my place as an outsider, I recalled from my experience in India that well-intentioned outsiders can unwittingly promote a cultural imperialism, our mere presence being a statement that our way of life was better than the lives of the native Indian villagers. Peace Corps volunteers were ostensibly there to assist the host country meet stated goals and many of us worked with local agencies and governmental entities. Although I cherished the lessons that I learned in those difficult years, did I learn them at the expense of the Indian people? I found this remark in a letter to a Peace Corps friend: "I don't know why they chose Risod as a site—of course any village in India probably needs help but Risod has two good doctors, 6 nurse trainees, and is pretty well staffed otherwise. I'm superfluous, so I go to the clinic mainly to get out of the house and to talk to someone else." My feelings about the people of India went to extremes from my suspicion of Indian men who were too curious about American women (based on movies they had seen) to the tenderness I felt for the untouchables who kept the Health Center clean. I suppose it was all part of living. I am just not so sure that I contributed anything of lasting value for all that I learned.

What is clear to me now are the similarities across rural areas where services are often second rate given that urban centers take the lion's share of resources. The women in both Risod and Pikeville taught me so much about kindness and generosity and inward strength. My experiences also taught me that I cannot judge by outward appearances: In India, arranged marriages where the new bride entered the home of her mother-in-law, obeying the rules of that household and tolerating her husband's occasional infidelity looked like slavery to me. Several Indian women corrected my misconception by describing the love that grew in the arranged marriage and how much they were able to accomplish. In Appalachia, I saw married women bowing to their husbands' wills in relation to the money they spent and the places they were allowed to go. My neighbor Connie, sensitive to outsiders' portraits of Appalachian women as passively accepting the rule of the mountain man, corrected my perception when we became friends. She had me look a little closer where I saw that although some women were abused, many women knew how to handle their men and make it look like they were in charge. Though we might decry those tactics, it worked for them, and Connie didn't want anyone else's pity.

I learned from my experiences in India and Appalachia to knock the feminist chip off my shoulder and look deeper into what women contribute in both societies. The female teachers in Risod; our second female public health officer, Dr. Thakkar, who was a rarity at that time in her field; the wealthy woman in the village who helped her husband with his farming even though she was Bombay educated; the Lady Health Visitor who had such tremendous rapport with the hundreds of families she worked with; Bainabai, our cook who took such good care of us and me for so long; and the sweeper in the clinic who befriended me and listened patiently to my dubious Marathi.

It was teaching composition at Pikeville College that taught me the most, especially when it came time to complete the research for my doctorate which I began late in life and completed before my 54th birthday. The women that I have met from the time I moved here, but especially the women I interviewed for my dissertation, *Whistlin' and Crowin' Women of Appalachia: Literacy Practices since College*, dispelled any stereotypes of illiteracy so common to this region. These bright and intelligent women were afraid to come to college but came out of economic necessity because their husbands were disabled in the mines or they were divorced. They were the least likely to come to college—two were high school dropouts—and attended against all conceivable odds. These women were remarkable: Lucy, whose husband would not allow her to bring her schoolbooks or any reading materials into the house; Jean whose in-laws made her feel awful for leaving her high-school-age children to take nursing classes; Sarah whose husband was so threatened that he eventually divorced her because she became too independent. These women shared their stories with me and in doing so made me a better teacher because they worked to achieve their goal of a college degree, which in turn improved both their lot and the lives of their children, whom I interviewed for a follow-up study.

When I look back at the immaturity reflected in my letters from India, I wonder at the wisdom of youth. At my current age, I could not have done what I did then. When I look at the sheer length of my letters, I wonder in this age of email and hurried multitasking whether I could ever have conveyed what I was observing without paper and pen. When I think of how long it took to reserve the phone for a long distance call home which had to be routed through Australia or London, I marvel at my ability to use my cell phone to call Mark's family in Germany as easy as I can call New York. I hear that volunteers are allowed to go home during their two year stint—India was too far away and it was too expensive to make the trip. The world is smaller now because of telecommunications and for better or worse, many Americans have seen the movie *Slumdog Millionaire* so they know more about India.

When I think of my India 44-A & B friends with whom I have become reacquainted, I marvel at what we have done. Whatever our experience was in-country, India touched us on the deepest level possible. How can I forget the sweetness of the beautiful children who greeted us daily with "What is your name?", the only English many of them knew, our Lady Health Visitor who named Sylvia, *Schoba*, which means beautiful flower, and me *Jhoti,* which means sunshine? How can I forget the smells of India—the flour in the mill, the betel nut after a meal, curry and cardamom in everything, chapattis hot on the stove, the hot season and the monsoons? And can I ever recreate the sounds of India: the tonga bell, the clomp of the bullocks, the popple of the wheat grinder, the vendors crying aloud in the market place, the crows gathering for breakfast scraps outside our door, monkeys scurrying on the roof and through the tree branches, static music from loud speakers blasting outside the movie theaters, donkeys braying in the front yard as they deliver their colts, and the water buffalo who always seemed to be in the path of the bus? How could any of us look at true poverty without remembering examples of what we saw: the leprosy survivor who used an old car tire to transport himself since his legs were amputated and who begged for money at the Risod bus stop daily? Can we explain to anyone the Indian sense of time: the bus or train is either late or, if it's on time, it's not your train? These are the images of the poetry of India of which fellow volunteer and spouse of Carolyn (Watanbe) Adler, Peter Adler, wrote about in the Gateway literary magazine in September, 1967:

The foreigner brings with him the mode of the West, his own ways and his own systems, and his eye views India through this but not exclusively. India snarls itself around the intruder just as it does around those who are native. As it does so, a mode of the 'new' and the 'old' is created. This is not a static thing, however, but a process which fluctuates and varies at its own individual rate. Poetry comes also for that very reason . . . .One does not squeeze India very hard, for already she does so to you, and the result in part is poetics, the image which we cannot explain but in which we can begin.

We are wise sages now looking back at our twenty-something selves, wishing we had been more aware of each other's talents and achievements. We were so self-centered—it's just developmentally what needed to happen. Six months into retirement, I am re-defining myself and feel just as unsettled as my letters and journal suggest back then. Looking back to this time in India, I have hope and confidence that maturity will finally come to me at this late date.

AN EDITORIAL NOTE

The three reflections that follow (chapters 8-10) touch upon events and choices that faced many of us in the turbulence and trials that were the 1960s. Peace Corps came of age when the U.S. was fully engaged in the Viet Nam war, a conflict that created deep divides within the American community. Some saw the military and Peace Corps as complementary strategies for helping the country confront the challenges of that age. Others were dubious of the Peace Corps concept, assuming it was little more than a way for young men to escape their obligation to serve.

The reality is that a few members of our generation wound up in India and other such sites as Peace Corps volunteers. While we sincerely believed we were working to make the world a slightly better place, we were also acutely aware of the hundreds of thousands of other young men and women serving and dying in the remote jungles of Vietnam ostensibly to preserve a way of life we all cherish.

In chapter 8, Jerry Weiss tells of meeting and befriending a young Vietnam veteran from his home town. Though their life circumstances were very different, their story suggests we are all much closer than appearances might indicate.

In chapter 9, Sam Rankin explores how he found Peace Corps from rugged Montana, and how that choice profoundly affected his life and his view of the larger world. Leaving India early, he soon found himself in the jungles of Vietnam as the only Medic in an infantry platoon. His unique perspective enables him to compare the sacrifices made by those who traveled these separate roads and to appreciate the commonalities across these two groups of Americans.

In chapter 10, Gareth Loy expresses his desire to absorb the Indian culture and to serve in the Peace Corps, a desire truncated by the PC decision to send him home early. There he confronts all the classic decisions of life facing young men of that generation. Affirming his conscientious objection to war and contributing in an alternative service role was the path Gareth chose as he sought to make sense of his Peace Corps deselection and find a way to serve some larger cause.

At first blush, so much separates those who served in the military and those who sought service in the Peace Corps. It is all too easy to see so many differences and to dwell on those things that might well keep us apart. For those who care to look more closely, however, one can also uncover some profound connections that bring us together. Sam Rankin served in both the Peace corps and the U.S. Army. Bob Proffit, another India 44 volunteer followed his Peace Corps Service with a career as a military officer. In the end, as these stories suggest, we are closer to one another than we might well imagine.

CHAPTER 8

An Untold Story

Jerry Weiss

During the twenty years between 1961 and 1981,
the Vietnam War claimed 58,000 American lives.

Two-thirds of them—nearly 40,000—died,
and another 200,000 were wounded during the 1967-69
period, while we served in India.

For every story told, there are a thousand untold.

My story is simple and ordinary. I grew up in Evanston, Illinois—five blocks from the Chicago city line: Howard Street, 1950s. On the Chicago side of Howard, there were liquor stores, bars, and those mysterious places called "Lounges".

On the Evanston side, it was dry.

On the Chicago side was the last stop for the "L" train. On the Evanston side, you had to change trains, take the bus, or walk. Unless it was snowing, mostly we walked.

I went to high school, college, joined the Peace Corps and went to India. Twenty years after my Peace Corps service, I met William.

His story is untold.

William was about my age, also from Evanston, but I never met him there. He lived on the other side of town.

193

At the end of 1966, at the age of nineteen, William joined the army. I finished college and joined the Peace Corps.

"Two years in the service of your country," they said, "will buy you the white picket fence for your new bride." Education, home loan, career—all these come with a good discharge. And she loved the way William looked in that uniform.

It made him proud: the uniform, the girl on his arm, new baby coming. This was everything good. William believed it all.

And when he got to Vietnam, Carlson, his best friend from high school, was there to greet him. They'd grown up together. Usually, guys from the same school weren't supposed to be assigned to the same unit. But there was a screw-up, and William got lucky.

Three weeks later, he watched his friend Carlson get blown to bits 10 yards in front of him.

"There was nothin' left but a pair of 'smokin' boots.

Oh, there was pieces of his body up in the trees, but I remember just seein' them smokin' boots."

At the end of his tour of duty, William volunteered to stay on.

"It's not so bad, once you learn to walk through the blood," he said.

William was no longer a teenager. And neither was I.

I had gone to Milwaukee, and then on to some great Peace Corps adventure.

"But why did you want to stay in that hell?" I asked.

"Drugs," he said matter-of-factly.

The bullet that finally tore through William in Vietnam shredded his pancreas. At the V.A. hospital he was put on Thorazine. They said he had emotional problems.

I met William in 1989 in San Francisco. My wife Andrea introduced us. Unlike myself, Andrea meets people wherever she goes. She was a volunteer at a local hospital when she met William in the darkness of his room. It was the morning after the "World Series" earthquake that October.

As he told the story, his bed shook violently during the earthquake, and he was thrown to the floor about 5:00 in the afternoon. The door slammed. He waited for help, but no one

came. Unable to rise without assistance, he spent the night there—on the hard floor, under a sheet.

Now crippled and with complete kidney failure, he ate pulverized meals with his remaining six teeth. A couple of months earlier, around his 42nd birthday, they took him into surgery to try to save his weakened eyesight. He woke up blind.

The psychiatrist said he adjusted very well.

Weight: 96 pounds.

Medications: Pancreas, Lomotil, Propoxyphene, Xanex, Diphenoxhylate, and more...

The doctors said he was still alive. This is when I met William.

I didn't know him before then, but I knew he was out there somewhere. I knew he went to Vietnam while I went to India.

And he knew about guys like me...

Surprisingly, William took a liking to me. I think it was because he liked Andrea. If I liked Andrea, too, then we must have still more in common. But whatever the source of our initial connection, something very close happened over the next eight months.

I started visiting him several times a week, sometimes bringing him food in the middle of the night. We talked, and we talked. He gave me his watch.

William's dad had been a reporter for the same newspaper I delivered as a kid in Evanston. I used to take the number 7 Oakton bus; he took the 3 Emerson. We talked about our schools, the music we listened to. (We both know full well what can stop the Duke of Earl.).

We talked a little about the war. But mostly we talked about our lives since then. We talked about our children, the way our mothers treated us, and the way the women in our lives...well, we talked about that too.

He was my age and from my town. But now, blind and bedridden, all he could do was talk.

He went to war. I went to Peace Corps.

—⋙—

August 8, 1947—June 4, 1990

SEIZURE, the doctor said, was the cause of death.

11:30 am, Monday, June 4, 1990, he said, was the time of death.

Of course, seizure was no more the cause of William's death than uterine contractions had been the cause of his birth. Seizure is a description of his dying. Cause is another question all together.

William's mother was Jacqueline. Her contractions on August 8, 1947, produced the man I met in 1989. In the 1940s, people on my side of town would say he was a colored boy. We were taught to say it like that, the nice way.

June 2, 1990

Franklin Hospital, San Francisco

"William, how are you today?"

""I'm proud to be Black! Are you proud to be White?"

It's come to this. I want a different story. I want ebony and ivory to be in perfect harmony. But the Black man from the other side of town went to war in 1967. And today, William is dying.

When I entered William's room that day, he was saying "I hear the slave ship coming."

I heard his voice. I know that's what he had said just before asking me about White pride.

Am I proud to be German, I wonder, looking at my Jewish wife?

I hesitate. I tell him that I'm proud to be myself.

"You know all the right words," he says, not complimenting me.

William and I shake hands warmly, going through the three-part ritual of handclasps that evolved during the civil rights years as a not-so-secret symbol of brotherhood.

"Are you still my brother?" he asks.

Again, I hesitate.

He and I had never done that brotherhood ritual before—-we were closer than that. Before, he had always just reached out for my hand, had held it for long minutes. William delighted in tell-

ing hospital personnel that I was his brother, leaving it for them to wonder about our parents.

But today, everything is different. Death is near. We both know it. (Is *that* the slave ship?). Today, ritual is important.

"Yes, of course. I'm still your brother." I tell him.

I know him now. And he knows me. He knows I'll come whenever he calls. We broke all the hospital rules together.

And I've been with him on those days when his real family would come round to mock him. They mocked him for his blindness, his diarrhea, his war wounds. But most of all, they mocked him for his total dependence on Whitey.

Whitey sent him to Vietnam. Whitey kept him in his neighborhood, got him on drugs, ruined his liver and kidney, took his eyesight. I am Whitey.

"I'm still your brother," I say again, still anxious about the meaning of his questions.

He smiles and reaches for my hand.

"You're all right," he says and holds it in both of his.

I relax for a moment, feeling like I had passed some unknown test, wondering if I had cheated somehow.

CHAPTER 9

Recollections of India and Vietnam

Sam Rankin

This is my story of India and my story of Vietnam. It starts, however, in the mostly rural state of Montana and with a question that I have always found perplexing.

How does a young person from Montana get interested in joining the Peace Corps? My first memory involving the Peace Corps was when I asked one of my friends sometime in 1965 to drive me to the post office to pick up an application for the program. His first reaction was to laugh heartedly. "Are you nuts? Why are you doing that?" he asked. In retrospect I think it sounded challenging and interesting. After all, who doesn't want to help other people?

I was always adventuresome: walking 10 blocks, with 3 corners to navigate, to my aunt's house when I was 3, without telling my mother. When I was fifteen and en route to Yellowstone Park with a friend for an overnight trip, we decided to drive to Las Vegas instead. Adding to the adventure we were going in a car I had put together from other junked cars. We called it a 'rail'.

Therefore, part of joining the Peace Corps was a natural continuation of trying to explore new places, doing new and hopefully exciting things.

I had a compassionate side but didn't know what it was called then. Some of my classmates in junior high and high

school, those seen as outsiders or not fitting in, made me feel I needed to be their friend, help them, or protect them from teasing by other classmates. Unfortunately, I didn't stand up for them often enough when they needed it. However, that intuitive feeling of wanting to help, along with my adventurous side, made it seem natural for me to respond to advertisements to join the Peace Corps.

In addition to the adventuresome side and wanting to help others, I, like many my age, was impressed with President Kennedy and thought he seemed to be talking directly to me. His exhortation to: "Ask not what your country can do for you . . ." was enough encouragement for me to act and fill out the Peace Corps application.

My father was born and raised on a homestead in central Montana. As a result of the Great Depression, he ended up owning and working in a clothing store in a small town. My father died while I was in elementary school. Consequently, I was raised in an urban setting, by Montana standards at least.

I believe if I had had more exposure to farming and ranching I might have joined the rodeo and tried bull riding to satisfy my need for adventure. Well maybe not, bull riding looks pretty dangerous but you get the idea. Joining the Peace Corps was an exciting way to find excitement that I didn't find in the town where I lived.

My recollection of India starts with the Peace Corps staff in Milwaukee giving me some bad news five or six days before we were to leave for New York and on to India. I wouldn't be able to go because I had a small opening at the base of my spine that hadn't closed properly during my early development. In most people this defect doesn't cause a problem. Nevertheless, it was a possible entry for germs and close to my spinal column so PC officials in Washington concluded that I couldn't leave the

country until it was surgically corrected. I've come to the conclusion that waiting to the last minute to tell me about my medical condition, while not necessarily planned, was something of
a calculated decision on the staff's part due to a 'readiness' classification that had been assigned to me by a PC psychologist.

I don't remember the name of my assigned psychologist (he
had a little battery powered fan on his desk) but he told me I was
classified as 'high risk.' As I understand it, the meaning of 'high
risk' went something like the following. If I were to undertake
my role as a volunteer as trained, I'd likely be a very good volunteer. At the same time, I might also follow an equally tempting
route (for me) and resign if my boredom level was high or I lost
interest. In other words, I was a high risk, high reward candidate
for Peace Corps service.

As it turned out it took more than a delay before our departure or a medical operation to bore me or cause me to lose interest. It took a near-death experience and lots of time to think in
a Bombay hospital.

While going to college I lived with my best friend's parents,
and his father was an MD. In a panic after being told I couldn't
go and wouldn't be able leave with my friends (plus not wanting
to go later by myself), I phoned him and asked if he could line up
the operation with one of his surgeon friends. He did and I flew
home the next day to have a pilonidal cyst removed. At the same
time, our group flew to New York for a few days of R&R before
heading to India. Little did I realize the operation is a serious
invasion of the human body and leaves a rather large wound that
is left open without stitches to heal from the inside out.

Not knowing what recuperating from the operation really
involved, I pleaded with the surgeon to allow me to leave his care
and get to New York in time for the evening World Airways flight
arranged by the State Department to take us to India. Unfortunately, my skills of persuasion were too good; he relented and
said I could go. This was only two or three days after the surgery.

I arrived at a gate on the same concourse, not far from where
all the India 44 people were waiting to board. After flying all
day from Montana, I arrived in New York in time and was happy

to be with my friends. I watched the loading of our trunks from the plane window and talked with everyone. I remember the excitement. I was tired but I was young and healthy and really pumped about going to India after all our training.

While the large pads (similar to a sanitary napkin) covering my incision had to be changed often, I did have Darvon for pain and discomfort. I couldn't easily care for myself because I couldn't see what I was doing. However, John Lievore and Mary Jo Dummer (now Clark) were brave enough to volunteer to help me change the dressings.

I remember eating breakfast in London's Heathrow Airport. I went to the men's room to change my dressing and came back and someone in our group had ordered for me: scrambled eggs and toast. Hmmmm, not bad! I don't remember who told me and I never did find out who ordered them, but the scrambled eggs were sheep brains. I'm hoping to find who it was at our next reunion. I'd forgotten this but Mary Jo reminded me at our reunion that she and I quietly went behind a statue at the Westminster Abbey where I lowered my pants . . . and she changed my dressing once again.

We landed in Tehran for refueling. I thought it was a little scary and odd to have the bus that was taking us to the terminal be escorted by two or three jeeps with mounted machine guns and a soldier at the ready. Of course it was only weeks after the Six-Day War when we lifted off. As I recollect now, I'm sure I saw 60 to 70 burned out, destroyed, and blown apart tanks lined up in a field we were flying over. Iran wasn't directly involved in the Six-Day War but may have supplied military supplies to Egypt, Syria or Jordan.

WAR . . . . . WHAT'S IT GOOD FOR? ABSOLUTELY NOTHING!

Somewhere over Afghanistan I looked out the window of the 727 and saw a flapping of the aluminum skin near the intake on one of the plane's engines. In a second or two it flipped over on itself and started peeling off backward. And then it was gone.

I think I was the first to see it, and I remember telling someone sitting beside me. A stewardess came and looked out my window and quickly disappeared. The plane slowed down and dropped in altitude but the remainder of the flight turned out to be rather uneventful. Amidst all this excitement, I continued to lose energy and was not feeling up to normal but I still felt motivated.

We landed in New Delhi, and I remember a number of fire trucks waiting beside the runway. In the airport, I realized what the words hot and humid really meant. We stayed at the International House for a day or two in Delhi and attended a few PC welcome briefings.

My lower back side was starting to ache. Moreover, I was very tired and my thinking was fuzzy. I was still committed, however

The train ride to Bombay was long, hot, and sooty from the coal powered locomotive. I think we were 3rd or 2nd class and therefore far enough back that we got a lot of the coal engine's smoke and soot. I know some of the group had talked about getting out near Agra to see the Taj Mahal and catching up with us later in Bombay.

I don't remember if anyone actually did get off and make the journey but I've always regretted not doing it. I believed I had plenty of time during my two years there to travel and planned on seeing it later. We arrived in Bombay and took taxis to the PC office where we met staff, one who was a nurse, ex-PCV, and who helped train us in Milwaukee. She took one look at me and said, "Come with me!"

I am no longer certain of the sequence of events but know I was taken to Breach Candy Hospital, a very *pukka* (first class) British hospital, within the hour. I had a massive deep infection in the wound and it was progressing fast to overpower my immune system. Days later I remember overhearing the head PC physician talking with a group of people by my bed making plans to fly me to a military hospital in Germany. He ended up by saying, "let's wait one more day and see how he progresses." I must have made progress because I never did leave Bombay. I was in a ward with approximately ten other males. One Russian sailor had received a shave/haircut on the street and had gotten an infection. His face and scalp were a mess. I think most of the men in the ward were all sailors from the cargo ships that ported in Bombay. Most were old, 30ish, and they were constantly looking, pointing at me, talking, and laughing.

I don't remember anyone coming to see me except John. I'm sure staff must have come but I can't recall anyone. When John came, he couldn't stay very long because he was supposed to be out in the training village, not in Bombay.

As I gained strength and the wound healed, I was allowed to leave the ward and walk around the grounds. Later I walked out into the neighborhood and saw firsthand the difficult living conditions for many people. One frail elderly woman stands out in my mind vividly. The few times I walked by her she had a big smile for me and she was always in the same spot, lying on a mat at a corner of a back alley. She had her head propped up with a rag and for two days had that big smile for me with red stained teeth (betel leaf) as I walked by.

The third day as she came into view I could see she was dead. She was unnaturally flat and ashen. I think she died not long before I came by because there was a large pool of urine beside her mat. I've always wondered if I had given her any-thing, would it have helped? I didn't realize how sick she was or possibly that she was starving. In that same general area where I walked, a couple of city blocks, I saw bullock carts that were used to pick up those who died on the streets. I now wonder if the people they picked up had tried to get medical help at the hospital but didn't have the money and were turned away.

During the month or two I was in the hospital and on the road to recovery, I was bored, very bored and very alone. I believe that's when I started to lose my motivation for being a volunteer. I think I lost interest due to isolation i.e. not being able to talk to the rest of my group with the support those interactions would provide. I also received no encouragement from staff, i.e. how everyone missed me and couldn't wait until I joined them or "it wouldn't be long until you're out" sort of discussion.

After visiting with everyone at our group reunion, I think many others experienced similar feelings only they were in a village. My hospital stay may not have been as big a factor as I had thought all these years. The staff may have viewed it as just more training (isolation) to see how I'd react once I was alone in a village. I may have expected too much from staff while in the hospital not knowing others in the group were having a similar experience.

While reading newspapers and *Time* magazine in the hospital, the U.S. involvement in Vietnam caught my attention every day, not in terms of the right or wrong of the U.S. being there, but in an intellectual-emotional way. I recall the cover of *Time* depicting American soldiers, bloody and wounded, riding a tank. They looked tired, lonely and scared. (I think the cover I'm referring to, which most Americans our age remember, actually came out a year or two after I was in India, but there were other similar pictures that had the same effect on me.)

The seed was planted: Maybe I could help those soldiers, and the Army seemed like it would be exciting and full of adventure i.e. I could be a medic (like in India) and help those guys. These weren't my conscious thoughts at the time but they were in my subconscious.

When I was discharged from Breach Candy, John came to show me the way to our village. We took the train North to Poona and went from train to bus to walking. As it got dark we were walking through a village and stopped to talk to a couple of old men sitting in front of a hut. The light was from a candle or oil lamp, very orange and dim. John did most of the talking as he had been interacting with the locals before, and, I thought, probably had a better grasp of Marathi and possibly had talked to these fellows before. I don't recall any specifics but John had an explanation after we left about why the one man had laughed so hard. He thought the old man was laughing at my answer to his question: "How long have your people (family) lived in your village?" It could have been because I answered: "My grandmother is thirteen years old and which way is the train station?"

Our quarters were on the second floor and I don't recall what was on the first floor. We were located in the middle of the village on a busy street and directly out our window we could look down the middle of another busy street which ended at our street in a tee formation. The first night I had a terrible time tying up my mosquito net and the next morning, after seeing one mosquito inside, I knew I was going to get malaria and die. The *bidis* (a local Indian form of cigarette) were great but I found my throat getting rather raw as I was smoking them like crazy. John and I went out each day to get our food. We had a cook but he couldn't come until the afternoon. The village had a rather large, even by American standards, developmentally disabled young man who would follow us around. I was somewhat afraid of him. No one seemed to be with him, and I thought maybe he'd want to come and stay with us, thinking if we said "no" he might get physical. Of course nothing ever happened. Most likely, he simply was not used to seeing any foreigners.

The village was on the Arabian Sea and one day a small group of us went walking out onto this long expanse of rela- tively flat beach which was not the normal color, light tan/white, but black sand. We all took off our sandals and walked barefoot only to find out later the area was part of the village latrine.

Later in the afternoon, most of the members of 44-A ended up at a home one of them was staying in. I was sitting on a large front porch with all of us talking and eating, when this huge raven flew onto the deck railing with this big swoosh, picked up a large piece of white bread with its beak, and flew off. I was not too far away from it and it scared the heck out of me.

I remember that during that meeting, I first began thinking maybe India wasn't for me. We were there for a reason, which I think was to give staff an ultimatum about something or other. I was a bit fearful of what lay ahead of me in India and I was still not mentally healthy, at least to the level where I was before get- ting on the plane in New York. Essentially due to my long stay in the hospital and slowly losing interest from not being 'out there doing something' I had slowly lost the will to be in India and to remain for the duration of my tour!

I do not recall to whom and where I said, "I want to leave".

Yes, PC was correct! I was a 'high-risk' volunteer. When I filled out the PC application in 1965 I was excited, and the thought of going to a foreign country was exhilarating. I checked the box that indicated I had no preference as to country. How exciting would it be for someone from Montana to be going to a foreign country and working? It was the ultimate! I was motivated. However, after the two summers training, isolation in the hospital, and possibly mental depression after getting out of the hospital, I was bored and had lost interest.

I don't remember very much of my four months in India and wonder how many remember the first months? Was it because of the 'culture shock' we were all told about i.e. just a huge change to our senses and thinking? Connie Robinson and I deselected at the same time and went through some of the same exit interviews and so forth. I stayed a night or two in the Taj Mahal hotel in Bombay and then flew to New Delhi for my final interview.

After a few days away from the group after I had voiced I wanted to leave but before I was on the plane in New Delhi leaving, I would have gladly said, "Can I come back" if anyone on staff had said anything like: "Are you sure this is what you want?" There was probably good reason for them not to say anything similar because my experience in the hospital was probably similar to what many of the group went through. My loss of interest while in the hospital probably was the equivalent of losing interest in a village and would have had the same effect: I would have wanted to do something more exciting and would probably have asked to leave. I thought I knew what I wanted but was really torn between wanting to go and wanting to stay.

I think Connie was with me on my way in the taxi to the PC office in Delhi. There was a food riot ahead of us, which I learned about by asking the taxi driver what the large crowd was all about. You could see the dust rising above the crowd. At least I think that's what he said. We were not in the mob but headed for it. I remember the deep instinctive fear I felt of that large a group. The taxi driver wanted to proceed but I was scared and remember making him go way out of our way around the crowd. It was somewhere near the Red Fort.

Not long after that I was on an Air France plane headed to Bangkok, Honolulu, Seattle, and Billings. My final Indian

legacy was a case of giardiasis (protozoa in your small intestine) and I had a heck of a time getting rid of it after I returned to Billings.

I returned to college to finish my degree. I attended for three quarters and graduated in June of 1968 with a Bachelor of Arts in Liberal Arts with a major in Biology and a minor in Chemistry. I received my draft notice two weeks after graduation. I was inducted into the U.S. Army on August 28, 1968 and discharged April 1, 1970. I was assigned March 9, 1969 to the 199th Light Infantry Brigade, 3rd Battalion 7th Infantry, as a combat medic, in Vietnam based just outside of Saigon, now known as Ho Chi Min City.

I was in a climate similar to Bombay with exactly the same visuals and smells of India. As a consequence, my adjustment to Vietnam was much faster and smoother than most of the other soldiers.

I was the only medic in the platoon of about 30 men. We all got along well but everyone had a small group of friends and we tended to stick with our own groups when we were able to mingle. While on patrols or ambushes we were placed in certain positions (order), depending upon our jobs, to efficiently respond should we walk into an ambush, be attacked, or come across the enemy in any fashion. As the only person with a drip IV, morphine and life-saving first aid essentials, I enjoyed, as all field medics, a certain level of deference. Who would want the medic, or "Doc" as we were all called, to be unhappy with you? No one! Very few knew our names but everyone knew who "Doc" was and what he could do for you if you were wounded.

I found the same satisfaction and fulfillment as an Army medic that I had imagined I would experience helping the people of India. As a medic, I was not required nor asked to be a 'fighting' soldier. My job was to tend to the wounded, friend or foe.

While I was in basic training at Fort Lewis, Washington in the fall of 1968, I received a package from my mother. The package contained an airline ticket and all the paperwork from PC to enter a training program with 27 trainees at Kansas State Teachers College beginning on September 28, 1968, learning to instruct Indian science teachers on how to conduct workshops for secondary students. I have a faint recollection that Connie Robinson entered this program but cannot recall for sure.

The day I received the package I asked the Army if I could leave! I was definitely getting bored and losing interest in what I was doing. In addition, being yelled at all the time and running to exhaustion each day proved tiresome over the long haul. The Army politely said "No".

I'll always remember the day I was discharged from the Army in Oakland. John came and picked me up! He'll probably never know how special and deeply emotional that was for me. My old friend came and picked me up! He could ask anything of me, anytime, and I'd make it happen. I was definitely confused, scared, and disillusioned to say the least. I distinctly remember meeting him on some street corner and him taking me to a store to buy some civilian clothes.

When Mary Jo told us that she stood on a street corner and felt lost, bewildered, and frightened after her arrival in Boston, upon leaving the Peace Corps, I became emotional, too. Like most of us, one can get very emotional remembering your return from doing something challenging, something that changed your life, that consumed your life, and then you get back home and realize that nothing really has changed and no one really cares.

In hindsight, I know now that I left India before I was physically whole. Several factors led to this questionable choice to self-deselect: having a doctor friend who cut through red tape to get me into surgery; convincing the operating surgeon to release me because I was in the medical field of the Peace Corps and they could care for me, and not wanting to go India alone.

However, after the reunion I think I might have decided to leave no matter what, given my high-risk nature. Even if I had not been in the hospital but out in a village exposed to the same isolation as others in our group, I might have made the same decision to leave. Who knows?

I have a unique perspective that I'm guessing very few other Americans have: an intimate knowledge and relationship with two very different groups of Americans—Peace Corps volunteers and the United States Army Infantry. Both groups that I served with, approximately 25 individuals in each, were tasked by the United States government with the hardest job either group was designed to confront. Yes, it was a given that we in front line infantry units faced death as part of our mission; however, that is not the most relevant comparison.

The better comparison is this: If you were in the Army, being in the field (front line) in Vietnam was the hardest of all the jobs to which you might be assigned i.e. cooks, clerks, transportation, drivers, police, Germany, stateside, etc. If you were in the Peace Corps, an assignment to India was the hardest job when compared to other Peace Corps countries. Surprisingly, nobody I served with in either organization seriously complained, which tells me both groups were idealistic, committed to a larger goal, and willing to make sacrifices. Both groups were thinking of a bigger picture and not of themselves. That "bigger picture" was different for each group but that's one of the strengths of America. It takes all of us with different opinions seeing a different big picture to make our country stronger and better than the sum of its parts. No one person or group has the 'true' picture.

My PC unit, India 44-A&B, was dealing with a country that had the highest attrition of PCVs (Peace Corps Volunteers) due to sickness and disease as well as a bureaucratic system that had no equal for delay, duplicity, redundancy and incompetence. Both groups were originally cross trained. 'A' (my group) focused on health education, with heavy emphasis on birth control, and trained at the both University of Wisconsin-Milwaukee and some at Milwaukee General Hospital. 'B' group was trained (initially, at least) in poultry raising and also trained at University of Wisconsin-Milwaukee. Its members also did hands on training at large poultry/egg farms in Wisconsin.

Before I arrived, my Army unit, 3rd Platoon, 'A' Company, 3rd Battalion 7th Infantry of the 199th Light Infantry Brigade was originally charged with urban security, house to house, of a section of Saigon (Ho Chi Minh City). After I arrived, our mission morphed into trying to stop infiltration of the enemy into Saigon and outer areas coming from the north along the Ho Chi Minh Trail. We accomplished this by day ambushes, night ambushes or 3- to 10-day missions in the jungle looking for hidden bunkers containing weapons, food, etc. The ambushes we set up attempted to catch the enemy moving between various locations.

My invitation to join the Peace Corps came in 1966, after applying in 1965. I'm not sure any of us who applied knew anything about Vietnam at that time. I know that Peace Corps later attracted some people who thought they could avoid the draft. However, joining the PC didn't absolve you of being drafted, it only deferred being drafted until your PC commitment was fulfilled. Our group had the distinction of being an 'ATP' group (advanced training program) because India had such a high attrition rate. It was thought that the extra training would solve the problem. My group was picked when we were juniors in college and we trained during that summer. We were sent lessons during our senior year consisting of language tapes and cultural and health-related information to keep us involved and learning about India. The next summer we trained briefly in Milwaukee and then flew to India. The extra time training was designed to (hopefully) make sure we didn't leave early. I believe for some of us, it had the opposite effect. When you're young, you feel you don't have enough time—period. I think some of the energy of my commitment was lost simply due to the long training time, which nearly equaled the amount of time one would expect to be in-country.

My invitation to join the Army came a few weeks after I graduated from college in 1968. As a college graduate I was constantly pressured to become an officer. I was still interested in going to medical school but it was becoming evident I didn't have the motivation or the money to go. However I wanted to do something in the realm of helping people. I wasn't sure our intervention in Vietnam was correct and didn't want to be in a position of leading other soldiers into a venture about which I was so ambivalent. As a result, I resisted taking a leadership role. During one discussion with a Colonel, I told him that they could put me in the jail but I wasn't going to Officer Candidate School and into one of the combat arms i.e. Infantry, Artillery, Armor, Combat Engineers or Special Forces. He smiled and said, "Fine". I believe he thought I was afraid of going into combat but knew I would probably end up as a medic in a front line unit anyway. And I did.

In both the platoon and India 44 A & B, groups about the size of a school classroom, there were some to whom I became close and others with whom I was not. Members of both groups watched each other closely in training and in the field. Whether or not you liked particular individuals, you respected them because you knew they would deliver and had been through exactly what you had experienced.

Both groups also witnessed others who wanted to be included turned away, or if admitted, moved when they didn't meet expectations. In the Army this meant that the best front line troops weren't the tough 'gung-ho' types because their aggressive thinking would get you in trouble. You needed soldiers who would focus on the mission and fight smart when they had to, who weren't prejudiced, who got along well with others,

who were intelligent, and who were aware at all times of their surroundings.

In the Peace Corps this meant you had to have an innate sense of compassion and tolerance, that you weren't prejudiced, got along well with others, and were intelligent. If you didn't have these attributes, you would set back the efforts of others trying to help the same people. In the Peace Corps, we were de facto extensions of the State Department and our country's diplomacy. We needed to be culturally aware and sensitive to how we acted as guests in the host country; thus, we had to watch our behavior very closely. For example, American culture surrounding interaction between the sexes and alcohol consumption is different than the cultural norms in India. Lapsing into the American way could get you into big trouble, endanger your effectiveness and, in the extreme, get you removed.

After my father died, I was lucky because my mother got a job as a secretary in the city library and was able to keep the home we had moved into not long before my father died. As a result, I was in a new area of town that was growing due to the oil and energy boom in eastern Montana. Therefore, the families around us were basically engineers, management types, and professionals. This meant that while all my friends could go skiing on the weekends, I couldn't because of financial limitations. Because of my interactions with them, however, the attitudes of their families about going to college rubbed off on me. Neither of my parents had gone to college for more than a short time, and they did not encourage me to go either. However, there are two colleges in my hometown and I had a friend who called one day and asked if I wanted to go along as he applied to the local private religious college. I luckily and thankfully said "sure!" While there, I happened to talk with a counselor and enrolled the fall after high school graduation.

I don't believe most of my friends in the Army had the opportunity to attend college. Most came from working class towns where patriotism and working hard are the American way, and serving our country is typically viewed through a military lens. As I think about who applied to the Peace Corps in 1965, the motivation of service to country was similar to those who joined the Army in 1968.

Both choices involved doing something for your country and not thinking of yourself first. Everyone with whom I interacted in either group was equally patriotic and all chose

an unselfish path, a path we know most Americans didn't or wouldn't choose. However, members of both groups know the contentment that comes from doing something audacious. It's sad that many of our contemporaries lack that satisfaction of choices made on behalf of our country.

I am grateful for the experiences I've had and am pleasantly surprised at how things seem to happen. I wouldn't trade my experiences of Milwaukee and India for anything.

We were a special group of young men and women. Unfortunately there aren't enough people like us in the world.

Post Script: I listened to a radio program recently where Army officers were talking about how to win the war in Afghanistan. They were convinced if they could build water-sewer systems, schools, hospitals, and so on, they would win the hearts and minds of the people and, therefore, prevail.

Is that, or is that not, what the Peace Corps mission was? Think where the world would be if all these years after Nixon severely cut the PC budget, the work of the Peace Corps had continued on the same scale as when we were involved.

CHAPTER 10

A Passage to Udaipur

Gareth Loy

Ask not what your country can do for you, but
what you can do for your country.
                                        John F. Kennedy

JFK's words fairly leapt out of the television as I watched his inauguration live that day in January, 1961. As a 15-year-old kid, soon to be of draft age, his words—and the Selective Service System—were heavily on my mind. The military draft would soon start shipping thousands of young American men every month to the killing fields of Vietnam as U.S. troop levels tripled in 1961, and tripled again in 1962.

As the son of a World War II conscientious objector (CO), I struggled with how to apply Kennedy's words to my life. Although there might be a justifiable war, the Vietnam War in particular seemed to me to be an unholy mix of opportunistic political aims and crass commercial exploitation. I valued my life more highly than to throw it away for some politician's career or some corporation's bottom line. A few years earlier, President Eisenhower had warned the nation about the dangers of the "military-industrial complex," and Vietnam seemed to be the quintessential example of his concern. Surely, military adventurism in a foreign land could not be the highest and best contribution I could to make to my country?

I believed, however, that simply being a war objector was a very limited role for me to play. I wanted to do something positive *for* my country, as Kennedy had urged!

A few months later (March 1st, 1961), President Kennedy created the Peace Corps and provided me with a plausible course of action. It was only a couple of years before I would be old enough to join. The fact that the Peace Corps was not an alternative to military service, merely a deferral, didn't bother me—I'd cross that bridge later. Meanwhile, I knew how I could fulfill JFK's challenge to my generation.

I signed up for the Peace Corps at my earliest opportunity in the fall of 1965, during my junior year at UCLA. I already spoke some Spanish and, therefore, expected to be sent to South America after graduation but was elated when I was accepted to go to India. I was already familiar with Hinduism through my father, a professor of world religions. The culture of India was rising in American popular culture through the influence of the Beatles and figures such as Ravi Shankar and Maharishi Mahesh Yogi.

Life gives each of us at least one moment with the power to change us forever. The Peace Corps was this moment for me. However, mine is not the usual "coming of age" story one might expect. I was ultimately "deselected"—a euphemism the Peace Corps used to mean "kicked out"—before I was able to serve. Given the enormous attrition rate of trainees, mine is actually the more common story: of dreams dashed, the return home, and the slow onset of the rest of one's life as the pieces are picked up, and other dreams emerge.

Altogether, I was "in" the Peace Corps from the beginning of training in June, 1966, through the day I came home in October of 1967, about 16 months later. How can it be that so much time went by if I was deselected? The answer is that the program I had been accepted for was a so-called Advanced Training Program (ATP), an experiment the Peace Corps set up to see if greatly increased training time would result in more effective service. So I spent the summer between my junior and senior years in full-time training. In my senior year, in addition to my regular studies, I took language classes, attended seminars, and took other coursework relevant to India. This was followed by additional stateside training the following summer and yet more training in India, followed by time spent in a temporary Indian village. Altogether, I was in the Peace Corps for about eight months short of a standard deployment of two years.

My shortened Peace Corps tenure experience was probably not so very different from many whose terms extended for the full duration of service, with moments of elation, fulfillment, disillusionment, boredom, confusion, rejection, and acceptance. There were also peak experiences that would last the rest of my life.

Let me briefly paint a picture of the times. The beginning of the radical 1960's, following on the impetus of the Beat movement in the late 1950's, saw the advent of a significant counter-culture, the likes of which, arguably, has not been seen in our society before or since. The most public events of that movement, such as the Free Speech movement at Berkeley, the Black Power movement, JFK's assassination, sit-ins, and the ever-present war in Vietnam, were merely anchor points for a revolution that was taking place in one form or another in virtually every individual's personal life. In my case, I took full advantage of the flood of information about the world that was newly available because of increased travel and media access to remote places.

I took up the guitar, sang and wrote songs, went to civil rights marches, participated in poetry readings and happenings, and developed a fascination with the ancient cultures of the world and their religions. I was constantly seeking inner and outer truth by attending religious gatherings and festivals, meditating, studying the I Ching (the ancient Chinese book of divination), listening to jazz, learning to play Japanese koto music at the UCLA School of Ethnomusicology, and generally swimming in the rich broth of social upheaval going on around me brought on by our ever expanding world horizons.

The Peace Corps program I joined melded all these interests into a single focus. I eventually became reasonably fluent in

Hindi, conversant with the broad sweep of Indian culture and society, and deeply immersed in Indian music. I formed deep bonds of friendship with other volunteers, and came to live and breathe the Peace Corps.

India 44

India 44, the Advanced Training Program I joined, convened in June of 1966 at the University of Wisconsin campus in Milwaukee right around the time of my 21st birthday. We studied Hindi, the history and culture of India, Hinduism, and ... chickens! Our original mission was to be "agribusiness specialists" focusing on improving the Hindu diet by encouraging them to eat more eggs, and encouraging farmers to raise chickens for their eggs. Our job was to convince the vegetarian Hindus that unfertilized eggs were not "alive" therefore not in contradiction to their religious teachings, and a valuable source of protein in their diet.

I became aware of the term "deselection" early on during a Peace Corps orientation, and even satirized it in a song I wrote and performed at a group event that summer. The operative couplet came from a Richard Farina blues song that I adapted for this purpose:

Well, they roll you in the morning and they roll you through the day and night

They've got a game called "deselection" and they play it in the broad daylight!

The training, for the most part, was straightforward, including language lessons, cultural history of India, and agribusiness. The training program also included a very odd collection of subjects. One of our field trips that summer was to an Oscar Mayer meat packing plant. We saw the Wiener Mobile, and some intrepid souls even ventured into the killing room (not me). Many of us gave up meat immediately. I suppose this could be considered a type of sensitivity training for sending us to a vegetarian country.

The Peace Corps continued to freely invent creative solutions to the problem of training us for our service. For example:

we were going to go to *India;* so, during part of the summer they sent us to an *Indian reservation* in South Dakota for training!

I befriended Mike Simonds, a fellow volunteer and, unhappy with the college I was attending (UCLA), agreed to switch to San Francisco State College (SFSC) for my senior year, and be his roommate. As it happened, our apartment was near the Haight-Ashbury district, and so I discovered the very tenuous beginnings of the hippie movement in San Francisco in the fall of 1966. This was just before the Summer of Love in the Haight so the movement was still small and regional, not yet exploited by main-stream television or other commercial interests. It was a lot of fun! I bought a Levi's jean jacket (which I still have) and some cool red fat-horizontal-striped bell-bottom jeans. I, and several San Francisco members of our Peace Corps group, attended the Human Be-In in Golden Gate Park on January 14th, 1967, when Timothy Leary famously declared, "Tune in, turn on, DROP OUT!" The Grateful Dead played. Michael McClure read poetry. Janis Joplin and the Jefferson Airplane wowed the crowd at the Fillmore Auditorium. "Peace & Love", always more of a motto than a fact, was nonetheless an excellent senti-ment for a social movement.

In those days, I played a gigantic 12-string guitar with a really deep sound. I wrote many songs and performed them in coffee houses on Haight Street and elsewhere around San Francisco.

I volunteered with the Diggers, a group that fed the homeless hippies in the Panhandle of Golden Gate Park. Mike Simonds turned me on to KPFK, the pioneer Berkeley public radio station that was (and still is) the mouthpiece of the nearby Berkeley counterculture. As opposition to the war in Vietnam grew, I attended anti-war sit-ins and lectures on civil disobedience at the Free University on the campus of SFSC. The radical movements burgeoning all around me mostly left me cold. My cause was the Peace Corps. I stuck resolutely to my dream of making a positive contribution to America by volunteering abroad. At the end of my senior year, I was committed to flying off to my destiny in India.

The second summer of training commenced on the Henry Seed Corn Farm outside of Madison, Wisconsin. We slept in tents in a field (rain or shine) and studied for our new mission of training Hindu farmers to improve wheat crop yields. (The chicken idea evidently had fallen by the wayside in policy circles inside the Peace Corps. Why we were being trained to grow wheat on a seed corn farm was never explained.) It was on that farm that I met Juda, who would later be my first wife and mother of my two children, Morgan and Greta. She was a friend of the Henry family and came to watch this group of crazy volunteers.

I remember falling asleep during lectures about the diseases of wheat at the University of Wisconsin Agriculture College. After a long-winded characterization of an obscure wheat disease by the professor, I asked, "So, what causes this disease?" Answer: "We don't know." "So, how do you treat it?," I asked. Answer: "We don't know." "So why are we studying this?" Answer (slightly irritated voice): "Because it's a disease of wheat." Oh... So I went back to sleep.

The Peace Corps did have a plausible humanitarian reason for our program. It was widely believed that parts of India would never be self-sufficient in food production. Instead of self-sufficiency, a better overall goal would be to improve crop production in relatively fertile areas, like parts of Rajasthan, and use the excellent railroad system put in during the British Raj to transport surpluses to other less fortunate areas.

The Peace Corps plan was to introduce American hybrid wheat in places like Rajasthan to develop an export market. Mike Simonds' recent research[3] showed that the particular hybrid selected was Sonora 64, developed in Mexico with Rockefeller Foundation money. This research had shown that when handled properly, Sonora 64 grew well in India, with yields many times higher than the highest yields of native wheat.

It was a risky gambit, because Sonora 64 had at least the following faults:

- Hybrid wheat required regular irrigation, which most farmers in Rajasthan did not have. It could not be widely adopted without first solving this problem, which our program did not address.
- Hybrid wheat required fertilizer and insecticide. In the 1960's, farmers would have to rely on expensive imports. [4]
- The local populace didn't like the taste of Sonora 64. Because it was designed to make leavened bread, western wheat variants contain abundant gluten; the local populace ate flat bread, and the gluten made tough and inedible chapattis.
- Hybrid wheat required capital to purchase it, and at that time there was no financial infrastructure, such as micro loans, to serve enterprising farmers motivated to expand their operations.

Our trainers freely admitted some of these problems. [5]

Of course, none of this was known at the time. We were left to wonder how—with virtually no credibility or experience, and with virtually zero financial or logistical support from the Peace Corps or the local government—we were supposed to overcome these obstacles? Perhaps the Peace Corps had some tricks up its sleeve we didn't yet know about that would make it all go swimmingly? We certainly hoped so.

To India!

The fateful day arrived; we boarded a bus for the airport, flew to New York City, London, Tehran, and on to New Delhi. I wrote this poem in the airplane just before descending into India:

In Transit
Then the sun did its morning thing
With the colors spread out,
 Together with the brown earth
Curving oh so slightly under the weight.
 When the sun rises, as it did
It sets for all my life so far lived.
 A light cloud layer
Like the surface of a lake:
 As though to see its bottom
I look downwards.
 The clouds came up to greet me,
Or am I descending?
7/29/1967

A brick wall of hot sun and humid air hit me as we stepped off of the airplane and out into the intense sunshine. The foreign nature of everything fascinated and repelled me. Bazaars were filled with people in bright costumes and headdresses. Three-wheeled scooter taxis careened down streets filled with dogs and people who stopped in their tracks, slack-jawed, to stare at us. Beggars flaunted the fetid diseases rotting their flesh for spare change. Parentless children roamed the streets in gangs.

I saw families of ten crouched in hovels six feet square and four feet high directly across the street from gleaming steel and glass hotels.

Conversely, I saw beautiful temples, awe-inspiring countryside, and sensed the ancient past very much part of the present. The next day, we boarded steam trains for a 24-hour ride to Udaipur, in Rajasthan state, which was to be the headquarters of our group.

I had brought my 12-string guitar, and committed myself to exchanging my music for theirs. The first opportunity for cultural exchange came when we arrived in Udaipur. I befriended a Peace Corps volunteer, Tom Purcell, who was finishing his stint by helping get ours started. Tom was a font of local connections and quickly introduced me to local culture. I began making field recordings of local musicians with the excellent portable tape recorder I'd brought along. [6] He introduced me to Sri Dagar, the owner and head teacher of the local music school, and member of the famous musical Dagar family of Rajasthan, and his brilliant tabla player, Ustad Hafiz Mian. I recorded them and some of Dagar's students on various native Hindu instruments, some I'd never seen before. One of these instruments was called *jal tarang*, a set of rice bowls laid out in a semicircle, with different amounts of water in each to give each a particular pitch. It was played (really well) by a child using two chopsticks to beat on the rims of the bowls. Another instrument, the *bulbul tarang* (also called an Indian keyboard dulcimer) had eight metal strings tuned in unison, but instead of frets, there was a set of spring-loaded knife blades with old-fashioned typewriter keys on the ends that could be pressed by the fingers to stop the strings at a particular pitch. Purcell introduced me to another local sitar player, whom I also recorded but whose name I did not preserve; and a famous local Kathak dancer who performed at the Lake Palace. He also introduced me to a tailor, who fashioned clothes for me in the local style: khadi's and pantaloons.

Being modestly fluent in Hindi, I could cruise the city and go wherever I wanted. It was glorious. The heart of Udaipur is the Lake Palace, an architectural jewel box set in the middle of a large man-made lake that was once the private playground of the Maharajah, and now was a tourist hotel catering to Americans and Europeans. You had to show your passport proving you were a foreigner to get on the boat to the island because they served (horrors!) alcoholic spirits in a bar there. In those days, alcohol was largely prohibited in India.

Famous in Udaipur

The pinnacle of my brief Peace Corps experience soon followed. The mayor of Udaipur threw a festival for the arrival of our group to his city. There would be native singers and dancers at the welcoming ceremony, and the word went out to our group to see if any of us wanted to make a creative contribution. Naturally, I signed up to play guitar and sing.

The day of the event, a sea of local residents (many thousands) filled the nearby parade grounds to hear speeches from the mayor and local Peace Corps mucky-mucks. Local musicians danced and sang, and then it came time for us. Gary Gruber played a Bach partita on his violin; David Bauer sang "The Hills Are Alive" from the *Sound of Music*, with my accompaniment. (Here's a photo of this moment taken by a local Udaipur newspaper photographer.)

Then it was my turn, but first a brief digression. I had been a fan of The Weavers, an American folk music group of the 1950's, whose most famous member was Pete Seeger (still going strong today at age 90). In one of their 1955 Carnegie Hall concerts, he had performed a 12-string guitar version of a Sanskrit song. I had this record in my collection when I joined the Peace Corps, and so I learned to play the song as part of my

language studies. It was this song that I prepared to play that day in Udaipur.

I stood up to the microphone, and began to sing,

Raghupati raghav rajaram,
Patit pavan sitaram

No sooner had I begun than I sensed the crowd stirring. They looked from one to another with startled expressions, then back

227

up at me. Was it because I was singing a song in their language, perhaps? Then they began to sing along. All of them! I had no expectation how the song would be received. Sensing their excitement, I played on more intensely. They responded by clapping along, some rising to their feet and dancing. I finished the song with a flourish, and they burst into enthusiastic applause.

Tom Purcell explained to me afterwards that this song, *Raghupati Raga*, was no ordinary song. It was considered to be the unofficial national anthem of India, because their beloved Gandhi-ji had himself penned a new verse for this ancient song—one of the verses I'd sung that day. This is why everyone knew it and why they all joined in singing it. The verse Gandhi added goes like this:

Ishvar Allah tero nam,
Sabko samadhi de bhagavan

The first word, *Ishvar*, is the Hindu name for the personal God. Loosely translated, the verse says that Ishvar and Allah, the Moslem name for God, are *the same name (tero nam)*. God (*bhagavan*) gives (*de*) peace (*samadhi*) to everyone (*sabko*). This is Gandhi's message to his Hindu and Moslem brethren in India: there is no valid reason for religious strife; stripped of superfluous cultural baggage, Hindu and Muslim worship the same god.

After this event, I was briefly famous in Udaipur. As I rode through town on my bicycle, people would break out singing *Raghupati Raga* as I rode past. This was a tremendously fulfilling experience for me, and one I cherish more than any other performance I've ever given. I went to India with the hope not just to improve agricultural practices, but to make a statement. I achieved an early and almost accidental triumph: Pete Seeger carried Gandhi's message of peace and brotherhood from India to America, and I had managed to carry it back as a gift of thanks to the people of Udaipur. Their apparent appreciation of the gesture felt very gratifying.

The rest of our training in Udaipur included some hands-on experience with local farming techniques. Here is a publicity photo taken by the Peace Corps of me behind the handles of a

native Indian plow, directing a pair of bullocks across a field as other volunteers look on. I actually look like I know what I'm doing! This was, of course, a complete fiction. I had taken the controls only moments before and would never touch such a plow again.

Lacowli

We were soon placed in temporary villages to get a feel for our permanent assignments. Don Nordin, Don Carter and I were dropped off in Lacowli (not sure of the spelling) village a few miles outside Udaipur. We were told someone from the local agriculture department would come by and let us into a padlocked government building.

A crowd of children gathered around us, staring unashamedly and chattering among themselves. Time passed, and then more time passed. The children sat riveted, staring. We had an uncomfortable stand-off with them that lasted an eternity. An

official rode up sometime later on a rusty bicycle and started fumbling with the lock. It was a standard Schlage padlock, but he couldn't figure out how to open it. I began to imagine having to sleep al fresco that night on the side of this dusty road. Eventually, we had to help him get the sequence correctly, and the door finally opened. This incident really gave me pause: our door unlocker seemed like a smart enough guy and he had a government job to prove it. Yet, he apparently had zero experience with even such primitive technology as a padlock. How was I going to teach someone like him the complexities of hybrid wheat, let alone teach it to farmers?

We dug a latrine in the backyard of the government office building where we were housed.

The *dud walla* (milk vendor) brought dreadful curdled milk in a dirty clay pot on the back of a donkey once a day. We had no cook. The crowds of children gave us no mercy, peering in through the open, unscreened windows at all hours of the day and night to see these freaks that had come to entertain them. Don Carter became increasingly morose and depressed. He took to his bed and wouldn't get out. He suddenly quit, and was back to the U.S. within a week, I think.

I was determined to make a go of it. I found that there were many delights to be had, despite the hardships. The village was fairly prosperous because the land was fertile, so there was not the grinding poverty I'd seen elsewhere.

It was picturesque, and the people—especially the women—wore extraordinarily colorful costumes. There was a beautiful lake (a "tank" in local parlance) where everyone bathed, somehow managing it without taking their clothes off, or even getting very wet.

Incense wafted from the door of an ancient Hindu temple. It seemed most residents were Brahmans, vegetarian, and highly religious. However, one night, the lone Moslem resident of the town surreptitiously invited us to his house and served us meat—an old goat he'd butchered that day. We slipped into his house under the cover of darkness, lest anyone catch us. It was almost inedible. My stomach rumbled for days after.

One day, a parade came to town. Dancers and musicians in festive costumes engaged the local populace in line and circle dances.

Later that week, the mayor and superintendent of schools for the village came and invited us to a *mela* (festival) taking place that day in the *jungali* (forest) nearby. We walked across plowed fields with people streaming into the jungle from all sides around us. A large site by a river had the same cast of characters who had recently visited our village—a man in a sun mask, and various other characters in costume.

There were amusements. A gigantic rope swing went out over the river; merchants sold jewelry; a young female contortionist climbed into a small wicker basket no bigger than her frame, sitting in the open on a thin carpet on the bare ground... and then disappeared, emerging a few minutes later from behind the crowd.

A circle of musicians played near a tea stall. As I stood enjoying their music, the mayor and superintendent of schools came up to me and invited me to have tea with them. We squatted on the ground in the customary Indian fashion, and were served proper British tea with milk in cups and saucers. The custom was to tip some of the tea from the cup into the saucer

and slurp it from there, the idea being that this way the tea would cool faster. I think I had consumed maybe two cups of this delicious tea when I noticed my brain start to develop a curious fizzy quality. I asked, "What kind of tea is this?", and was told, "Oh, sahib, you like?! This is bhang tea, sahib, *bhang tea!* Veddy good bhang tea, sahib! Here, you must have *more!*",

233

and they grinned and waggled their heads from side to side as they poured me another cup. The mayor and superintendent of schools were getting their respected foreign guest stoned on marijuana tea. They later asked me if I wanted to take some with me and told me they could get me kilos of the stuff.

At this point the drums for the line dances took up a heavy, enthusiastic beat and everyone leapt up to join in. I have many photos of this day; it was magical.

At dusk, I went up to see the sunset from the top of a nearby hill. The people I'd met that day at the mela were friendly and waved as I went by their houses. The incense and chanting poured invitingly out of the temple. I began to feel a bit at home.

Later that night I wrote this poem:

To my vantage point
On a hill above the village
Human beings below
*   With a billion faces*
Doing what it takes to be Indian
*   "Hare Rama, Hare Rama*
Hare Krishna, Hare Hare"
As I came down
One of them, with warm smiles
Hailed me into his house
And I
One lone American
With one hundred ninety million faces
Doing what it takes to be American.
*   Om, shanti, shanti, om.*
We regard each other with innocent eyes
Through the looking glass sun.

I had experienced life in a rural Indian village, and I began to think again about what I would do when I received my final placement. I doubted whether the Peace Corps would support anything beyond proselytizing for hybrid wheat and I continued to have doubts about how this was going to succeed. I wanted so badly to do what I was sent here to accomplish.

Just before leaving the temporary village assignment, I wrote this rather sardonic poem about my prospects as a Peace Corps Volunteer:

Present Compound Verb
The noun, with his plow,
Watches his verbs grow
In his sentence-field.
Enter the modifier,
An "adjective of change",
With adverbs in hand,
And new roots for his words.
We live in a predicate,
The direct object's indirect friend
And we exchange meanings.

I worried about loneliness. What would I do when stuck in the hinterlands of India all by myself, with no English speakers, no society that I could relate to? I had no answers but I was determined to find out. I figured that my life up to this point had been incredibly lonely so would this really be so different? My solace against loneliness had always been my music; and I always had my guitar with me. Perhaps that would be an entrée into village life, or at least something to keep me company.

Four Blows

The next part of the story is sad, punctuated by what I call the "four blows." The first blow came when we returned from our temporary village assignments. The trainers, some of whom had been with us throughout, were preparing to hand us over to the local Peace Corps officials who would supervise our work in India. The local officials were a very dour, conservative Midwestern couple. I felt a cold wave come off of them. I couldn't tell if they were hostile or just reserved. I basically have no sensible explanation for why, at that last possible moment, they deselected me. Perhaps my hippie tendencies rubbed them the wrong way? I'll never know.

All I know is that the meeting where I was supposed to receive my final assignment was the meeting where it all came to a premature and very sad end. In retrospect, it just seems even more bizarre. I'd passed all previous tests; I'd never wavered in my commitment; the Peace Corps had invested by then about fourteen months of training, far more than their regular program, and I was now so highly trained it was foolish, near-sighted, and plain stupid for them to even consider tossing me away. But they did.

Of course, I was upset, and ready to do whatever was necessary to continue with my group. I was told the most they would do for me was to try to find another program in India somewhere that I could join. They told me that if I fought this decision, even that option would be withdrawn. I was deselected; conversation over. I returned to my room trembling. After a long night of soul searching, I wrote the following poem:

Catharsis
Gareth, I think it's about your mind we are talking
Sitting here on the riverbank
That runs so deeply.
Is this your river?
It isn't, is it?
A bubble, deep under the surface
Races and fights its way
Desperately to the surface:
"NOW!", it shouts, as it breaks away.
And the gravel of a thousand roads
Rushes up at my feet.

The next day (second blow) I became violently ill with fever and diarrhea, and took to my *charpoy* (bed). When my fever headed north of 106 degrees, the local doctor decided to evacuate me to a hospital. They packed me up, drove me to the airport (that's me getting into the car; that's Mike Simonds standing next to me), and flew me to New Delhi, where I spent a week in a hospital with bacillary dysentery, amoebic dysentery, and

possibly hepatitis. I was very, very sick, and had really vivid and remarkable fever dreams.

Ten days later, when I was finally discharged from the hospital, the Peace Corps began processing me for another assignment. I was so bonded with my group that the prospect of starting over just made me sad. It eventually turned out that there were no other assignments available in India for me to join anyway.

Next (third blow) a letter arrived from my draft board (that later turned out to be an error) ordering me to show up for induction. How could it be, I wondered, that my draft board knew so quickly that I'd been kicked out of the Peace Corps? Because I was deselected, the Peace Corps said they would pay for my return trip to the US, but only if I agreed to go straight back after my convalescence. I had no other prospects and little money. Depressed, freaked out about the draft, and still very sick, I decided to pack it in and return home as soon as I was able.

Gullible's Travails

I think I spent about two more months in New Delhi recovering enough to travel, but the timing is rather vague. The Peace Corps put me up in a hotel near their offices. They sent me to virtually every hematologist in New Delhi trying to figure out what was wrong with me. I felt like a pin-cushion with the amount of blood being drawn.

I was completely alone in this very foreign place, waiting for what I did not know. I walked and walked all over Delhi at all hours of the day and night trying to figure out what to do with myself. I was a freak of nature to the local populace—an albino giant dressed in *khadis*, completely out of place. Some were kind to me, most just stared.

Somehow, I met a man who was an artist and musician. He took me to a concert of Ustad Vilayat Kahn, an extraordinary sitar player who could, among other things, make his instrument keen like a woman. I wanted to buy a sitar to take back with me, so he took me to Rikhi Ram's store in Bhagat Singh Market in Delhi. They made an instrument to my specifications which I picked up the following week. This fellow then taught me some lessons to get me started.

Next door to my hotel room were some world travelers (WTs, as we called them) who had traveled overland from Europe through Turkey, Iraq, Afghanistan and finally India (sadly, a route no Westerner can safely travel anymore). I befriended them as fellow Westerners. I was so naïve that, when a couple of weeks later my room was broken into and 300 rupees were stolen, I didn't immediately suspect them. How could it be them, they were supposed to be my friends?

I was so trusting that I even told the WTs how to reach me in the States. A few months after my return, they visited me. Still desperate for friendship, I welcomed them. A week later, they (I have good reason to know it was them) broke into my apartment and took everything I had of any value, including my beloved 12-string guitar (fourth blow). Naturally, I never saw them again.

After the theft of the rupees in New Delhi, I was broke. My sitar-playing friend deserted me as well. About this time I wrote this dark song in my New Delhi hotel room.

Delhi

Through darkest nights I walked alone
Delhi's streets of cobbled stone
The passing crowds gape at my eye
While restless animals run by.
>   *And the day turned into the night*
>   *As the weeks went by*
>   *I saw the sky turn as black as coal*
>   *Heard the streetlamps cry.*
Down through the corridors of rhyme
I felt my soul was trapped in time
To where we're going in the end
No one stops, no one begins.
>   *Kali stands on Shiva's chest*

> *While she gazes nigh*
> *With her sword the dead are blessed*
> *And their fates untied.*
> *Taking the loss of stolen rupees*
> *I returned unto my land*
> *The draft is brimming in my country*
> *Young the soul that it commands.*
> *Turn around your backroom lie*
> *Let the spring begin*
> *Put the blame on no one else*
> *Don't come again.*

The song showed me some unsettling truths about myself. I think the "backroom lie" was my belief that I could hide out in the Peace Corps, not just from the draft, but also from myself. I had no idea who I was! I had joined the Peace Corps so I could wrap myself in the identity of a good cause for a while, to get some relief from the crushing emptiness I felt inside. I had hoped that, in a sleepy Indian village somewhere, life would calm down enough that maybe I'd be able to sort myself out. That was not to be. Instead, I saw that my altruistic aims came along with baggage; joining the Peace Corps was way more about my needs than it was about helping anyone else. This seems so straightforward now, but then it was a shameful epiphany.

The next line of the poem is, "Let the spring begin." Somehow, I knew that if I could accept complete responsibility for my current predicament, perhaps things could get better. And if I didn't learn this lesson now, I would surely be doomed to repeat the same mistakes.

These realizations, though painful, were a turning point for me. I knew I was now finished with the Peace Corps. I told them I was well enough to travel. Meanwhile, my mood lifted, and I began to enjoy my last days in India. I went to visit Mahatma Gandhi's shrine in Delhi, and read his autobiography. His conviction to nonviolence reinvigorated me to follow through and become a conscientious objector on my return from India, regardless of the price I might pay.

240

With my last few rupees, I took a day trip to Agra to visit the Taj Mahal. On the return train ride, I began to feel some gratitude for the experience India had given me through the Peace Corps. India's gifts to me were not its monuments and palaces; rather, it was the ancient spirituality that I sensed somehow organized everything. I bought an abridged copy of the *Upanishads* (early Hindu philosophical texts) in a book stall, and began reading them in my hotel room. I came across a copy of the Gospel of Sri Ramakrishna and stayed up late many nights reading it. Ramakrishna's teachings have had a profound influence on my life ever since.

One day, I returned to New Delhi International Airport with my guitar and my new sitar cradled in my arms to fly home. As I buckled into my seat, I remember hearing the stewardess recite the following familiar litany,

In the unlikely event there is a sudden loss in cabin pressure, oxygen masks will deploy from the compartment located above you.

Immediately extinguish all cigarettes. [7]

Pull the mask towards you, and secure the elastic band around your head so that it covers your nose and mouth.

Breath normally.

Even if the bag does not inflate, oxygen is flowing.

Please be sure to secure your own mask before assisting others.

Her last sentence captivated me and reverberated in my mind throughout the rest of the trip. *How could I realistically expect to help anyone else until I'd first taken care of myself?* I resolved to let go of President Kennedy's maxim, even if only for a while, and dedicate myself to healing the one person I knew I could definitely affect... me.

Shame and Redemption

Along with the other baggage I brought back with me from India, I also carried strong shame for my failure to deploy with the rest of my group. I also felt a tremendous emptiness; my fellow PCVs had been pretty much all the friends I had at that point and now I was bereft of them all. The Peace Corps had been what I believed in, even if the dream was highly improbable, and its loss was very traumatic. I found it too painful to talk openly about what really happened with anyone. When people asked me about my Peace Corps experience, I'd be vague in my response and then try to change the subject. This effectively meant that I never had a chance to heal from the trauma. I remained stuck in the shame, loss and failure for years, and couldn't move on.

Of course, who knows whether I would have fared any better had I managed to stay in India? From the stories I've heard from those who stuck it out, there were many opportunities for things to go sideways—or downhill. However, I would have had the comfort of knowing that I was with my comrades who were also trying to make some kind of magic happen, even if it was only enduring 'til the end. I was completely isolated with my pain. I know now that unprocessed shame crystallizes into a hard, toxic substance around the heart that cripples the spirit. It poisoned me for a long time.

But now, four decades later, the Internet has finally allowed some of our group to reconnect. Originally, I was very cautious because of the shame. As I recover their friendship, and hear their stories—including their own struggles with shame and failure—I now see that there was more than enough frustration and shame to go around; my story is not so special in this regard. It is tremendously healing to hear all the stories—triumphs and tragedies—because doing so ameliorates my pain and returns me to full membership in the flawed human race. As I narrate my own story, I have recovered the truly virtuous impulse that led me into service: JFK's vision that a handful of American college kids sent to volunteer in foreign lands could somehow make a positive difference in the world.

The Wanderer

The Peace Corps had been my first post-collegiate foray into the adult world, and it had been very shattering. The life I returned to was hardly any better. I was still sick when I returned to the US and was under my doctor's care for months before I was able to pick up the thread of my life. I had never been that sick before (or since, knock on wood...).

I remember how strange American culture seemed to me when I first got back. Before leaving, America had been to me like water to a fish. Our culture now seemed crass, superficial, and immature. I was repelled by it. This just increased the isolation and alienation I felt.

I had no money and no prospects for work. My friends had scattered to the winds after college. I had to move back to my father's house, there was no place else I could go. My mother had died when I was 17, and my father had remarried (badly) to a woman who, if she didn't outright hate me, at least had no interest in having her husband's 22-year-old son hanging around her house for any length of time. I had to begin looking for a job that would qualify for alternate service but I was so flattened I could barely get out of bed. This seemed to my new stepmother equivalent to being a sloth; the tension in the house was palpable, further increasing my isolation and alienation.

Shortly after I returned, my draft board reclassified me 1-A as a precursor to drafting me. I was afraid for my life—quite realistically, as this was at the height of the Vietnam War, when thousands of men my age were being killed every month. The whole thing was enough to make you crazy and the justification given by the government for the war was certifiably and transparently insane. However, the killing machine was just ramping up and would eventually destroy the lives of hundreds of thousands of Americans and Vietnamese. Surviving soldiers would not be welcomed back; Agent Orange would kill them slowly; many would end up broken shells, shunned by the society they had supposedly "protected", living on the streets, their lives shattered by what they had endured.

What should I do? I had to save myself before I could be of use to anyone else. Filing for CO status was the only legal option available to resisters, but it had a vanishingly small chance of success. Obtaining a CO was even less likely in the redneck district I lived in. Other bad options included fleeing to Canada, crippling myself somehow to fail the induction physical, going to jail, or even suicide. I had friends who settled for each of these options.

Gandhi's words about the futility of violence came back to me: "I cannot teach you violence, as I do not myself believe in it. I can only teach you not to bow your heads before anyone even at the cost of your life." Anger rose up in me as I watched hundreds of thousands of lives torn apart by war. I railed at the collective insanity of it all, for blood needlessly spilled, lives wasted for political gain. I swore to myself I would not be a casualty of this madness. This anger finally motivated me to get off my ass and act. I steeled myself, filed for CO status, and began to prepare to battle my redneck draft board. I would not go quietly into that dark night.

Soon after I returned, there was a tremendous fire in the chaparral-covered hills behind my father's home, driven by the hot, dry Santana winds of Southern California. The fire burned ferociously, blasting through the canyons like an enraged, shrieking orange tiger. The fire did not scare me, it felt attractive and exciting, like a dangerous friend. I felt a curious kinship to the flames that swept up the hillsides; they lived only in the present moment, burning from canyon to canyon, wandering whither they would over the hills. I walked out on the charred hillsides that night, over the scorched earth, trailing along behind the flames, treading on the blackened bushes while nearby tree stumps still smoldered. I felt no fear.

When I got back, I pulled out my copy of the I Ching, the Chinese book of divination, and consulted it by throwing coins, as I had been doing already for years. The reading I got was titled The Wanderer (hexagram 56), consisting of the trigram for fire above, and the trigram for mountain below, in other words, "fire on the mountain." I was floored by the synchronicity of receiving this reading while there was a physical fire still raging on the hills outside my window. It was clarifying to see so sharply the archetype I was living out, but devastating to realize that the wanderer indicated in the hexagram was none other than me.

That same night I wrote this song:

The Wanderer
Fire on the mountain rises high
Grasping reaching fingers to the sky
Wandering among the flames I go
As the story of my life unfolds.
On the shadow of a flame I see
Many faces of myself to be
Then the shadow rises into smoke
Into the depths of which I cannot look.
With a burning ember in my hand
With its smoke inside my lungs expand
As I sing this song the smoke pours out
Rising from my burning flame of doubt.
Sunlight burning off the morning dew
Evaporating memories of you
Now the glowing coals of dawn combine
With fire on the mountain of my mind.

Shortly thereafter, a woman did a Tarot reading for me. The first card she drew was The Fool, showing a young vagabond, eyes fixed in the heavens, striding confidently but directly off a cliff. My stomach churned. It seemed that the die was cast; I saw clearly that I had been and would continue to be a wandering fool.

Many tumultuous years of wandering (and foolishness) did indeed lie directly ahead of me. Music was at first my boon companion, eventually my destiny. Of course, a benefit of foolishly wandering about is that you end up seeing a lot of life. I hoped that the acquired experience from this vagrancy would eventually wring out at least some of the foolishness so that the wandering could subside.

Moving On

My first move was to appear before my draft board in person to qualify for CO status. It was in San Bernardino County

245

which, next to Orange County, is the most conservative Republican district in California. This was, after all, home of the John Birch Society, the core of the arch-conservative movement. My father had been a CO in World War II and had then become a Methodist minister. He was now a professor, and through his connections, I got draft counseling and letters of reference from some well-known local objectors.

The law required belief in God to obtain objector status, because the original war objectors were Quakers, who objected on religious grounds. (A lot of them spent time in jail resisting conscription before allowance was finally made for them in the law.) Luckily, being a preacher's kid, belief in God was no problem for me then. Along with my application for CO status to the draft board, I included a short but passionate essay titled "Jesus, the Prince of Peace" that included quotes from the Bible and Mohandas Gandhi. The tone was respectful, but pulled no punches about what I thought of the Vietnam War and my pacifist beliefs.

On the day of my interview, I put on a suit and tie, and slicked back my longish hair. I was ushered into a nondescript room with a few old guys sitting around a table. They worked me over a little to see what I was made of but it was actually not as bad as I expected. I remember one of them asked, "So, are you content to let these other boys go over and fight for their country while you stay out of harm's way?" I replied, "I will perform alternative service." My aim was to hold my ground while avoiding provocation. Another asked, "What if everyone believed the way you do? How would our country defend itself?" I avoided the bait and replied as calmly as I could, "I am a conscientious objector to war. All I am asking is for you to recognize me for what I am." I told them about my visit to the Gandhi memorial in New Delhi and the commitment I felt to non-violence. They listened quietly. That was about it. I got a provisional CO status in the mail a few weeks later. I now had to find a place to perform my alternate service.

Through my father's ministerial connections, I landed a "job" in a church on the Sunset Strip in West Hollywood that was ministering to the young hippies who were starting to flock to the Strip. (A similar phenomenon was already starting in San Francisco.) The job paid nothing, but the church gave me a place to live; I'd have to find paying work to eat. I applied to my draft board to make this my alternative service. I was every bit as lost as the hippies and stoners were, but I was put in charge—the blind leading the blind. We had a soup kitchen and crafts activities. Pretty tame stuff. I lived in a house the church owned with a very beautiful woman (a former Playboy bunny) and her child who were down on their luck. We threw our lot together for awhile. I learned a tremendous amount from her for which I will always be grateful.

I later fell in with one of the hippie chicks, also a musician, at the soup kitchen. I gave her some of the costumes I had brought back from India. We wore them to local Hollywood parties and looked very stylish, given that India was now all the rage in American popular culture because of the Beatles.

We inevitably rubbed up against Hollywood actors and directors. I was introduced to Dennis Hopper and we became friends for a while. I didn't know he was such a famous actor. He came a few times to my house just to hang out and talk about spirituality. We shared an interest in the recently translated Gospel of St. Thomas, from the Dead Sea Scrolls, a fourth-century cache of early Christian documents found in a cave in the Egyptian desert. My father—a serious scholar of the Dead Sea Scrolls—had turned me on to it, and Hopper was eager to study it. Given my thorough biblical training in my father's church, Hopper and I had a lot to talk about. I enjoyed his rants about the poisonous way religion was being used in our society. We both approved of St. Thomas' emphasis on personal transformation. He was a really interesting guy.

Hopper introduced me to another actor whose name I can't recall who decided he wanted to put on an improvisational play in the sanctuary of the church where I worked. I went out to USC and UCLA recruiting acting students; he went out and raised money. We started buying lighting equipment, musical instruments and props before we even had much of a clue what we were doing. Our idea turned out to be a kind of improv theater where we would select people from the audience to share a traumatic experience from their lives. We would then dramatize it on the spot with them in the lead role, and hope to reshape it into something transformative. To say we were ahead of our times is understating it by decades. Although television programs like "Dr. Phil" have made personal catharsis a national pastime, in the 1960's this was not the sort of thing audiences were ready to experience as entertainment, so naturally it fell flat.

However, it led to more introductions. I met a couple of guys who were floating a proposal around Hollywood for a feature-length film, eventually titled "1A", about a draftee who got killed in Vietnam. They were set designers by profession and actually had some money. They wanted me to do the music for the movie. This was way beyond my abilities at that stage, and I knew it—but I didn't tell them. Fortunately, the project didn't come to fruition for several more years, during which time I became a much better musician. They eventually used me to compose the music for some dream sequences in the film, which allowed me to buy audio equipment and studio time.

Something's Happening Here

At a superficial level, Hollywood seems to be all about good stuff, like self-actualization and realizing your inner potential; finding your voice; polishing your craft. But if you do not have the persona or the luck that the institutions of Hollywood demand, then the culture of Hollywood allows its denizens to fabricate a few credible illusions that are passed off as credentials. This could even be something as slight as the conspicuous way one dressed. I soon realized that the town was filled to capacity with people who'd settled for this arrangement. I remembered the parable of Pinocchio, and realized that if I stayed among them I'd soon enough turn into one. I had to get out.

I began thinking of returning to San Francisco. Out of the blue, a letter arrived from Dell Fitzgerald, an old friend who now lived in Berkeley. I stuffed my belongings in a backpack, put on my jean jacket and my bell bottoms, and hitchhiked up Highway 101 to visit her. With my thumb out by the side of the road late that night in downtown Santa Barbara (back in the days when the freeway didn't go all the way through downtown) I got lucky: a hippie van—an old bread truck—picked me up and dropped me off at dawn the next morning in Golden Gate Park. I drifted around from place to place in San Francisco looking for somewhere to perform alternate service, at one point sleeping for a week in Louella Sommers's parents' basement until they politely told me to move along.

Once again my father's connections came in handy. Through a friend of his at Union Theological Seminary in Berkeley, I got an introduction to Robert Johnson, the director of Intersection Theater for the Arts at 756 Union St. in San Francisco. The theater was founded around 1965, and then housed in a tiny desanctified Methodist church in North Beach. The aim of Intersection was similar to what I'd been doing in the church in Hollywood—only ever so much more brilliantly conceived—so I was a shoe-in.

The place was a 24-hour-a-day artist's happening. Virtually everyone who was anyone in the Beat movement, and many of the emerging poets and artists of the hippie movement were involved at some point with Intersection. The rent on the building was $1/year. Johnson was later quoted in the San Francisco Chronicle saying, "One of the first things we were able to do was get legal status so we could get conscientious objectors to do alternative service in place of going to Vietnam. I had three working for me: typing in the office, cleaning up the bathrooms, sweeping, whatever." [8] I was one of those three. I slept behind the stage or in the basement. I had no money; the gig paid nothing. I found that there were many ways of surviving in North Beach on nothing. For example, I could buy a cup of minestrone soup at the US Restaurant on Columbus Avenue for 20 cents, and could plead for extra crackers. The old-time North Beach Italian family that ran the joint understood poverty; they had no compassion for bums, but if you had even a little money, food would come.

I was essentially a street person, but I finally had alternative service I believed in. However, my draft board disagreed, so I had a fight on my hands. A year-long struggle with my draft board ensued over what constituted acceptable CO job placement. As a back-up, I needed another CO gig I could take if this one was declined. I also needed to make some money so I could fight my draft board in court if needed. A counselor at the Department of Employment set me up with a civilian job with the Coast Guard as a gardener on Yerba Buena Island (the island the Bay Bridge goes through) that would qualify for backup alternative service. That way I (hopefully) wouldn't have to start over from scratch with another two-year assignment if the draft board officially declined to approve Intersection as my CO job site.

I took the gardening job and moved in with Stephen Mitchell who had a tiny apartment near the Panhandle of Golden Gate Park, on the edge of the Haight-Ashbury district. He was another Intersection CO. I would ride to work up Market St. on the street cars (then still 15 cents a ride) to catch a bus to Yerba Buena Island where I tended the rose garden of the Coast Guard Admiral by day. I would return to Intersection Theater to help out at night. Eventually, I saved enough from gardening to be able to buy a very used VW bus. I constructed a platform bed in the back of it and built a wooden roof rack on top. In those days, all my worldly possessions fit comfortably into that bus with still enough room for me to lie down in the back and sleep.

Crazy times ensued at Intersection. Poetry readings, fringe film festivals, happenings, wall-to-wall hippies, Hells Angels, Beat poets, dancers, painters... we put up a café downstairs, which lasted for a while; but everything was in flux—flux *was* everything. By day, I was a gardener for the Coast Guard; by night, I was incandescent with the flood of energy that was the confluence of the Beat and Hippie movements.

It was about this time that another India 44 member, Betsy Stephens, who had switched to a program in Turkey, came back to San Francisco and looked me up. We began dating, and were together and apart, on and off, for the next several years. She accompanied me on many of these crazy adventures, and can attest that they really happened.

The sitar I'd brought back from India turned out to be quite playable. I took lessons for a while from Pandit Bannerjee who was then teaching at the Society for Asian Arts in Berkeley. I played well enough to find semiprofessional work as a sitarist. [9] I got a gig accompanying Ann Swearingin, a modern dancer active in San Francisco at the time, in a show at the Palace of Fine Arts Theater. I was introduced to an eccentric *Bharat Natyam* dancer named Ishvani Hamilton. Ordinarily, sitar does not accompany *Bharat Natyam*, but Ishvani had made a career of finding rules that needed breaking. In the 1940's and 1950's, she'd been one of the first to bring *Bharat Natyam* to the West.

Ishvani married an ambassador and led a very Bohemian life. We toured colleges along the West Coast and concertized around the San Francisco Bay Area for a couple of years. Then one day I woke up and realized, "Hmm, how is playing sitar a winning career path for a white American kid?" I wanted to return to western music... but what genre? I saw the great San Francisco rock-n-roll scene unfolding all around me, but I wasn't particularly attracted to it. It was too loud, too crazed, and too druggy. I wanted something different... but what?

After struggling many months to get my draft board to accept my CO job, it started to look like I might have to appeal, which could stretch things out indefinitely. Meanwhile, my life was on hold and I couldn't even start counting the time served thus far. A draft counselor had an idea. She pointed out that my draft board must have hated awarding me CO status in the first place. If I gave them the slightest excuse, like sending them my Peace Corps medical records showing the diseases I had brought back from India, they would kick me out of the Selective Service system altogether and say good riddance.

I kind-of liked the idea of getting some good out of all that sickness I suffered through, but this didn't seem like the honorable pacifist stance I'd envisioned for myself. This felt more like I was cheating the system. I dithered about it for a while, but eventually realized that my draft board was also playing a cagy

251

game with me—and they had the upper hand. Their game was to string me along until I buckled. I felt trapped, like a caged animal. I learned a big lesson about the power of freedom. Eventually, I followed her advice, and sure enough, lickety-split, a shiny new 4-F classification with my name on it showed up in the mail.

At first I was euphoric; I had survived the valley of the shadow of death. I felt like I was floating. I could start to come alive again but I had guilt and remorse; I'd beaten the draft, but in that one year alone 16,592 young Americans of my generation died in Vietnam, and many thousands more would come home crippled in mind and body. Every day, images of the violence and carnage filled the radio, television, and newspapers.

I felt confused and upset; why was I spared while so many others were killed? I had no idea what to do with the life I'd just been handed back. Survivor's guilt made a wicked cocktail in my heart when mixed with my still-bruised feelings about the Peace Corps. I had no center. Like a leaf driven by San Francisco's foggy wind, I kept wandering.

Prodigal Father

A year or two later when I was 23 or 24, my father called and invited himself up from Claremont to see me. His second marriage was on the rocks, although he didn't tell me that. I was living by myself (one of the "apart" phases with Betsy) in an apartment on Congo St. (owned by the wife of Irving Berlin), still gardening by day and working at Intersection at night.

My dad began spilling out stories about the early life of my family: how my mother had had a "nervous breakdown" when I was less than 3 years old; my brother Tom and I had been separated from our parents and, at that tender age, shipped off to Kansas to live for a year with separate sets of grandparents. His stories triggered my recall of the dream-like state of my earliest childhood and helped to piece together what had happened. I began recalling my mother's increasing disconnectedness and despair, the long spells during which I had to stay at other people's houses, followed by the long, heartbreakingly painful abandonment in Kansas, which I now understood was the time during which she convalesced from her mental trauma in Los Angeles.

The trajectory of my early family life was emotionally like the letter "U", a precipitous decline triggered by the deterioration of my mother's mental health, followed by several years at the bottom, and then a gradual climb out of the abyss as my parents got psychological help, which was rare in those times, in the late 1940's and early 1950's. The "U" started down when I was three, and started back up when I was about ten. I sometimes think the experimentalism in my own life derives from the unbelievably daring experiments my mother and father engaged in to recover their own sanity during these times.

My father had been studying for a Doctorate of Divinity at Yale Theological Seminary when the Great Depression carried away the hopes of so many. Dreaming of being a professor of theology, he had to settle for being a minister. My mother hated it. She was a fine singer and pianist, and longed for a musical career. She felt trapped by the church—much as she had felt trapped in her family of origin, having to step into her mother's shoes when she'd died, and become the entire feminine support system on her patriarchal father's farm in rural Kansas while she was still but a child. When her own babies came, the combination of our utter dependence and the rigid moral demands the church placed on her as the minister's wife reminded her so forcefully of her childhood trauma that it gradually drove her into a suicidal despair and massive depression.

It was a terribly painful journey, but over the course of my parents' recovery, I experienced what I called the "golden age" of my family. They changed everything, mostly for the better. My father got off of his career-advancement track, moved to a small parish (Chino, CA) and focused on raising my brother and me, at the same time working on himself and his marriage. My mother took herself out of the job of minister's wife and became a schoolteacher. My father, a fine rag-time pianist, accompanied her on a program of Negro spirituals that they toured around to white protestant churches in Southern California, promoting racial harmony. (This was during the early 1950s—a time *way* ahead of the civil rights movement).

Then, tragically, when I was 13, my mother developed breast cancer and died when I was 17. Her last request of my father before she died was that he leave the ministry and become the professor they'd both always wanted him to be, teaching psychology, world religion, and sociology at a nearby college. It was a very tough time for us while she spent four years dying. When the cancer metastasized into her brain, and morphine couldn't control the pain any longer, she had a lobotomy. My mother spent the last year of her life as a vegetable. As soon as he graduated, my brother disappeared off to college, got married, and finally moved to Alaska. My dad was preoccupied with changing careers and burying his mate; I was struggling to stay focused in school. The family basically broke into splinters.

My dad started dating a couple of years later. He remarried about the time I went off to UCLA in 1965, the same year I careened off into the Peace Corps, desperate for a little structure in my life. (Hah!) The woman he chose was the one who gave me the cold welcome when I came back sick from India.

What! Me Worry?

My father's visits and the stories he told put me into an intensely reflective mood. With the Peace Corps and the draft behind me, I enjoyed the breathtaking musical and artistic vistas opening up around me. I was in my mid-twenties and I should have been on top of the world, but I was not thriving. My relationship with Betsy was unraveling, and I was spiraling down at work. I felt dead inside—a head unconnected to my body.

Although music had always been a big part of my life, I'd stopped playing after I got back from the Peace Corps. I had been a singer-songwriter in the Folk Music movement of the 1960's, but the musical circles I'd traveled in were long gone. The wild swings of cultural change in San Francisco had kept me off balance, and I had lost my sense of direction. Yes, it was an intoxicating environment, but the word "toxic" is in that word too.

In a perverse way, I think my struggle with the draft had kept me going in the long months after I returned from India. With that behind me, the air went out of my sails, and I had no idea what to do next. I became increasingly depressed, which scared me. I was in a vicious spiral. I saw only emptiness where a sense of purpose and youthful enthusiasm should have existed. I was both nauseated with my life and terrified of change (which didn't take rocket science for me to know was a bad combination). I became afraid that I might slip into the same suicidal despair my mother had faced, only without her support network. It occurred to me that I might already be headed in that direction.

These depressing thoughts made me yet more anxious, and my insomnia worsened. One night as I lay awake thinking about my plight, I remembered a saying from the Gospel of St. Thomas. I couldn't remember it exactly, so I dug out my copy from a box and read:

"Jesus said, if you bring forth what is within you, what you bring forth will save you. If you do not bring forth what is within you, what you do not bring forth will destroy you." [10]

Have you ever momentarily been dropped in an elevator? You know what a clarifying experience that can be even if the drop is just a couple of inches. Suddenly you remember you are alive, and that there is something vital at stake. I had just been jolted like this, as though Jesus had spoken the words directly to me. What did the words mean? The saying was a perfect koan for me, an impossible paradox on its face, like "What is the sound of one hand clapping?", but urgent for me to understand. It could cost me my life if I failed. This was my koan based on Jesus' words: *How can I bring forth "what" is within me if I don't know "what" is within me?!* If I understood correctly, this "what" could either save or destroy me, depending on whether I could bring it forth or not? Yikes!

At first I recoiled from this idea, rejecting it. It seemed nonsensical and dangerous. I then realized, NO, the danger is *in me!* I am not bringing forth anything, and I am going down in

255

flames! Was it possible that my lack of direction—my inability to bring forth "what" is within me—was the very source of my destruction? My anxiety increased two-fold.

It occurred to me that what Jesus said would only be true if his corresponding assertion—that I would be saved if I did manage to bring forth "what" is within me—were true. I could test it if I could only figure out "what" to bring forth! I didn't know what the "what" was! Augh! I was going mad!

While it seems somewhat comical now, like some existential version of the old Abbot and Costello skit about "Who's on First?", it most certainly was not comical at the time. There was a life-or-death quality about it, and I sensed there was a truth I hadn't yet discovered, a truth that might matter a great deal.

I declared a time-out. I threw on a coat and went out for a late night walk a couple of hours before sunrise. I walked around the city feeling miserable and wishing I were anyone but myself. The cold San Francisco fog screamed silently across the night sky, dampening the dust in every alley and seeping into every crevice of my coat. Stars winked here and there, only to be blotted out again by the racing fog. It seemed to come down to this question: What is the "what" I would have to bring forth in order to find out if it would save me? How would I know what the right "what" is? What if I choose the wrong "what"? What if the right "what" that is not brought forth still ends up destroying me? What does it mean to be saved anyway? Saved for what? What is "what"?!

I walked until sunrise and ended up in an industrial district by the Bay, far from home. As I turned back, I passed a line of workmen standing outside a closed liquor store. I realized they were waiting for it to open before their shift began so they could buy six-packs of beer to numb them up so they could survive their factory job and get through their day. I wondered if I'd end up living some equivalent of that kind of life. I figured I might if I couldn't sort myself out. What would I settle for? What would be my version of a six-pack to get me through the day? What would my excuse be for settling for it? When I returned home, I collapsed in bed, sickened and exhausted.

Over the course of the next several days, things started falling into place. I had to find out if Jesus was right. There were only two ways to do it: 1) I could keep going the way I was headed and see if I crashed on the rocks. This seemed a likely outcome. Or 2), I could try to dig something out of myself and see if it "saved" me, whatever that meant. It seemed evident that the later course of action might be less painful in the long run. Being "saved" sounded vaguely promising. My father never talked much about "being saved" the way revival preachers did so I had no idea what it meant. I decided I would actually have to run the experiment to find out whether Jesus was right. I might come to know what it meant to be saved. What a bonus!

A plan gradually formed in my mind.

The Little Room in Berkeley

I quit my gardening job (right before they fired me), quit my relationship with Betsy (just before the door would have hit my backside on the way out), let go of most of my friends (not that I had many left), stopped watching television, listening to radio, going to movies, and reading newspapers. I moved into a little room in a boarding house south of the Berkeley campus. With Food Stamps and my meager savings, I figured I had enough money to live for about nine months without working. I would spend that time studying how to bring forth what was within me.

I hit on a plan for how to do the work. I vowed to myself that for the next nine months,

I would do only what I was personally motivated in each moment to do.

If no direction arose from within, I would stop and wait until something came up. I wanted to find something—anything— that could reliably spur me to action. I also wanted to learn to tell the difference between what I wanted for myself and what others wanted for me, or from me. And if I felt an impulse arise, I would, if I could, act on it immediately. I was seeking to cultivate a dialog with my opaque soul.

My early efforts were sometimes comical. I might stop at a street corner to decide which way to go and stand there immobilized for what felt like an eternity as I wrestled with myself. I could see people glance at me nervously as they passed by, perhaps wondering if I was a nut case. At first I felt ashamed, but I kept on. I willed myself to hold still until I could reliably start to feel like myself.

One of the odd things I learned about myself was that my natural sleep-wake cycle greatly exceeded 24 hours. I'd sleep solid for 10 hours and then be wide awake for 18. This meant I woke up four hours later every day. This could prove inconvenient if, for example, it meant I woke up just after the grocery store had closed for the night and I needed food... so I sometimes had to temper my vow for expediency. I did stick to my program whenever possible.

It was not easy. I had no guru to help me except my own empty center. The key was to stick strictly to my program. If I could leak out into old habits, or space out, or freak out, then I remained stuck. When I was able to just face my emptiness, I discovered that it wasn't really empty; it was me.

After a couple of months of my practice I started to relax a bit. Taking some time off was itself very healing. This was more than a vacation, however. By examining my default responses and cultivating my authentic impulses, I could tell that I was gradually freeing myself from the cultural and emotional noise that had governed me. Gradually, I felt myself begin to spread out into my body.

As I relaxed into myself, I became interested in music again. Did I want to play music? If so, what kind? Could I remain true to myself and not be swept away by the fickle winds of fashion? I decided to do an inventory of what I liked and had a talent for.

What were my natural gifts? I began at the beginning: opening my ears and listening uncritically. I found I could distinguish each instrumental voice in a symphony, even the inner parts—such as the violas and English horns by listening carefully. That would certainly be a useful talent for an arranger or composer. One day on a long drive, I started playing a Mozart symphony in my head (the "Jupiter", as I recall). As an experiment, I started it in my mind from the beginning and listened internally to every note and nuance from start to finish, including the complicated fugues in the final movement. A good memory for music would be an asset as a performer.

As I continued listening uncritically, I began to hear details in the sounds all around me that I had never noticed before. I was sitting at a frog pond one night and I found I could shift my attention from hearing the chorus to hearing each individual frog, and make out its particular location in the pond. I listened that way for quite a while, distinguishing the individual calls. When I shifted back to hearing the chorus, the organic rhythmic quality of it stood out. When I concentrated, I began to hear a mesmerizing music in it I'd never heard before. I became aware of the tapestry of sound woven together by the individual voices, phasing against each other to create an undulating sound that was much more than the sum of its parts.

Soon, I began wandering around Berkeley making recordings of whatever sounds attracted my attention, and would go back to my room and listen intently to them. Then I would splice and mix them together to make sound collages. Late one night after a violent storm, I drove to Lands End in San Francisco and dangled a microphone on a long cord over the cliffs directly above the ocean to capture the waves crashing below. Another time, I found a box of broken sheets of glass. I set up several microphones in the driveway, and spun the panes so they would shatter as they flew past the microphones, making a dancing, shimmering, rolling crash. I laboriously spliced all the individual crashes together to make a continuous rolling thunder of breaking glass.

I came back from the public library with Helmholtz's landmark book on acoustics, John Cage's book *Silence*, and Harry Partch's book on music composition, and devoured them. I started to construct new electronic musical instruments, wiring contraptions together to alter the sounds I'd recorded. I met someone who had built an Altair 8800 digital computer. I began to think about how I could use computers musically. I figured out for myself the basic theory of digital sound sampling. I also got out my guitar again and started playing again. I found I was drawn to playing classical guitar, and began to study and practice. I started to get very excited and a little worried.

A compulsion to create had now begun to replace my former ennui. I increasingly felt gripped, even driven. Music became ever more numinous, more filled with energy and meaning. I began to be flooded by hot, enigmatic creative urges that drove me through long sleepless nights. I would wake the next day exhausted, only to pick up and begin another eighteen hour day of creative work. As isolated as I was, I began to worry. Were my creative preoccupations benign, or was I starting to go off the deep end again? But I didn't care, my creative voice enchanted me, and I labored on…

Beginning of the End

I was finally rescued from this dizzying enterprise by running out of money. I realized I had no way to fund the dreams that were now shouting in my ears. I desperately longed to dream! I could not go back to my former life, but I had no idea how to go forward, and funds were getting scarce. I began to feel a desperate sadness, as though I'd emerged from a coma, only to feel it threaten to come on again. Would I have to abandon myself again and return to the work world where the dreams of others seemed to be all that mattered?

As funds dwindled, I started missing payments on my VW bus. My dad, who had cosigned the loan, heard from the bank that I was in trouble so he paid me another visit. He looked around me at the musical instruments, weird audio gear and tapes, and scratched his head. He reminded me that I hadn't finished my BA degree before going off to India (I had missed graduating by 5 credits). He made me a proposition: what if I went back to finish my degree by studying music? He'd pay me a (very modest, but livable) stipend for every month I was enrolled full-time in college. I agreed to try. At first, I was worried about reentering society because I had been so isolated. But

I quickly found that I was spring-loaded to rejoin the world, and I began to find my way.

And so, the era of The Wanderer came to a close. The experiment I had conducted on myself in that little room in Berkeley proved a critical turning point for me. Forty years later, I am still guided by those dreams, still fueled by the energy that they released. Although I may now have more skill and craft, and my horizons have certainly expanded, much of what I have achieved is grounded by my experience in that tiny room. Years later, I wrote this poem about my experience of those nine months in the little room in Berkeley.

Good Lost
When the sadness takes you
Or you lose your way
Just stop
Listen—until the sound of your own voice
Finally reaches you
Let go of the world you know
Fall into this breath, this moment
Step forward within yourself
Until you come to recognize that sound—that steady flame
The one that holds you, that is you
There is really nothing else worth hearing
And longing opens your heart
Now, when your still small voice rings out
You know how good it can be to be lost
And though demons remain
You remember the sweet sound
The world makes when it is new again.

The Myth of Askeladden

How had I gotten myself so stuck? It's not like I had always been so blocked. Why was this time so fraught with possible self-immolation? The answer is that this time it really mattered, because I knew that whatever I chose to pursue at that point had to launch me into, and carry me through, the rest of my adult life.

I could change course, but whatever I did from that point forward would be the portal to whatever the future held. If I got it wrong or missed it entirely, I could end up shipwrecked, especially considering the emotional headwinds I faced. The stakes were high.

I'm convinced by my own experience, and from watching others go through similar episodes, that the hardest thing the young have to do is to cook up an adult self. Think about it; when children are born, their parents are their entire world. Gradually, children learn that they have an autonomous will. My son Morgan learned this at the age of two. He was reaching for some candy and I said, "No!" to him. He stopped for a moment to see what his hand would do, and to his delight, he discovered that it continued reaching for the candy!

Big problems come during adolescence, when kids face the task of creating their adult selves. It is a life-or-death matter. It is literally a life-or-death matter. They must succeed or die, but they have no idea how to go about it. At that point, their parents *are* their world; all they can do to start with is to define themselves in *opposition* to their parents, producing the archetype of the sullen, resistant teenager. Normally, this lingers on until sometime around age eighteen. If all goes well, they then realize that, by defining themselves in opposition to their parents they are still defining themselves *in terms* of their parents. This horrifies and embarrasses them, but gives them the final kick in the pants they need to find a way to define themselves in terms *of themselves.* Guided by the inner light they have awakened in themselves, they can (hopefully) find their own way.

That is what should happen normally but didn't happen in my case. There are many ways into adulthood and some of the pathways are very strange. The path I followed is like the Norwegian myth of the ash boy. In this story, the ash boy (Askeladden, literally "ash lad") gets his name because he always just sits by the fireplace, playing with the ashes. He appears to do nothing all day but sit and stare at the fire, and so he is thought to be a simpleton. He is the younger brother of brash older brothers, Per and Pål, who seem much better prepared for life. In most of these fairy tales, the three children come from a poor family (as did I). His parents despair of him (as did mine); his older brothers constantly ridicule and belittle him as a slacker and weirdo (as did mine!). Although their ridicule is painful, ash boy keeps his thoughts to himself. He sits at the hearth all day long, lost in thought, playing with the ashes until he is covered with them from head to toe. The old wise ones of the village secretly keep an eye on him because they suspect that he is really the Golden One, but they keep it to themselves—after all, saying anything about it would only make everyone laugh.

Indeed, something truly amazing comes out of this ash-boy eventually. The Norwegian stories show him to be a 'trickster' figure, effortlessly able to work his will on trolls and princesses alike, and winning half the kingdom in the bargain, succeeding with his creative intelligence where his brothers fail with their conventional thinking and brawn. This is the crucial insight: his ways are inscrutable, even to himself. His powers are revealed only in the moment fate requires them of him and then magic happens. After all, what is magic but a hidden power suddenly revealed?

My life was like the ash boy, except that as a child, no one let me just sit by the fire and stare into the flames. Life was too full of trauma and emotional noise for that so it was necessary for me to find a way to do it for myself as an adult. I spent nine months in the little room in Berkeley metaphorically "staring into the flames." My powers were only revealed to me in the moment I exercised them like those of the ash boy.

Epilogue

At this point I'm about 25 years old, on the cusp of artistic and technological achievements that launched me into my adult career, combining music and technology. I auditioned for the classical guitar program in the Music Department at SFSU and was accepted. I quickly branched out to include composition and electronic music in my studies. My composition professor, Dr. Herbert Bielawa, and I founded a student organization for new music. I played classical guitar professionally, and started

a classical guitar duet with Jim Colgan, a fellow guitar major. I developed a concert of electronic music with Hale Thatcher and Stephen Mitchell that we called *Hermes* and performed around northern California and nearby states. I received a Doctor of Musical Arts degree from Stanford in computer music, became Apple Computer employee #77, taught for a decade in the Music Department at UCSD, married Juda, raised two kids Morgan and Greta, and published two volumes on the mathematics of music... but I'm getting ahead of myself.

Of course, what was to come was not all triumph and mastery, far from it. It is important to know about Askeladden that, despite his ultimate triumph, he coped with a tremendous emotional deficit, as did I. We humans are social animals to our core, and when any are cut out of the herd like Askeladden and I were, over and over, a hole opens up in the heart that is hard to fill. The road back to health began for me with first finding a way to make my life worth living—not an insubstantial accomplishment. Eventually, through lots of hard work, I have developed what is called in the literature "earned secure attachment." I am very grateful for this, but mindful that I must earn it anew at every turn.

Alhough it felt like wandering in the wilderness, I was actually on a path that eventually led to my own heart. That is what life is: a path to the heart, if you'll take it.

Oh yes, and I decided that being on that path must be what it means to be saved.

Namaste.

CHAPTER 11

Reflections on a Prior Life

Tom Corbett

You must become the change you want.

Gandhi

The Air India flight now seems like a dream and yet, some images remain indelible—musing over expressive, high topped clouds through the plane window as the reality sank in that I was not in Worcester, Massachusetts anymore. Looking out, I physically sensed a kind of transition, a faint anticipation of the coming challenges tarnished by a tiny dread of the unknown and the unknowable. If I recall correctly, we dropped off another Peace Corps group headed for Iran which, from the air, struck me as a reasonable representation of the far side of the moon. "I sure feel sorry for those bastards," I mused as they departed. Ignorance of one's own destiny can be a blessing.

When my wife and I were driving Sam Rankin back to the hotel after the Sunday gathering of our weekend reunion, he posed what I thought was an interesting question. How the hell did we all get on that plane? Why did each one of those kids back then, from diverse backgrounds and from varied community settings, sign on to spend two years in a situation that promised such physical deprivation and emotional challenge? The easy answer is that it was the 1960s, or the call of the Kennedy mystique, or (for the guys at least) a somewhat more palatable alternative to Vietnam. But I suspect, as did Sam, that there were as many answers as there were 'kids' on that plane.

My own choice appeared predictable and, at the same time, quite remarkable. I grew up in a very Catholic, very ethnic, and very working class world. For those needing a translation, cultural relativism was not the norm. A kind of fierce tribalism prevailed. Upon being introduced to someone new, you were likely to be asked, "What are you?" While a reasonable response might be along the lines of, oh, let's say "Gee, I am a human being," such sarcastic literalism would generate either a blank stare or a punch to the nose, depending on the size and IQ of the enquirer. Irish, Polish, Italian, or some acceptable mix of the tribes was the response demanded. You then became a known entity; and the questioner could fill in the blanks.

Prejudices were not confined to the simple distinctions of White or Black, Gentile or Jew, WASP or ethnic group member. Believe me, although all the common stereotypes were alive and well, my childhood world was more nuanced than that. Your response to the question "what are you" positioned you in a far more complex mosaic of national, political, and class distinctions. It framed you in a web of status and expectations that went far in defining who you were and how you were to be treated. I still recall, as a little tyke, being asked the Big Question, perhaps for the first time. Pondering over a response, I applied the incisive logic that would later bring me some success in the world of academia. I speak English, I calculated, so I must be English. Unfortunately, my very Irish father overheard my response and, to say the least, was not amused. I learned much about Celtic-Anglo history and relations over the next several minutes.

There is no obvious reason why I should not have been like everyone else I knew growing up, tribal and provincial. Yet, almost from the beginning of my memory, I seemed tugged in a different direction. Instinctively, I rebelled against the 'fill-in-the-blanks' world where you knew someone based on their race, religion, or ethnicity. We lived in what was called a three-decker and, even though I was no more than 12 or 13 years old, I recall getting into an argument with visitors from Virginia who were related to the elderly couple that owned the building and who lived on the first floor, or deck. The *Brown vs. Board of Educa-*

tion Supreme Court decision, laying the foundation for school integration, was still controversial and I heard them ranting about it one day. You know, "what right did this damn Supreme Court in Washington have to tell us how to run our lives?" I still recall getting upset and arguing that of course the Supreme Court had a right to rectify such an obvious injustice. Where did those feelings come from? It is inconceivable that anyone else in my immediate world felt that way.

I recall running across something called the World Federalist Society, a one world organization that probably was, in fact, some kind of Communist front. It made perfect sense to me. I used to think about our excess agricultural production and wonder why we didn't share it all with those who were without.

I recall being enthralled by mythical figures such as Albert Schweitzer, who labored to bring basic medical services to Africa
many decades earlier, and Mahatma Gandhi, who very aptly cor-
responded to my image of sainthood. In my high school years,
I particularly responded to a medical missionary of that era, Dr.
Tom Dooley, who was a contemporary saint among Catholics
for his work in Indo-China just as the French were pulling out
of Vietnam. I can still remember listening to the radio as he gave
spell binding speeches on the need to save the third world from
the inexorable advance of the godless Communists, heady stuff
for an impressionable young Catholic lad.

Simplistic thoughts for sure, but emblematic of the way I
organized my emerging conception of the good society. I lived
in a world that prized small tribe thinking—my tribe (ethnic,
working class, and Catholic) or my neighborhood or my family.
I was handed an immutable world of givens. It was a world of
black and white, good and bad, evil and redemption. And yet, I
instinctively found myself responding to issues in a big picture,
non-traditional way.

Troubling signs that I was drifting off the tribal reservation were observable early on. Sitting in religion class at my
all-boy's religious high school, I absorbed the Catholic dogma
on birth control while the rational side of my brain kept saying, "that doesn't make sense." The conventional argument was
that birth control wasn't 'natural.' Well, neither was open heart
surgery if God was, in fact, responsible for heart disease in the
first instance. And where the hell were we going to put all these
people? Surely, such rebellious thoughts were a sign of Satan
making early inroads.

After observing how individuals constructed their world
views over many decades, I eventually concluded that, while
much of what we believe is a product of nurture and experience,
quite a bit of our personal architecture is hard wired. It is built
in from the start. I am not talking about political affiliation or
positions on specific social issues necessarily but rather how we
think about things on a more fundamental level. Do we respond
from a narrowly tribal perspective or can we easily get outside

of our confining conceptual boxes? Can we deal with ambiguity or do we need certainty? Do we see the world as a threatening place that needs to be controlled or as a positive place where the good only needs to be nourished? Do we see people as evil and lazy, thereby demanding negative incentives (or punishments) to do the right thing, or as basically decent folk who sometimes go astray? Is society inherently competitive or is it naturally cooperative—Wall Street or Woodstock? These, and other foundational beliefs, constitute a kind of emotional palette we draw upon to fill in the canvas of our personal worldviews.

By the time Kennedy and the vision of Camelot emerged, I was pretty much ready to save the world. The question was, how? Peace Corps now existed but not as a realistic option. So, I did the next best thing, at least for someone still comfortably ensconced within the Catholic cocoon. I entered a Catholic missionary order, the Maryknollers. They were in the business of saving souls, and sometimes people in Asia and Africa and in various places in between. It seemed like a good idea at the time.

I would follow the footsteps of Schweitzer and Dooley, helping the dispossessed and vulnerable in ways that only the irretrievably innocent can believe makes sense. After about a year-and-a-half, this grand plan encountered a problem. It dawned on me there was a basic job requirement for being a priest—you had to believe in God—really believe. At some level, I knew that belief was not there. I was more interested in addressing the physical and political needs of the poor, not in harvesting their souls for an entity about which I harbored substantial doubt. My rational side never could accommodate the institutional fidelity that Catholicism, or any absolutist belief system, demanded. Forgoing women for the rest of my life might also have been a factor. Then again, I really only knew Catholic girls, which pretty much was like taking a vow of celibacy.

The road to the Peace Corps picked up speed after leaving the seminary. I enrolled at Clark University, a small liberal arts school located in my hometown of Worcester and thus, with luck and hard work, a realistic possibility financially. Sounds like a routine choice, but it was not. I had attended a competitive Catholic all-boy's high school where every single graduate went to college. Yet, despite the close proximity of the two schools, not a single graduate from my high school had ever, ever matriculated at Clark even though it was a pretty good institution academically. Clark boasts that is was the second graduate school established in the U.S., the place that Freud chose to give his American lectures, the birthplace of the American Psychological Association, and the place where physicist Robert Goddard launched the space age by developing the liquid fuel rocket, among other distinctions.

Why is this, you might ask, unless you suffer from a deplorable lack of curiosity? Well, Clark was widely considered a pinko, leftist school where nice Catholic boys would forfeit their faith and, if lucky, their moral compass. But I held out against the invidious and corrosive effects of rampant secularism with great bravery for at least two weeks. Ok, maybe a week.

The Clark experience constituted an epiphany for me. This was not my usual Catholic, ethnic, working class world. Suddenly, I was exposed to cultures and ways of thinking very diverse from my own. I was expected to think things through on my own. But even better, I met non-Catholic girls and, for the first time in my life, began to believe that miracles could happen even to a schlep like me.

And it was, let us not forget, the sixties. I remember a classmate named Carol (one of two girls I got close to in college) and I deciding to attend the first anti-war march in Worcester. Carol was emblematic of my break with my past. For one thing, she was Jewish, which caused my parents (my mother in particular) extraordinary *angst*—what would people think? She was also safe, in my view, since she was more or less attached to a fellow who had the misfortune of getting himself drafted. Thus, little was expected of me. Best of all, she was smart, ranking first in our class (I googled her once and found that she was a Dean at a well-known college). To this day I can envision calling her the night before finals to ask when our exams were scheduled while she screamed in response, probably in abject despair that she actually wasted time on this total goof who seemed destined to drift aimlessly through life.

In any case, anti-war sentiments were still tantamount to treason in 1964 (or was it 1965?), so the 150 or so protestors gathered in front of city hall found themselves surrounded by thousands (it seemed) of home-brewed patriots. As I looked around, one thought overwhelmed me—I am going to die. I did survive but it was close, very close. The protest march stopped at one point and I could sense a group of bikers straight out of the Brando movie—*The Wild Ones*—staring at me. Lets kick the shit out of the tall one with glasses, the one with the steroid-fueled muscles sneered. As far as I could figure out, I was the only tall one with glasses in the vicinity. For the first time in quite a while I tried remembering the perfect act of contrition that just might help me sneak into heaven. Fortunately, the line started moving again and all I had to worry about was ducking eggs and beer cans.

Obviously, I did not die on that day, but the simple truths of my childhood were quickly withering away as my working class parents looked on with dismay at the inexorable decline and fall of their only child. The 'big' fear always lurked in the background, what would the neighbors, relatives, and anyone else that counted, say? During my seminary tenure, I was ready to enlist in the armed forces during the Cuban missile crisis to help thwart godless Communism. By my junior year at Clark, I was heading the campus leftist organization (which I helped found), leading anti-war marches, and even joined the Students for a Democratic Society group (more as an intellectual statement rather than as a revolutionary). We called our leftist group the 'Student Action Committee' or SAC, you know, just like the Strategic Air Command, those guys that flew 24/7 so the Russkies could not sneak in a quick attack. Our cleverness knew no bounds.

My long-suffering parents did enjoy one consolation. Their decision to stop at one child now appeared prescient. They must have looked at what they wrought early on and concluded no more of this. But then again, they never did seem to like one another so perhaps there were other explanations.

Beyond my dalliance in revolutionary politics and my work to envision the just society, my impulse to do good never flagged. Being relatively poor, I needed to work through high school, and college would be no exception. So I found a job working the 11-7 shift as an orderly at a large Catholic hospital. The regulatory environment must have been weak in those days, because on many nights there would be just a senior nursing student, an aid, and myself to look after an entire floor of patients—and the place was generally packed in those days. Now hospitals kick you out four hours after quadruple bypass surgery AND a lobotomy.

It is hard to look back and not wonder how we managed not to kill off more than I can recall. My most serious crime, as I remember, involved little more than giving an enema to the wrong patient. This should have been a clue that any ambitions of becoming the next Albert Schweitzer may have been a bit of a stretch. However, the night shift at an urban hospital remained a great learning experience. I would get called to wherever problems broke out anywhere in the hospital resulting in things like wrestling with disoriented patients who decided they wanted to go home at three in the morning. I still remember one night getting called down to the emergency room to prop up a guy who kept fainting. As I looked at the seal of St. Vincent's above the emergency room door which proudly proclaimed that God Is Charity, the nun in charge kept screaming at the poor man during his brief, non-comatose moments. "Do you have health insurance?" Perhaps *He* was charity but St. V's fell just a bit short.

Despite myself I managed to graduate, a rather remarkable feat given that I showed up for many a morning class suffering from sleep deprivation after working all night, given my more or less persistent and quixotic pursuit of social justice, and given that I spent a disproportionate amount of time chasing women who were remarkably swift of foot. A word of wisdom: don't listen to those who tell you to pursue fast women. The truth is, they can too easily outrun you. As I stumbled forward in life, the prospect of the Peace Corps loomed larger. One of my friends

273

at the time was Cornelius (Neil) Riordan, a graduate student at Clark whom I had known loosely from the old neighborhood. Neil had done a PC stint in Iran and we talked about it a fair amount. Besides, let's get real, what was a psychology major with no visible skills (some things have not changed) to do as his draft board eyed him with increasing fervor?

So, I weighed two options—graduate school and Peace Corps. When I asked my faculty advisor where I might pursue a PhD in psychology, he rattled off Harvard, Yale, and Stanford. I thanked him but that plan was a non starter at the time. Hell, I was a working class kid who could not even keep his final exam schedule straight. It would take many additional years before I realized I was not quite as dumb as I thought, or looked. So, the battle over my next step in life was fairly brief. Somewhere I ran across some literature about a program in India in public health. Perfect, I thought, since my hospital career of emptying bed pans, giving enemas, and other wise keeping the crazies at bay during nocturnal full moons certainly gave me a heads up for this program. After all, I could realize my long held dream of being a contemporary Albert Schweitzer (or Tom Dooley), and in exotic India no less, the home of Mahatma Gandhi, a personal hero. It was, as they say, a done deal.

I have this memory that there was a conflict between the Graduate Record Exam (the GREs) and a Peace Corps exam with both being given on the same day. In my memory, I signed up for both and would decide which exam to take after weighing the relative merits suggested by the hypothetical life trajectory associated with each alternative. The more I reflected the better India and public health looked. Perhaps that is just a convenient memory that lends some drama to the choice—the path not taken and all that—though it is true that I took the GREs in India. In any case I was Milwaukee bound.

Training Days

For a Worcester boy, even Wisconsin was an adventure. You have to remember that Bostonians believed that civilization

ended at Route 128, the main artery that circled the city in those days. We Worcester folk were far more cosmopolitan; civilization extended all the way to the Hudson River. Perhaps you think I exaggerate. But I recall the Worcester train station as a kid, in the days when people actually traveled by train, where a sign read "Albany NY and *the* West."

If it had not been for my brief seminary experience outside of Chicago, I probably would have anticipated that cows would be meandering down Wisconsin city streets and indoor plumbing to be a luxury enjoyed by the wealthy few. Despite my trepidations, it was off to Milwaukee. Little did I know that I was destined to spend my adult life in the Badger State and to fall in love with Madison, home to the state capitol and to the flagship campus of the University of Wisconsin system.

I marvel at those who have photographic memories though, at the same time, I do feel fortunate at having the ability to repress a few painful childhood recollections. Still, some images of PC training did stick. What remains, though, are rather random, almost idiosyncratic snapshots of selected events. I do not, however, vouchsafe for their accuracy and certainly not their relevance.

I clearly recall being told that it would not be public health for me despite all my experience at St. Vincent's hospital. No, I was to be a poultry expert. Though my initial thought was to protest and point out my years of service to the sick and dying, I hid my disappointment for fear of deselection perhaps. My silence was quickly rewarded by learning skills that I just knew would benefit me in the coming decades—like de-beaking a chicken (if you have to ask, you must be citified). To make matters worse, all the gals eventually were assigned to the other program and would be sent to a different province in India. For obvious reasons, this seemed a rather grim prospect, though the gals might have been somewhat relieved. It would appear that gender profiling was alive and well—boys are chicken farmers and girls are nurturing nurses.

I remember the physical exercise program. In my mind physical training would involve heroic challenges such as traversing deep chasms over rushing rivers on a rope. Somewhere in my imagination were pictures of such training feats. Others recall demanding swimming tests which required us to dive to the bottom of a pool to retrieve an object with our feet tied, presumably an anti-drowning exercise. All I can recall, though, is running around the track at the University of Wisconsin-Milwaukee. That alone was enough to almost kill me. Somehow, drinking a lot of beer in college, while plotting the revolution, failed to shape my body into a finely honed machine. I made it half way around the track before collapsing, lungs screaming for mercy.

I was trying to keep up with one of the gals. I think she was from Kentucky and had done track in college, or did I make that up to assuage my rapidly disappearing ego. As I collapsed to my knees desperately sucking in all available oxygen within a square mile, her trim, athletic body receded down the track. Well, I thought, if this is my last earthly image, it could be worse.

I remember our first Indian movie. It lasted, like all Bollywood productions of the era, three days, or so it seemed. Even *Gone with the Wind* mercifully ended after 18 hours. Somewhere around the end of the second day, the male and female leads were running toward each other across an open field. Yes, this is it, I thought. So did the male lead, you could tell by the way he was drooling. But oh no, just as they were about to embrace, the ground between them opened up and they were separated by an earthquake. We had 7.4 more crises to go before they were to finally connect, at which time we saw a wonderful ballet of butterflies, a somewhat pathetic proxy for the real thing. I mean, after all, this guy put his life on the line about a dozen times to get the goodies. But it was good preparation for the deprivation in 'companionship' we would experience once we got to the sub-continent.

I remember Dennis Conta, our training director, whom I was to help just a bit get reelected to the Wisconsin State Assembly a few years down the road, and who rose to a position of some power in Wisconsin politics. I remember Hindi classes and culture sensitivity classes and the Tuxedo Bar, but not Buddy Beaks as others do (I am assuming that everyone told me the Tuxedo was the meeting place and then headed for Buddy Beaks). A few things still resonate, like being pushed to recognize our own prejudices and stereotypes. For example, I recall one of the PC staff asking if we ever thought about why we call part of the globe the Mideast, east of what? I remember doing very well in Hindi class and getting puffed up about that. But when we got to India and the real world, I watched Haywood's fluency soar, while I flat lined. And I certainly recall the technical content of our poultry training. To this day, I can still distinguish a chicken from a cow. But a lot of Milwaukee remains a blur.

I remember little things like walking down the street with Carolyn Adler (Watanabe, then) and Nancy Simmuel. A car with a couple of young black men screeched to a stop and they asked if this was some kind of protest. Seeing a white male walking with an Asian and a black female apparently stood out. Like a lot of places, Milwaukee was seething with racial unrest, some of it organized by an iconic Catholic priest named Father James Groppi.

At some point, I recall being at Dennis Conta's house during a period where a prominent Milwaukee judge's home was being picketed for belonging to a whites-only social club. Four of us, including a congressional aide who was visiting Dennis decided that justice required that we join the protestors. We arrived late and the National Guard tried to keep us away. The visiting congressional staffer, who had been most reluctant to come in the first place, now totally lost his cool and started screaming about his constitutional rights at some twenty-year-old kid sporting a rifle and looking scared shitless. We got to join the march. Ironically, the judge turned out to be the father of my future wife's best friend, though that particular piece of information was unknowable to me at the time.

Some of my most vivid training memories were off site. Racial tensions followed us to our brief stay in Houston during the Christmas break. A few of the 44-B group will remember this, I am sure. One evening, a small number of us went looking for a 'private club' where you could join for an hour or so to get a drink. We ran into some others of our group who had just been refused admittance to such a 'private' club, ostensibly because one or two of them were black. They can't get away with that, we thought, and back we went. To get 'proof' of discrimination, we put some white guys at the front, and they paid the club membership fee and went in. I recall being right next to the first black member of our group, John Alexander I believe. The fun really started when our little interracial group reached the front of the line.

Instead of the nominal 'membership' fee, the very large man guarding the door pointed to our black member and said, "for you the fee is $20" or some other outrageous amount for the time. When the guy saw that he was going to pay it, he said, "No, for you, the fee is a million dollars." Then, after a few

more words, the pushing and shoving started. The locals were not impressed that we represented the Peace Corps, responding to that bit of input with a few expletives attached to the less than complimentary attribution that the Peace Corps was nothing but a bunch of commie pinkos and/or fags. I recall David Lubbs, a veteran of civil rights marches in his native Virginia, dropping to the ground in the entranceway. Eventually, we were pushed out to the street and surrounded by a rather large group of menacing looking rednecks, the size of which has grown in the intervening years. To tell you the truth, I thought their entire heads looked red, further brightened I believe by an intense desire to beat the shit out of us.

For the second time in my life (well, third if you count my one attempt to run around the track at UW-M), I thought I was a dead man. Thankfully, I saw a police vehicle coming down the street, the cavalry to the rescue. When they pulled up I asserted with righteous indignation that a violation of the civil rights act had just occurred. I can still recall the look of total disinterest and disdain on the cops face when he said to me, "I don't give a fuck about civil rights." He then rolled up the window and cruised on down the street. Now, I thought, we are really dead and went back to work on that damn perfect act of contrition. But we survived and some of us dutifully trooped down to a federal agency (FBI?) the next day to file some form of complaint. On hearing the story, I seem to recall one of the Black trainees, from Texas I believe, sort of laughing at us without mirth. "What the hell were you thinking, this is Texas." Whether we knew it or not, some of us white kids were growing up quickly.

Two other cross-cultural experiences remain with me. First, we had our Waunakee Wisconsin farm experience. Waunakee, as you may recall, is located just north of Madison and touts the fact that it is the only Waunakee in the world. Apparently, no one else has felt moved to compete for that moniker. This may have been my first experience in a tent. Whatever, it became clear to me that I have a lot of my father in me. He always thought outdoor living was overrated. Even picnics were off limits. If God wanted us to eat outdoors, my father would huff, *He* would not have created restaurants. Dad was not an educated man but had considerable wisdom, which he shared with me and anyone else who might listen. My favorite T-shirt for visiting national parks was the one proclaiming "my idea of roughing it is when room service is late."

I cannot recall what I learned on the farm, other than it deepened my appreciation for being born and raised in a city. I do remember people being very nice to us and the farm family's neighbors coming over for some kind of party. They looked at us as if they were doing research for a *Scientific American* article on discovering a new, alien species. My memory is that we could see interstate 94 from our tents, and that the farm had a sign along the highway saying Henry's Seed Farm, or something similar. Returning to the area some years later, I thought about stopping to ask if they remembered our little group but then feared that they would. You hate to dredge up bad memories for folks. Over the next several decades, when traversing along I-94 on the way to the Twin Cities where my in-laws lived, I would pass that sign and strain to see the place I thought our tents had been pitched. Then one day, not all that many years ago, I realized with a strange sadness that the sign was gone.

The second highly memorable training experience was the Indian reservation in South Dakota where we were exposed for several weeks to a real cross-cultural environment. I always considered most of Indiana as a vast wasteland that even God ignores. Let me tell you, Cherry Creek South Dakota truly is the end of the earth, or was until I got to my village site in India. On the way there, or maybe the way back, we stopped in Aberdeen South Dakota. We had trouble getting served in a restaurant because one of the dark skinned Indian PC staff was with us. This just went to prove you could get screwed anywhere in this great land, at least back in the 1960s.

It was blazing hot the day we arrived in Cherry Creek. We applied our usual cleverness to erecting the tents in some kind of overlapping configuration so that it could serve as a big shelter. Frank Lloyd Wright would be duly impressed at our sense of architectural innovation. Once we finished, everyone else went off to a swimming hole while I stayed back to keep an eye on things and do what I do best, take a nap. I have always been strong at napping. Sure enough, a storm blew up, and so did our tents. I ran around for five minutes or so holding onto tent posts and then said the hell with it and went back to my nap.

The biggest edifice in the town was some kind of community center/church most likely built by the Mormons. At some point, the local boys challenged us to a basketball game at this center. After three minutes, it was clear we were going to get our asses whipped, which is the equivalent of losing badly, very badly. The big difference is that they could run and we couldn't. I had not made much progress in the physical shape department since my aborted run around the UW-M track. So, as I would huff and puff my way to one end of the court, the flow of the game would be going the other way. Death once again stared me in the face, as did the first line or two of that act of contrition. In my last moment of consciousness, someone rushed into the center yelling "fire, fire." That's right! I was saved from sure death by a direct act of the same deity I had discarded casually in college. Go figure!

We rushed out to see a brush fire heading toward our tents. I am sure those conspiracy theorists who argued that it was set deliberately to hasten our departure were wrong. After all, we had to be the best entertainment of the year, hell, the decade. After bravely putting out this raging conflagration, we were congratulating one another when we noticed another brush fire up on the hill near a house. We raced off to play the hero one more time. As we were crushing out the last embers a woman came out of the house and quietly asked why we had put out her fire which she had set, as I recall, as a way to keep snakes away. We gave her a match and sheepishly wound our way back to the camp. For the remainder of the day, though, I worried about what was keeping the snakes away from 'our' tents.

Of course, there were lessons to be learned and insights to be gained everywhere. Toward the end of our reservation visit, I recall asking a teenager what he was going to do in the future. "I am going to college," he exclaimed, although with mild conviction. It seemed to me that he had never thought about that possibility before our visit, it was just too far beyond his experience. He probably never went but at least the thought crossed his mind. Looking around, I wondered where inspiration or ambition might be found in this hardscrabble, desolate piece of earth.

Even the river that wound through the village betrayed you. Looking for relief from the heat, you would immediately find your legs coated thick with silt pushed along by the current. As modest as my own circumstances had been growing up, they were infinitely fortunate compared to those kids growing up in the midst of such impoverished isolation. Clearly, anyone who thinks life's starting line is equal has never been to Cherry Creek, South Dakota.

In any case, I survived despite the fact that the side of my face blew up with a delayed infection from a dental procedure to extract my impacted wisdom teeth. All I recall from the procedure was the 'dentist' grunting and straining as he hacked away at my mouth, blood spurting up on his glasses. Every once in a while, he would utter a 'damn' or 'shit,' suggesting even to my untutored understanding of dental practice that all was not well. Perhaps I should have used a licensed dentist. That crisis, too, was survived after a trek to the government health clinic that served the reservation.

It rained the day we were to depart but quite a few of the villagers gathered to see us off. A great cheer went up as the bus lumbered down the slick, muddy road. An even greater groan erupted as the bus slid off the road into a gulley. The whole village now joined as one in pushing us back onto the road to make sure we got back on our way. The prospect that our stay might be extended galvanized them into decisive action. For many years I wondered if anything has changed in Cherry Creek, or even if it is still there.

The other big training surprise was that India no longer needed poultry experts. This was a good thing, because there were none in our group. India now needed agricultural experts. This was a bad thing; we had none of those either, although I think a couple of the trainees had seen a farm at one point in their young lives. Of course, we had enough hubris, and ignorance, to believe that we could make a contribution in any case.

In the summer of 1967, stateside training was over and we were bound for India. So many shiny, hopeful faces that started out on the Peace Corps journey were now gone. Someone in our group estimated that only 1 in 4 that started on day one were still around at the finish of our two year stint. Most had chosen other paths, but a number had been deselected (bureaucratese for being involuntarily cut from the program). I had gotten close to one gal who was deselected, I believe at the end of the first summer. I could not for the life of me see how she differed from the rest of us. Hell, I couldn't even run around the damn track, not even when chasing an attractive female. I questioned Dennis Conta about it but of course he could not talk about it nor, in truth, did I protest too much.

India

In some respects we were well trained. They told us India would be hot, and it was. In other respects, we were not. They tried to prepare us for all that separates our cultures but that was really impossible. You can be told there is a difference in how time is calculated and you can appreciate that as an abstract

283

piece of knowledge. However, when someone tells you the bus "…is just now coming," you are simply grounded in a western expectation to look for the bus. The fact that 'now' might mean five minutes or five hours or five days is beyond us. Time is more than an abstract concept. It is a way our minds, and even bodies, work. This is just an obvious example.

I am getting ahead of myself. Our in-country experience started with, guess what, more training. I struggle now, over four decades later, to recall what I learned about cutting edge agriculture. But frankly, I draw a total blank. In fact, my reflections on India are twofold, a set of discrete, almost random images that I cannot even put into context and a smaller set of more generic lessons that, for better or worse, I took away from the total experience.

One significant lesson is that you cannot turn a bunch of urban bred and raised kids into farmers in a few weeks. Farming is very much a craft, a complex undertaking where experience and disposition play key roles. Peace Corps invested lots in us (ok, sometimes training us for things we would never do) and the staff were top notch. I still remember Usha and Amar, two of our language instructors, with great fondness. Bill (Whitesell), Haywood (Turrentine), and I became close to Amar's family, visiting them over at the Radio Colony section of Delhi. At some point, we were invited to the wedding of her brother (cousin?) up in the Punjab. It was a lavish affair and an unforgettable cultural experience. I wonder where Amar and Usha are today.

I recall a couple of isolated images near the close of our endless training. We stayed at some school (the dormitory for a local Udaipur training school perhaps) for a bit. Each night when we returned to our room, the biggest rats I ever had the misfortune to meet greeted us, and I do mean rats of the rodent persuasion. We would chase them around the room, eventually realizing that some would take refuge in the drainage pipes that dumped excess water out into a courtyard. With vengeance in mind, we poured near boiling water down the pipes—a temporary defeat for the rodent kingdom but an important victory for us. God, in my memory those rats were huge, surely able to devour a city bus, or a PC volunteer who might stray from the rest of the pack, if it were moved to do so.

I also remember a conversation with several students, probably at the same school. "So, what do you eat in America," one asked? We were always getting such intellectually provocative queries. Running out of meats and vegetables whose Hindi equivalent I could recall, I threw beef into the list. It was one of those moments, a word thrown out that could not be retrieved. As the student's faces twisted with horror, cows being sacred to most Indians at the time, I realized two things. It is very hard to explain a concept like cultural relativism with a 4th grade command of the local language. Secondly, for almost two years there would be no such thing as a casual conversation.

What I most remember about those final training days were the basketball games. Somehow, several of us (Bill Whitesell, Haywood Turrentine, Tom McDermott, Mike Goldberg, and maybe some staffers) wound up playing a short series of games against the local boys from the university. This quickly became a popular spectator favorite with local fans supporting the 'home' team and the PC family cheering for the stalwart Americans. Hah, Naismith (the creator of the game) would have been proud of the way we demonstrated the superiority of U.S. round ball skills. However, showing up the local youth may not have been our smartest move.

One day we arrived for a scheduled match but the opposing team had been switched. In place of the local college kids was some kind of military team, or so we were told. My guess is that they were lifers from the local prison. I don't know how the rest of our team fared, but every time I moved to the basket, or tried for a rebound, my midsection would be rearranged by an opponent's elbow, or fist. The locals in the crowd enjoyed the mauling, perhaps our one contribution to US-Indian relations. I can still recall our mild-mannered agriculture instructor from some western state screaming at the officials to call a foul on them, just once. Visions of a headline screaming 'Peace Corps group ejected from country after basketball brawl' danced in my head.

Our local college opponents must have forgiven us for the beatings we had inflicted on them since several of us later were asked us to join their local team to help represent Udaipur at the all-India tournament in Jaipur. Well, we thought, how many points would we score for Peace Corps and America if we brought basketball glory to Udaipur? One problem, Udaipur was a basketball backwater. Most of the other teams partici- pating in the tournament could actually play the game. While my conditioning had vastly improved since our debacle on the South Dakota reservation and my aborted marathon around the track during training, we were out after one game. It was not even close. We played one more game against some other losers and were quite competitive as I recall. I believe we may even have won, though fortunately no discoverable record of our overall performance remains. Our days of athletic glory were over but the trip was great fun.

Eventually the day of reckoning arrived. After a seemingly endless period of preparation and one final celebration at the Lake Palace, we were to be dumped off at our sites one fine morning. The Lake Palace, by the way, is a very romantic hotel, a former playground of the last local Raj of pre-independence India, situated in the middle of (you will never guess) a lake. Many celebrities have stayed there, like Jackie Kennedy, and at least one James Bond movie, exploiting the site's exotic beauty and charm, used it extensively in making the movie *Octopussy* (I believe). In retrospect, this final party had the feel of a con- demned man's last meal.

Randy Stoklas and I were scheduled to head south out of Udaipur to a place called Salumbar, I am guessing about 40-50 miles (kilometers?) away. Steve McKenzie would be dropped off at his site even further south, way beyond the reach of civi- lization. Our worldly possessions were packed on a back of a truck and off we were on a rather hair-raising trip down a twist- ing road that settled out of the Adravelli Hills before reaching the bleak, desert-like terrain that was to be home for the next two years. And I had felt bad for the Iran group.

That would prove to be the first of many trips between our site and Udaipur over the next two years. These sojourns took place on the local mass transit system, buses that surely were

constructed by the vehicle maker Henry Ford forced out of business way back in 1903. Of course, it was always a pleasure to share your motoring experience with locals suffering from motion sickness and to share your seat with various species of livestock. I always wondered, though, why goats got seat preference before me.

The trip up to Udaipur typically brought doubts whether this sleek motoring machine would make it or whether the duct tape would split and the engine drop to the road. The trip back down always raised a different concern—the vision of hurtling over the side of the mountain, or was it just a hill, to oblivion thousands (hundreds) of feet below. One day, sure enough, the brakes failed and we hurtled around curves with increasing speed. Women were screaming (or was that me screaming) as I frantically tried to recall the 'perfect act of contrition' one more time. By now, unfortunately, I could only remember the first few words. My prospects for getting to heaven were dim indeed. Our intrepid driver saved the day, however, by ramming the bus into the side of the mountain at a brief point where the elevation went up, not down. I decided to write out the perfect act of contrition for future reference.

Our first trip down the road from hell, however, proved quite uneventful so Randy and I looked forward to being greeted by a group of excited locals. Surely, I thought, the arrival of the Peace Corps miracle workers would warrant some visible display of anticipation, or at least one lonely greeter. The truck pulled up to a few isolated government buildings situated along a lonely stretch of road surrounded by...nothing. No sign of life was visible, no town, no welcoming banners, no brass band, in fact, no people at all. There was just hard-packed dirt punctuated by small bushes and an occasional dwarf-like tree. This looks exciting, I thought.

While Randy guarded our worldly possessions, off I went to find civilization. The town of Salumbar was a mile or two further down the road, depending on whether you took the short cut or followed the main highway. It was of decent size and still had a remnant of an old Raj palace that was now a school. There was a bank, post office, a restaurant, a gas station, numerous small shops, and a variety of government buildings and schools. We were to be housed in the government buildings located on the site from which a variety of rural community development activities were administered. There were accommodations for four or five government workers on site but none ever chose to live there, preferring to live in town. Of course, it is possible that our presence had driven local real estate values down. All in all, the accommodations were not bad, once we swept out the scorpions, put up some screens, and the electricity eventually arrived. We had been told that the availability of electricity was 'just now coming" and it did, after about six months.

The PC experience in India took place on two levels. There were sharp vignettes and experiences that stand out even after 40 plus years, sometimes incidents so seemingly small you wonder why they endured. And then there are deeper lessons, or at least impressions, that emerged from the accretion of experiences over time.

An early insight was that I had absolutely no idea what the hell I was doing. I still remember standing with a local farmer as we looked over his wheat crop that had recently broken the surface of the soil. He asked me how it looked. I was actually surprised the sprouts were green. Why aren't those damn things brown, like the 'amber' waves of grain in that patriotic song? Or when a local farmer asked me if his soil would be good for these new fangled, high-yield seeds we were peddling. I picked up a handful of his dirt, scrunched it in my fingers, and threw it up in the air before turning to him with supreme confidence, saying, "Yes, your soil is perfect." How the hell would I know? My only farming experience was a 20 X 10 foot garden plot in the backyard I tried as a kid growing up in Worcester on which I successfully grew seven scrawny radishes.

This lack of confidence was more than just a personal shortcoming. Our primary mission was to help spread the use of newer, high-yield varieties of seed, part of what Norman Borlaug and others launched as the so-called 'green' revolution. The choice farmers faced was stark. They could throw their usual seed stock into the ground and be relatively assured of a crop, even if this approach resulted in a rather meager yield. On the other hand, they could try this fancy new stuff, even though it was expensive and required careful attention to every detail— planting at the right depth, using fertilizer at correct times and spaced the appropriate distance from the seed, and watering at proper intervals. Even if you did all this correctly, you still risked that someone earlier in the seed distribution chain had stolen the good stuff and replaced it with some worthless substitute.

No problem you say, just encourage the local farmers to engage in a little US-style entrepreneurship. No risk, no reward, right? Not quite that simple, unfortunately. Most farm plots in that area were tiny. Complicating matters furthermore, successes in public health were evidencing positive, yet complicating, outcomes. Children were surviving in greater numbers. At the same time, rural family patriarchs yet assumed that many children were necessary to ensure that male offspring would be available to support them in old age. The resulting imbalance between progress and perception was overly large families surviving on the thin thread of postage stamp size plots situated in a marginal agricultural area.

If a poorer farmer tried to be entrepreneurial, and any one of a number of things that could go wrong did go wrong, the consequences were more than a write-off on this year's taxes. It was devastation for the family. So, you almost unconsciously worked with the better off farmers who spoke English or at least Hindi (as opposed to the local dialect of Mewari) and those who had the wherewithal to survive disaster. On a micro-level you knew you were exacerbating the kind of inequality that was anathema to crypto-revolutionaries like myself. But the possible guilt associated with failure was simply too overwhelming.

We did have successful demonstration plots. I still have a picture somewhere of brilliant, thick waves of 'green' wheat growing next to sparser yields from local seeds. We planted a local garden outside our modest abode to encourage similar efforts locally. We built a chicken coop on top of our house to encourage that cottage industry. The garden worked well until some thieving goats somehow breached our impregnable security. The chickens laid eggs until they all died while we vacationed somewhere and had put our crack household staff in charge. I even convinced some of my former professors at Clark to get their current students to raise money to buy books for the local school library.

At the end of the day, it was hard to say that we influenced the course of history in India, much less the town of Salumbar and environs. Somewhere, though, I ran across the somewhat apocryphal 'fact' that India went from a grain importing nation to a grain exporting nation sometime during our tour, between 1967 and 1969. I certainly like to take credit for this; you can't dispute the numbers.

Our quality of life, if not survival itself, depended on our faithful staff—Rooknot and Cutchroo (phonetic spelling). Rooknot served as a kind household chief of staff, while Cutchroo, a teenage boy from a local tribe, did the actual work. This involved the shopping, cooking, boiling water, identifying which local creatures would kill us, and so on. The boiling water part was crucial. The dreaded guinea worm resided in the local step wells. These cysts would situate themselves in your body and grow to considerable lengths before erupting through your skin. Your option then was a local hospital, think Marquis De Sade, or the local barber/surgeon who would slowly twist the worm around a stick, hoping it would not break and disappear back under your skin to form a painful abscess. One story is that the current striped barber poll is a stylized version of a worm encircling a stick, a form of medieval advertising from the days when step wells and guinea worms existed throughout Europe. There are, of course, competing stories.

Rooknot was a character, always with a mischievous smile. He always reminded me of Zorba the Greek, from the movie about how a poor Greek villager opens up a visiting Englishman to new experiences. I recall he definitely thought Randy and I needed female companionship, which of course was obvious to anyone noting our twitching and drooling. He kept saying how he could sneak in the women without anyone knowing. However, our sense of caution prevailed, barely. Our Hindi did improve through our long, philosophical dialogues with Rooknot. One that I remember was prompted by his interest in how many times we had enjoyed intercourse in a 24 hour period. I have no idea what we said to him but his number was astounding. He assured us, using sign language to graphically hammer home the point that his last effort during that day of carnal achievement never came to full fruition.

Our female deprivation plight was dramatically illustrated when we got a cat (let me finish the story, pervert) an acquisition motivated by the fact that I awoke with a rodent on my chest one night. God, Randy had to peel me off the ceiling. We would hear rodents running around our place each night, and each morning we would empty the daily catch from our mousetraps. A resident cat was the answer, indeed. After all, they torture rodents, don't they? Actually, it turned out to be one of our few successful endeavors, no more nocturnal rat visits.

Then one day, a stray cat in heat visited us. Billie (after the Hindi word for cat, sort of) leaped halfway up the screen and began to wail. There was nothing to do but let him out, after which he disappeared for several days. We would hear the cat wailing in the distance followed by silence and then even more wailing. We thought, alas, Billie might be gone for good. To our delight, though, Billie returned, looking like shit, but seemingly very happy. He slept for about three days straight. Damn cat, I thought, getting a lot more than I am. Then again, who didn't?

Rooknot did keep us supplied with local booze which came in a variety of appealing colors. We did not ask many questions about its origins, but stories about poisonous additives to the bathtub gin from our own prohibition era kept circling my head. Nevertheless, it remained an irreplaceable anesthetic after long, hot days. During the dry season, the thermometer in our place hit about 106 or 108 on a regular basis. In the evening, thankfully, a cooler and refreshing breeze might blow off the desert. We could sit on our roof and enjoy quiet time appreciating the sunsets of rural India. I remember the serenity in particular, the almost glacial pace of life. One day, I looked out and felt something was missing. I spent that day looking out over the bleak landscape across the highway. Around evening I had my 'aha' moment. Someone had cut down one of the few small trees on the horizon and carted away the remains. This was a big change.

You became much more sensitive to the rhythms of life, the cycles of the moon, and repeated patterns of daily routines. Here and now, I never pay attention to things like full moons. There and then, it was a blessing. At a minimum, it was easier finding the outhouse after a night of local brew if the moon were full and the sky cloudless. Calming patterns played themselves out everywhere. We would watch a water buffalo wander down the highway. Every once in awhile a bus would roar by and we would begin to count—one, two, three. At a count of six or seven, the buffalo would suddenly react, long after the bus had moved on. Apparently it took that long for its brain to be engaged. I thought, gee, I have a lot more in common with these creatures than I would have imagined. We kept somewhat engaged by writing books (well, I wrote one book and I know

Randy started one), devouring every piece of literature we could find and desperately savaging every letter and magazine from home.

Not all letters from home were equally prized. I recall getting a classic Dear Tom letter from my one real college girlfriend. Randy was chatting away as I read but I quickly lost track of what he was saying. The girl I left behind had met a post-doctoral student while working at a Harvard lab and they were soon to be married. Lee was Greek-Irish, quick witted and feisty while, at the same time, quite shy, with an aura of vulnerable innocence. She had long black hair and deep, soulful eyes. I had always been quite ambivalent about marriage, if ambivalence means viewing marriage as something akin to daily root canal work absent any numbing anesthesia. I was, however, weakening on the topic. India was, after all, a lonely experience and memories of her remained deep.

I had started to even mention the M word in my letters to her by the beginning of 1968. The truth is, however, that I had left for India without asking her to wait and without making any kind of commitment to her in return. She saved many of these missives and shared them with me not long ago (the wonders of Facebook). The letters I sent sounded more like the demented ravings of some lunatic losing what was left of his mind on the edge of the desert. Besides, communicating by mail back before email and modern communications was primitive indeed. Someone sent something to me in India by ground mail and I think I got it in 1987.

It is clear she made the right choice given her options— Harvard post-doc or raving madman running around the edges of India pretending to be a farming expert. No brainer there, as they say! And she did well for herself in life, eventually obtaining a PhD. in molecular virology, something I have trouble spelling, never mind understanding. Nonetheless, the news hit me very hard on the day I got the letter, yet another road not taken and another price to be paid for my decision to go overseas. One good thing came of it, though. It gave Randy and me an excuse to get even more blotto than usual that evening.

I have always liked history, visiting famous sites, reading historical books, and the like. Historian Doris Goodwin, talks about imagining, as a little girl growing up in Brooklyn, what it was like living in far gone times. I too feel that pull of the imagination. Walking through parts of Salumbar, I would imagine I was in Dodge City, circa 1880. I can recall a herd of water buffalo kicking up dirt as they were driven through town by tough looking men riding camels, carbines slung over their shoulders and bandoliers strapped around their chests. One could easily imagine Matt Dillon of *Gunsmoke* fame lurking around the next corner waiting on the Dalton gang.

So much of what we saw and felt would fit nicely in a time capsule—the women who beat their clothes down by the lake that bordered the town, the simple farming tools and techniques used for generations upon generations, and the feudal customs and cultural mores that shaped interpersonal interactions.

If you looked closer, however, change was palpable; subtle transformations were both deep and profound. I would look at the generation of elders. They typically spoke Mewari (the local dialect), had grown up during the British Raj and thus were governed for all practical purposes by local nobility, and shared a world-view that seldom looked beyond their local experience. Their children, the adults of that period, typically spoke Hindi, read newspapers, and had a world-view that stretched to Delhi and beyond. The young, for the most part, were in school, learning English, and would likely have access to technologies that would broaden their world view significantly. If you looked very closely, one's sense of the world, and the individual's place in it, was evolving in dramatic ways and at a quickening pace.

At the same time, you could sense that so many were trapped in more traditional ways of understanding their world. One thing the British did not leave was the order and sense of the queue. If ten Indians met at the entrance of a 500 seat movie theatre, a riot would break out, even without a scarcity of seats. There would be pushing and shoving which I suppose emerged from a sense that there simply would not be enough to go around. I often felt the same about these small farmers who had far more children than they could support on their meager assets. Siring fewer children risked not having anyone to care for them in a society where no public safety net existed. While many more of their children were surviving and reaching adulthood, it was hard to take that risk. India would have to make a profound, almost unimaginable leap forward if it was to absorb all the kids who would be pushed off the land in the coming decades. It struck me at the time as a Malthusian apocalypse waiting to unfold.

I remember mentioning the lack of anonymity in India in a conversation with a black fellow student during my graduate studies back in the States. Wherever you went, particularly outside major cities, you were an object of curiosity. Children would stare and follow you. You were subject to endless and repetitive questions. Sometimes you were made fun of, not surprising given how many mistakes we made. Sometimes you were treated with a deference and respect you did not deserve. The inescapable reality was that you were always on display, always visible, and always on stage. He smiled and said, "Then you do know what it is like being me."

In India, you were always 'on stage' in a continuing play with a set of complex characters and a convoluted plot. In our ordinary lives, we exist more or less unconsciously ninety-percent of the time. In my case it may be ninety-nine percent of the time. Life is a repeated series of well-scripted interactions where the social and interactional rules are second nature. You realize at some point that, in India, everything requires thought. That society is an incredibly complex and chaotic canvas of caste, color, class, religion, language, history, ethnic identity, political disposition, and on, and on. You continuously had to calculate with whom you were interacting and what rules and conventions governed those specific interactions. Virtually every social interaction contained at least the possibility of misunderstanding and hurt feelings. You simply cannot imagine what it takes out of you to actually think about what you are doing all the time.

Obviously, mistakes were all too frequent and sensitivities hurt more than we liked. Over time, the effort to negotiate the labyrinths of this social web wore you down; however, it was more than that. There was nowhere to go to 'blow off steam'—to just relax. You couldn't go drinking with the boys, because the boys didn't drink (at least in public). You could not find comforting women to soothe the weary spirit since the potential cost was a lot more than a few rupees. You stuffed it in, plodded on, and did your best not to leave with the local's perception of America worse than when you arrived.

Recollections of India are mostly small memories that crowd in, sparkle for a moment, and then are replaced by others. Those memories that still glitter after four decades include disparate images such as the following: A group of farmers encouraging me to go ahead and pet that cute baby camel and then laughing as the mother charged while I ran for my life. Fortunately, I could actually run with some celerity by this time. I recall being offered sugar cane juice squeezed fresh at harvest time. Nothing is sweeter, trust me. I think of the time I was about to put my hands into the water pot we used to wash our hands when I heard something splash around. I jumped back to the merriment of our household staff. When they looked in, they yelped, swept up the pot, and rushed out the door midst a great hue and cry. I never got an explanation but I apparently escaped something very bad. I remember cycling on our Superman bicycles over dirt paths that would suddenly turn to sand that would send me flying over the handle bars. Years later, my wife could not understand why I did not share her romantic vision of riding our bicycles into the sunset.

I recall wandering through the streets of Salumbar where, over time, our presence evoked less and less curiosity. I had some favorite locals, with whom I would sit in their shops and pass the time of day. It was a good way to get a sense of local life. After the fact, I realized I spent about equal time with a Hindu merchant and a Muslim merchant, instinctively seeking cultural balance. Nevertheless, as eager as each apparently was to have my company, neither ever invited me into their homes or for dinner. Some degrees of separation were hard to overcome.

I fondly remember doing some fun things, attending local celebrations or refereeing games of basketball at the local high school, which was more like herding cats than calling fouls. On days I tried real work, I used to travel to a village outside of Salumbar, the name of which I can no longer recall. I would chat with the local farmers and walk around with the local development officer. It was never totally clear what my role was but no one seemed to mind my presence. Periodically I recall filling out some forms outlining all that I (we) had done and all that we intended to do. If only intentions were reality. Although Randy typically went off in a different direction from town, I suspect his experiences were roughly the same as mine. I regret that we didn't keep in touch after our tour; he is one of the few volunteers that could not be located for the reunion.

I especially recall losing copious amounts of weight, even though my appetite for food and drink never slacked in the least. In fact, I grew to love Indian food, even okra, a love that remains today. My vision of heaven has evolved over time. At that time, I think heaven had more to do with having access to an unlimited number of women with no standards. Today, heaven is having access to an unlimited variety of curries and *naan* (bread) which bring with them absolutely no calories whatsoever.

During my tour, my weight bottomed out somewhere in the 140s, not very substantial given my 6'1" frame. Some pictures of me show a rather cadaverous guy with thick, black hair, sporting cool Buddy Holly glasses. No wonder the women were throwing themselves at me. The culprits responsible for my weight loss turned out to be an assortment of intestinal parasites with which I shared my daily sustenance. Looking at pictures taken during my tour, it is no wonder that my poor mother, looking at these same pictures, thought I was at death's door and came close to contacting our Congressman to save me from destruction.

I doubt I look much like that guy anymore. Maybe it's the extra 60 pounds, maybe it is misplacing my hair somewhere, or maybe I should find another pair of cool Buddy Holly glasses. As our PC reunion approached in 2009, I passed around a group picture taken during our India training days, and asked a number of my contemporary colleagues and friends to pick me out. Only one did so successfully. Some of the choices were, well, choice!

You think I look like HIM? Often, when I pointed out the correct choice, the subject of my little experiment would exclaim with incredulity, "that's not you, no way." What really hurt was my wife guessed wrong, and then muttered for weeks afterward something about how cute I was back then and wondered what had happened.

I vividly recall 3rd class trains, particularly during the hot season which also was the marriage season. Half of India seemingly was on the move, so the trains were packed inside, with additional scores perched on top of the cars or hanging off the sides. Remember the movie *Dr. Zhivago* when the family was fleeing Moscow after the revolution along with thousands of others? The huge crowd rushed to the train as it pulled in, pushing and shoving their way into a car until a soldier started beating them back when the car was full. That scene pretty much captured the train experience during marriage season except there was no soldier to beat back the surging crowd. I recall hurtling through a window to get aboard and enjoy the luxury of riding in a packed train in 100 degree plus heat while village women threw up next to me, if not on me.

For most of the year there were two kinds of heat, the dry, scorching heat that ran from March to June and the wet, humid heat of the monsoon season. You thought the first was bad until the second arrived. Every crawling and flying creature imaginable emerged with the rain. After a while, even drinking water from a cup involved challenges. You always covered the cup with a book or some suitable covering. Without thinking you raised the cup to your lips, lifted the covering off, looked at the liquid, and only then imbibed. Failure to follow the recommended sequence could result in the ingestion of some unknown insect that had landed in your drink during an unguarded moment, no matter how brief. Of course, insects in your drink might prove fortuitous on occasion. When imbibing the local booze, the death of a flying pest upon contact with the liquid might prove to be useful information, much like the canary in the mineshaft warning system.

India also involved colorful festivals and sights you would never experience again. A sect of holy men visited Salumbar and I watched one of them literally rip all his hair out as an exercise in self-mortification. I am well on my way to achieving the same hairless state on top of my head, but in a more natural way, absent the physical pain at least. Old pictures reminded me of other memories. There is a photo of a band that visited our house and pictures of many government officials with whom we worked, some who were appreciative of our presence and others who tolerated us. One photo that elicited a smile involved Cutchroo milking a goat in the entrance way to our place. His appropriation of the goat's milk clearly was without the permission of the owner, as could be detected from the mischievous smile on his face. Randy and I never inquired too closely into their shenanigans.

I spent two years in India and never did get to the Taj Mahal. Then again, I never visited many of the historical New England sites until I brought my wife to see them. I did get to one of the hill stations in the foothills of the Himalayas and to Goa, the former Portuguese colony on the west coast of the subcontinent south of Bombay. The hill resort was cool with magnificent views; however, my clearest memory was less inspiring. I recall sipping my drink on a veranda overlooking the majestic mountains in the distance. My sweet reverie was disturbed, however, by the sight of smallish local men with cases of Coca Cola and other drinks on their backs. They hauled their burdens up the side of the steep mountains to our idyllic hotel. Apparently, human labor was cheaper than trucking the liquid up to us pampered westerners. Good to support the local economy and all, but my drinks never quite tasted the same after that.

Goa was paradise. At that time, the best places in the world had been discovered by the international hippie community— Nepal, Negril Beach in Jamaica, and Goa, just to name a few. My memory was that the beach was perfect and unspoiled except for a couple of small hotels. The landscape was dominated by local fisherman plying their trade, cool breezes, and spectacular sunsets. At noon we would amble down to the small restaurant and tell them what we wanted that night for dinner and then dine rapturously on marvelous cuisine to the beat of the surf just yards away. Or, we might have a lobster lunch for what amounted to something like 40 cents as I recall. That is not all, though. During our stay it turned out there was to be a special viewing of the uncorrupted body of St. Francis Xavier in celebration of a visit of some papal official. I thought St. Francis looked a bit worn, but not all that bad considering he died several centuries ago. I should look so good now and I am, technically speaking at least, still alive.

On the boat back to Bombay, we snuck up to first class, one of the privileges of being a westerner and at least 'looking' affluent. There, we met an official representing the government of (then) Czechoslovakia. We sparred for a bit about which of us were the real spies, but he concluded that American spies would not need to sneak into the first class section of the boat. After a few drinks, we became fast friends and he insisted we visit him on our way back to the states. In the months that followed, we exchanged correspondence with our Czech friend who inquired what kind of liquor we enjoyed, what kind of car we wanted, and what type of women we preferred. The last question was easy—women with non-existent standards. He seemed intent either on making our visit memorable or recruiting us as red spies. Unfortunately, we will never know which or how cheaply we might have been bought. All this occurred during the days of what was known as the 'Prague Spring,' when Alexander Dubcek was experimenting with a liberalization of thought and speech. One day, we heard that Soviet tanks had crushed the hopes of the reformers. We never heard from our friend again.

Our need for western contact was satisfied by periodic visits to Udaipur, where one or more of the other volunteers could often be found. We stayed at the same hotels and ate at the same restaurant, and occasionally saw English movies shown on Sunday mornings, if I remember correctly. Udaipur was a lovely place with lakes, hills, and a rich history. The city stood at the frontier and traditionally stood guard over the country protecting it from periodic invasions from the northwest. Traditionally, Rajasthanis were fierce warriors.

One historic Salumbar legend was the story of the local Raj who was called to battle by the big man in Udaipur or perhaps an even bigger man in Jaipur. As in any feudal society, it was his duty to go to war; however, he had just married and could not make himself leave his beautiful wife. Several times he left, only to return to ask for another remembrance of her. She would dutifully hand over some clothing or other personal remembrance, all to no avail since he kept returning. Fearing total shame, and in despair, she eventually had her servant bring her severed head to her warrior prince. There would be no more excuses for him to shirk his sacred obligation. Stories like that reminded me of how lucky I am to be born in this time where personal honor is a bit less exacting, like not cheating on your golf score. I do wish I had learned more about the place in which I spent two years of my life. Perhaps I was too busy surviving.

I suspect we did some good in the end but as I have heard so many volunteers say, you take away far more than you ever contribute. I was always amused, somewhat at least, by the prevailing rumors as to why we were there. One explanation is that we were CIA spies, perhaps only believed by the friendly man we were introduced to as the local communist. I doubt that particular rumor had much traction. What the hell could one spy on in this godforsaken place? The second explanation was that we were there to learn agriculture so that we could be better farmers when we went back to the US. Few, it would appear, believed we were there to advance farm production in India.

Despite the challenges, the experience of India was priceless. As our adventure came to a close, I recall arguing that PC should not assume that college kids, with a little training, could contribute in technical areas where they had little or no real expertise. At best, it was patronizing to the host country. On the train to Delhi for the last time, I recall many of the other volunteers expressed similar views about the need for more real expertise as opposed to good intentions. We would make sure PC understood the realities on the ground, you betcha (as Minnesotans would say).

As we actually did this roundtable debriefing, however, one after another talked about their India experience in what I recall as rather glowing terms. So much for searing honesty, I thought. Perhaps my fellow volunteers were right, and I just came across as a whiner, a personal attribute my wife claims I have mastered all too well. My lingering reservations were swept aside, however, when an Indian official gave us certificates thanking us for our contributions to the country in the area of… poultry? I think it would have looked more sincere if they had gotten the program area right. All was made worthwhile, however, when we received the thanks from a grateful America on a piece of paper signed by President Nixon himself (before he was impeached, of course).

It was over. We were going home. But what kind of home would greet us? For two years, we witnessed what looked like, from afar, the dissolution of American society. There were the assassinations (Robert Kennedy and Martin Luther King), the urban riots, and the increasingly savage and violent debate over the war in Vietnam. For better or worse, this is what we faced.

Coming Home

I suspect that reentering civilization affected each of us in idiosyncratic ways. Personally, I recall the blessing of anonymity. First stop for Bill (Whitesell), Hap (Pedigo), and I was Istanbul, which still felt like Asia. The airline put us up so we stayed at a fancy hotel overlooking the Bosporus Straights. To this day I can remember standing on a balcony mesmerized by a romantic vision of this link between Europe and Asia. The world I grew up in was so close I could taste it and yet I knew I was not back yet. It hit me that I did not even own a pair of shoes, just flip flops, and was refused entrance to the fancy hotel restaurant due to my untidy and decidedly unhygienic appearance. Civilization, or at least the version of it I best understood, would have to wait a day or two.

Athens began to feel like the Western civilization that was embedded in my memory. I recall getting excited by an escalator, feeling the comfort of walking the streets without attracting attention, and buying a pair of shoes. We could not have been too anonymous because we were hustled by some guys trying to acquaint us with the virtues of several young ladies whose interest in us, it would appear, was largely pecuniary. I know, I know, hard to believe they were not overwhelmed with our good looks and charm. I must say, the offer was tempting.

The reentry process was surreal in many respects. Literally days earlier, we lived in isolation on the margins of a desert. Now, armed with an open ticket (as long as we kept going in one direction), we felt like jet setters, at least just a little bit. Several times we got up in the morning and chatted about where we might fly that day. Athens was followed by Rome, and then Geneva, and then Frankfurt, and then Paris, and so on. We began to experience on a grander scale what we sometimes encountered during brief trips to Delhi or Bombay. The contrasts between the modern and feudal worlds were stunning; rural India could be like a slap in the face. I remember once splurging on a breakfast at the luxurious Oberoi Hotel in Delhi and overhearing a fellow westerner whine about the orange juice not being fresh. "No whining," I wanted to scream, "don't you realize how privileged you are?" At that point I realized the transition was permanent. We were leaving India behind, and I could soon return to my own whining ways without any guilt.

I ran across attractive women in each city but encountered a bitter truth—they remained as fleet of foot as always while I had slowed down perhaps a bit more as my youthful vigor evaporated. I should have taken up that offer in Athens. By the time we arrived in Germany, it was just Bill and I; Hap had gone his separate way at some point. We made our way to Frankfurt to visit Mike Simonds, who had undergone urgent eye surgery at the U.S. military hospital there. On the train to Delhi for mustering out, Mike had mentioned a problem with his vision. It seemed minor but we jumped all over him to mention this *before* cutting loose from PC. Sure enough, it turned out to be a detached (or detaching) retina and he was shipped off to Frankfurt. He could easily have lost sight in that eye. I can still recall him lying in bed with his head immobilized. Unfortunately, his mouth still worked, but we still managed a pleasant visit for a couple of days before heading off for a trip up the Rhine.

Paris held some vivid memories. We were there on Bastille Day, France's 4th of July. I recall walking toward the Arc De Triomphe at night as crowds of revelers packed the streets. Bill and I rescued some young American gals from overly amorous Frenchmen, and we spent the night with them enjoying the sights and sounds of Paris. The morning sun was a hint in the eastern sky when the last café still open kicked us out. I marvel at my stamina in those days; staying awake for the 10:00 pm news (CST) now is an achievement worth celebrating. The 11:00 pm local news on the East Coast is beyond the pale.

I can still recall that these gals could not really believe that we had spent two years in a celibate state which, while not strictly true, was true enough to claim without too much guilt. While it struck me as an overly transparent plot to win their sympathy and convince them it was their Christian duty to help us out, they almost seemed convinced to do just that. Two years, they squealed in disbelief. How did you last that long? And we didn't even have cold showers... I had a hard time believing it myself. The appeal to their Christian charitable sensibilities fell short, unfortunately, since they turned out to be Jewish.

Bill took off at some point, I cannot recall if it was in Paris or London, but he was anxious to get home. I had one more stop to make—Ireland, land of my ancestry on my father's side. My mother was Polish but that would have necessitated back tracking and thus cost real money at this point (Peace Corps paid for our airfare by the most direct route but we could stop anywhere along the route without extra cost). It would also have involved complications like getting a visa to a communist country when they would naturally conclude that all PC volunteers were CIA agents.

Dublin was poor and shabby back then, this being well before the country became known as the Celtic (economic) Tiger. However, it seemed very romantic to me. There were plaques and monuments all over the place commemorating this or that event in the cause of Irish freedom. You know, Billy

O'Toole fell off his bar stool on this spot in 1912 while singing songs of Irish heroes.

I must admit, the tug of my Irish roots remains strong, and I had a good time there. One day I spent with a nice young gal from Sweden. I dropped her off at her hostel in the wee hours of the morning and somehow made my way on foot back to my place. As I walked into the hotel I saw a television on in the small room that served as a bar located just off the lobby. A small crowd was intently watching something. It turned out that Neal Armstrong was about to take that first step for mankind on the moon. I watched history being made in a Dublin hotel bar around three or four in the morning. I can always say that I knew where I was when man first set foot on the moon.

One other night, I sat at the bar and struck up a conversation with an Irishman who was killing time before heading off to see his girlfriend. We bought each other several drinks and then he left. I thought I could hold my own but he seemed perfectly sober while I was desperately trying not to fall off the bar stool. I truly doubt they would have erected a monument to me, as they had for Billy O'Toole. At this point, the bar maid was looking extremely fine to me, as was the coat rack adjacent to the front door. Two years really is a long time. She was spared, however, by my inability to move at the critical moment. I had an early morning train reservation which I somehow managed to make. How I managed not to barf my way across the Irish countryside remains a mystery to this day. What a hangover!

Many years later, the pattern of steady and increasingly excessive imbibing would become more a way of life than a cheap joke. In truth, I had to admit I suffered the ethnic curse of my Irish ancestors, an over fondness for all things alcoholic. My future wife, Mary, was a rock of support and I can now count over a quarter-century of sobriety.

Home

My Aer Lingus flight landed at Logan International in Boston. My parents were there, but they had talked an old high school buddy into driving them to the airport, which you would understand if you ever tried negotiating Boston traffic. My wife wonders, to this day, what happens to her husband when we return to the Boston area. I transform from a mild-mannered Midwestern driver into a wild maniac, veering in and out of traffic with my hand constantly pressed on the horn. I explain that it is a matter of survival or the aggression additive they put in the water.

It turns out my father had just been released from the hospital. His lungs were already shot from smoking too many cigarettes and the foul air of pre-OSHA factory work. Both of my parents died prematurely of lung-related diseases and other problems—the consequences of hard lives and hard choices made in a lax regulatory environment. Let no one be fooled on this point, we do (or did) sanction outright corporate homicide in this country through our lack of attention to workplace hazards.

Shortly after my arrival back in Worcester, Don Nordin visited me at my parent's apartment. I thought this a wonderful way to recapture those precious memories of India as we transitioned to what we considered to be normal life. I dragged out my several hundred slides to rev up our trip down memory lane, dimming the lights so as not to lose anything in the moment. All went well for awhile. As I approached slide 300, however, I noticed that Don was no longer responding, not even issuing the occasional grunt that accompanied every tenth slide or so. Turning on the lights revealed Don in a deep sleep, head plopped on his chest, his face twisted in a look of absolute torture. I have noticed since then that I have had that effect on many folks over the years. Now that I think about it, perhaps I should have rented those slides to Dick Cheney for interrogation purposes in the war on terror.

Someone once told me that I tend to let life come to me, that I don't pursue it with any particular force or sense of direction. I suspect there is a modicum of truth there. I had heard about this Urban Affairs masters program at the UW-M when we trained there. This naturally became the one academic program to which I applied since I kind of knew about it already. As a result, I was back in Milwaukee in the fall of 1969. In retrospect, I should have been more proactive. I thought Urban Affairs would teach me how to seduce city women but it was all about politics, economics, and sociology. Nevertheless, I enjoyed the program very much, made great friends, and had the pleasure of getting to know one of the most unforgettable academics in my experience, and I have known many. Warner 'Bud' Bloomberg intimidated and inspired, and I wished I had kept in touch with him when he moved to California.

It was during this period that I achieved my highest level of popularity. In addition to having research assistant positions, I worked as a ticket taker at a local theater (anyone remember the Downer Theater?). I am proud to say I have seen the Woody Allen movie *Bananas* some 732 times and would still laugh at some of the scenes. In later years, my wife would catch me laughing away at Rocky and Bullwinkle cartoons and shake her head, "but you are supposed to be so smart, how can you watch that stuff?" But I had the last laugh when a good friend, and now the Dean of Letters and Sciences at the University of Wisconsin, told my wife he bought the entire set of Rocky and his Friends. The important part is that back in Milwaukee, the manager actually let me run the place on Thursday evenings. We never sold many tickets on Thursdays but, depending on what was showing, the theater might be quite full. I finally was a very popular guy.

One of my new friends was Mary Rider. I had no idea that free movies could be so persuasive. We had one date and I sort of moved in. She was funny and smart and never came across as trying to trap me into marriage, which of course was the perfect way to trap a confirmed bachelor like me into marriage. As I recall, I proposed in the bathroom, always the romantic. Cary Grant had nothing on me.

It was one of my better moves. For some totally inexplicable reason, she must have been motivated to marry me. We wanted to get married before a scheduled trip to her parent's home at Christmas, but my birth certificate was late in arriving. She started harassing postal workers and civil servants back in

307

Worcester. We both can imagine the conversation around the water cooler back then. Boy, this desperate woman called yesterday, she must have a live one on the hook and does not want him to wiggle off. In the end all was well; never underestimate a motivated woman. We have laughed over those days for many years now. Remarkably, she has put up with me for over four decades, through thick and thin as they say.

Despite her deplorable choice in husbands, Mary is quite accomplished in the work world. She had one of those meteoric public service careers. Mary started out as a limited term (temporary) employee managing a study of the career patterns of women in Wisconsin state government. After accepting an entry level 'real' state position in the Division of Vocational Rehabilitation, she began her upward climb. In a remarkable short period, she became a division administrator in the department that governed employment relations for all of state government. Not long after that, Mary assumed the position of Deputy Director for the Wisconsin State Supreme Court, which effectively managed the entire state court system. Somewhat later, she took a leave to secure her law degree from the University of

Wisconsin, from which she graduated with honors. I loved that since it gave me an opportunity to drag out all my sophomoric lawyer jokes—what do you call 100 lawyers at the bottom of the ocean….a good start.

My career was less meteoric but an enormous amount of fun. And, like a lot of my life, it came to me, I did not pursue it. Although I had finished my masters program at the University of Wisconsin-Milwaukee in the summer of 1971, I continued to help a professor with his research. This, in turn, resulted in my meeting several Wisconsin state officials. Had I ever thought of a career in state government, one asked? I barely knew we had a state government but dutifully filled out the forms I was sent. One evening, the professor called and said I had an interview the next day in Madison. What is the job, I asked, but all he had was the address of the interview. When I showed up, it turned out to be a civil service panel interview for a position described as "research analyst-social services."

This should be mercifully short, I thought, as I knew nothing about research or social services. Never discount the capacity of government to make inscrutable, even bizarre, decisions. I came in third on the civil service hiring list, the last position that the hiring supervisor could interview. Surely, she would discover I am a fraud, I thought. Alas, no, I got the job, which exposed me to the fascinating worlds of research and of human services. She told me later that, for some reason, the second candidate was better than the first and I was better than the second. "Good thing you could not get to number four," I exclaimed, "they must really have been special."

I enjoyed government work. I was surrounded by some pretty smart folks. Wisconsin had a reputation of cutting edge public service governance back then, and we were doing interesting things. Among other projects, we started to automate welfare and human services and thus revolutionize the management of these systems. However, opportunity knocked on the door four years later in 1975. Irving Piliavin, a professor at the University of Wisconsin-Madison (UW) needed to get state support for a research proposal on assessing the role of front-line discretion in the making of welfare decisions. The source of federal funds he was seeking required that state government make the official application, not the university. Even though the distance between state government and the university was only a mile, they were universes apart. No senior state official thought an egghead from the university could possibly contribute anything to the proper management of welfare. So, they found a lowly functionary (me) and told me to work with this clown.

I did so, spending a fair amount of time working to make the application something my employer could support. Off it went and I forgot all about it. One day, the phone rang. It was Professor Piliavin, saying he got the grant and wondered if I would consider moving to the university to manage it on a day-to-day basis. As with all great decisions in my life, I thought it over for six or seven seconds and responded with a "sure, why not?"

Actually, it was one of those spontaneous decisions with life-changing consequences. Piliavin was smart as an academic but clueless about how government worked. Although he was a professor in the School of Social Work, the study was to be run through something called the Institute for Research on Poverty (IRP). IRP was, at the time, the only academic-based national research center funded by the federal government to assess the causes and cures of poverty. It had been created as part of President Johnson's War-On-Poverty. Years later, when I testified before a U.S. Senate sub-committee chaired by Senator Daniel Patrick Moynihan, the welfare expert in the Senate, he mused that the Poverty Institute was one of the best legacies of Johnson's so-called poverty war. Of course, Pat was known to engage in a bit of hyperbole from time to time.

Two years later, as the study wound down, I looked around and concluded that this academic life sure beat working for a living. However, I needed what is considered the union card for an academic, a Ph.D., and therefore enrolled in the doctoral program in social welfare (i.e., social work). And that was that! Except for a one-year stint in Washington where, on leave from the university, I worked on Clinton's first welfare reform bill, I never left IRP. I did eventually accept an appointment in the

School of Social Work later in my career and, over the years, taught a variety of social policy courses at the graduate and undergraduate level. For all practical purposes, though, my career was centered at the Poverty Institute where I served as associate director and acting director for the last decade or so of my academic career before partially retiring in 2002, I fully retired in 2010.

They had a big party for me when I stepped down from teaching and administration (I still dabble in some project work). In my remarks at the gathering, I reflected on the good fortune associated with my more or less accidental academic career. I gave special mention to the lessons I learned from my hard working parents who labored in real jobs like factory work and waitressing. What I learned from them was a key life lesson, which I was happy to share with the crowd of well wishers that day—never take a job that involves heavy lifting.

What did I do for most of my career? I flew around the country to struggle with incredibly challenging and fascinating issues while working with a bunch of very smart people. What amazed me most of all is that they paid me to do this. As one of my cousins always says, is this a great country or what? It was like being a perpetual kid with a license to steal in a candy store.

I never forgot the laborers who carried caseloads of drinks up the mountain side to my hill station resort. I never forgot the emaciated looking farmers holding body and soul together by pulling small yields from the parched soil of Rajasthan. I never even forgot the hopeless futures facing the young Native American's on the isolated reservations of South Dakota. So, I was never totally sympathetic to the whining from privileged faculty at a research university like UW-Madison. One apocryphal definition of the modern university is "… a bunch of academic entrepreneurs held together by silly disputes over parking and office space." I thought I was a master whiner but some of these folk put me to shame. India taught me just how damn lucky I was, a lesson I hope never to forget.

Of course, working on welfare and poverty issues over the past several decades proved stimulating and even provocative.

These were what we call wicked social problems where goals were contentious, underlying theory and values were conflicted, and solutions were debated ad nausea. Welfare reform definitely was not a topic for the faint of heart. I was on the speed dial of media folks around the country and always tried for objectivity in a content area where opinions were deeply held and quite emotional.

I recall a conversation one day with a top Wisconsin official, appointed by Governor Tommy Thompson, twice presidential hopeful and later Health and Human Services Secretary under Bush, the son. Thompson's appointee thanked me for supporting a controversial idea that the governor was pushing, and which was being savaged in the press at the time. I chuckled, noting that I call them as I see them. I pointed out that, in the case of welfare reform, I only felt I was approaching the truth when no one agreed with what I was saying.

Doing policy work, even as an academic, had moments of drama. One example must suffice. The 'learnfare' concept was an early effort to link welfare to appropriate behavior on the part of recipients. As such, it was at the forefront of the emerging social contract approach to welfare design and management. Not surprisingly, it was hugely controversial. I had written about 'learnfare' and thus was asked to testify in DC, a place that was like a second home in those days. Although I thought testifying was a bad idea given the likely political fallout, the IRP director at the time gave me a stirring speech about academic freedom and all that rubbish. My fear was that all our remaining contracts with the state of Wisconsin would be terminated, which at a minimum would have thrown a lot graduate students out of work.

I was lobbied fiercely, even on the plane out to Washington. A former Republican legislator from Wisconsin, who then held a high Food Stamp position in DC, looked me right in the eye and said, "Tom, you know what happens to people who try to stand in the middle of the track?" "Yeah, I know, the train runs right over them." For one of the few times in my life, I really prepared my remarks. After the testimony, a Thompson appointee came up to me and said, "Well Tom, those remarks were fair. The child support research contract is coming up for review next week, and I think you will like the outcome." To this day, I cannot tell if my testimony was totally truthful or whether I slanted things for political purposes. I certainly did not do so consciously.

One thing was certain, life was interesting back then. On another occasion, then Governor Thompson yelled at me from the podium at a public meeting hosted by a Chicago-based foundation. This was years after he personally put a crony on a review panel to make sure IRP did not get a contract to do a federally mandated evaluation of one of his nationally touted reforms. In the convoluted world of welfare, as it turned out, even a Governor's personal attack might prove beneficial. As his tirade ended, the President of the host foundation walked up behind me and whispered in my ear, "Tom, in our eyes your stock has just gone up." Her assessment apparently was correct since they proved quite generous to me over the years. A few years later, I happened to be at the Foundation on her last day. She was moving on to the Presidency of Second Harvest, a huge national charity that helps feed the poor. As I expressed my best wishes, she told me that she used the Thompson tirade vignette in her interview that won her this new position, but did not explain exactly how. No matter, I am always happy to be of service to my fellow do-gooders.

At the end of the day, there was always something both comforting and frightening in the fact that I could be my own man. I was always in a position (perhaps except for my year in DC) where I could come to my own conclusions about what was right and about how I should conduct my professional life. I tried not to be an ideologue, nor partisan, nor predictable. Searching for my own personal truth remained a precious opportunity, and burden, for me.

All in all, it was an enormously satisfying, if exhausting, career. Admittedly, I was never a great academic, nor did I aspire to be. The real world was always much more fascinating to me than publishing technical pieces in peer reviewed journals to be read by a handful of colleagues. However, I would say I was a pretty damn good teacher and undoubtedly inspired a number of students over the years. I found that you never knew what kind of impact you were having on the kids you taught. Once in a while I taught undergrads and recall a young gal who complained mightily how hard my course was and how she was going to have a breakdown from all the studying she had to do, etc. She complained so much that I actually stored her name in my memory in case I ran across it in the newspapers under tragedies or she returned to campus sporting a semi-automatic weapon. Years later, a colleague who taught Public Policy at Johns Hopkins University approached me at a conference and asked if I remembered a certain former student. Oh my god, I thought, he uses his academic position to front his real job as a hit man and she sent this guy to track me down and exact revenge. I admitted remembering her. "She is my stepdaughter," he went on to say, "and she still talks about you as the best professor she had at UW."

I also believe I can say I was a talented policy wonk which is good because I always thought of myself first and foremost as one of those. I had the pleasure of working with the best and brightest from academia, think tanks, the philanthropic community, top evaluation firms, and government officials at all levels. I gave perhaps hundreds of talks all over the country and in Canada (a colleague came up with an estimate once when she was introducing me at a conference and I was stunned at the number), had my writings entered into the Congressional Record, served on a National Academy of Sciences expert panel and, most importantly (to me at least) had the respect of both my academic colleagues and policy practitioners at the local, state, and federal levels. One project that especially pleased me involved setting up peer assistance networks among regional groupings of senior state welfare officials. At one point, three such networks functioned, a Midwest group (called WELPAN), a West Coast group (called WESTPAN), and a Southern group (called BUBBAPAN), just kidding on the last acronym. Among other things, this gave me a front row seat to reform on the ground and a vehicle for nudging thinking in creative directions.

It all could be exhausting, though, between teaching graduate courses, helping administer a poverty research center, raising
money, managing multiple projects simultaneously, and traveling continuously. In the old days before power point (BPP), I
used to carry around a huge file of transparencies that I would
continuously update. When I got on the plane to fly somewhere
to give a talk I would pull out the file and start sifting and win-
nowing and reordering. By the time the plane landed I would
have my talk prepared, sort of. I never really knew what I would
say until it was time to say it. Colleagues would comment that
they were preparing for a talk they were giving three weeks later.
Three WEEKS! I felt ahead of the game if I was ready three
hours before the talk.

I suppose I began running out of steam a few years ago, too
many mornings of getting to the office at 5:30 AM, too many
flights (particularly through O'Hare on Friday evenings), too
many hotel rooms, and too many battles. I still have a bit of
project work on my plate but have largely left the policy field
to the young and the restless. Mary and I now winter in Florida,
living on one of those golf course communities where we can
watch the cranes and the golfers from our lanai and passing
judgment on which looks more awkward and silly, the birds or
the golfers. Most importantly, I read voraciously. With some
exaggeration, Mary says she never saw me with a book that did
not have a colon in the title. You know, books like *Poverty: The
Curse of the Working Class*. Now I have a surfeit of one of life's
most precious commodities—time—and a pile of unread books
high enough to last a lifetime.

Post Script

I had not seen most in our group in 40 years. When we got
together that weekend in May, 2009, it felt more like 40 hours
since our last time together. Toward the end of the second day,
as the reunion was winding down, I looked around the room as
people chatted and shared with one another. Of course, body
parts dragged and drooped in awkward ways, a few extra pounds

could be found on most, and a bit more grey coursed through the hair that remained. However, I could easily think back to those bright and shiny faces that gathered some 40-plus years earlier in Milwaukee. Although I am, by nature, a pretty detached guy, someone who skips through life with a bit of wit and a joke or two, I couldn't quite ignore the very real emotion that surged through me. "I really do love these guys."

Recently I used Google Earth to look up Salumbar, my old village. This was a feat for me since I am terminally challenged technically. The clock on my VCR still blinks at 12:00 AM. From the satellite image taken from above, my old site looked oh so familiar on first glance. I could see the main artery where it ran past our government housing and curved into the town a mile or so down the road. I could see the lake that was located over the hill in back of our place. I could see the outline of the old Raj palace.

On closer look, some things did surprise me. Peering close, Salumbar looked bigger and different. If I was interpreting things right, the desert that existed outside our little home was now filled in with buildings that bordered the main highway out of town and, beyond them, with farms that were not there 40 years ago. I could not locate where we lived, but that may be my fault or because the government housing was torn down years ago. Similarly, I could not find any monument to our service to the community, or perhaps my lack of command over the technology explains that. Nonetheless, what struck me most is that a recurring dream I've often had of Salumbar with American-type suburbs might not be totally far-fetched after all.

Salumbar has changed. India has changed. I have changed. Perhaps it is time to return.

CHAPTER 12

Ghosts

Bill Muhler

I was nearing the end of my three year stay as a Peace Corps volunteer in an Indian village when the Day of the Dead occurred. On this night, somewhat like our Halloween, ghosts were supposed to come out. These were not kids dressed like ghosts but purportedly the real thing. Not far from where I was staying, two night watchmen were guarding some cows in a corral. One of the men came to me and said that his partner had seen a ghost and that I should come and check it out.

When I got to the cattle pen with my flashlight, the first watchman had a look of terror on his face. I was asking him what had happened when he suddenly jumped into the air and fell down, beginning to thrash around in the dirt as if he were wrestling with an invisible opponent. I aimed the flashlight beam through the rising cloud of dust mixed with the pungent, acrid smell of dried cow manure. I tried to see if there was any evidence of some kind of epileptic seizure and if I should try to protect his teeth or tongue. I asked the colleague if this had ever happened before, and he said no, so I just decided to wait it out.

After a minute or so, the fellow calmed down, got up, and shook himself off. I asked if he were all right and if the ghost had gone. He said yes and that there was nothing that I could do for him. I thought that maybe this was some kind of attention-getting display, but the anxiety seemed genuine. Neither man asked for anything, so I attributed the incident to some kind of latent fear exaggerated by the power of suggestion. I had already seen village people in trances, beating themselves in other agitated states, so I decided that this was an aspect of traditional folk culture difficult for a westerner to understand. I went back home and went to bed, unsettled, but certainly not believing in ghosts.

Thirty-five years later, because of this ghost story and other reminiscences, my twenty-year-old son Nate was convinced that a good portion of his father's weirdness could be attributed to his experiences in India. He expressed a desire to visit the scene of the crime. I had very much wanted to return to the village so his request provided the opportunity to make the long, difficult, and expensive trip.

On our way to my village, we stopped in Udaipur, the district headquarters for my PC group. My volunteer group started with 45 candidates and through attrition, failed FBI background checks, and terminations, we were down to about a dirty, but dedicated, dozen. Each of us was assigned to a village, ten to forty miles from the city, but Udaipur was the rendezvous point and source of personal needs and agricultural supplies not available in the villages. We almost always met someone in the group, and it was exciting to speak English, catch up on the latest news, and get project ideas.

There was only one non-vegetarian restaurant in the city and it was our meeting place. Meat was very difficult to get in the villages and the modified form of British cooking was faintly reminiscent of home. We stayed in local, three to four room, family-run hotels near the restaurant that cost about 45 cents per night. In winter, we used to take the curtains off the windows and curl up in them. There was a store nearby where you could buy peanut butter, jam, and *Newsweek*. We would buy the magazine and memorize every page of news including the advertisements. When we met at Berry's restaurant we would discuss the latest magazine by page number. "Did you see the new car on page 16?" "Sure, what about those pictures of the moon?" on page 63.

I thought that it would be fun to take Nate to the old restaurant, if it were still there, and see how the menu had changed.

We found the place, just as it was, with the same blue-lettered sign overhead. I walked in expecting to remember the good old days, but before I could even sit down, I realized the place was filled with ghosts. You hear of people seeing ghosts or hearing them, but I realized now that sometimes you have to wrestle with them. This was not the kind of physical contact that I had seen in the cattle pen but a very real coming to grips with aspects of the past that had been long forgotten and repressed.

First, there were the ghosts of the departed, those who could never come here for a reunion. John, my supervisor, who was just a few years older than I, had returned to Oakland and lived not far from me. John was a big guy who had played football in high school. He came off as a jock, but he had great social skills and could get along with anyone. I envied his sociability and ability to communicate. As a supervisor, he was always clear in his rules and demands and fair in implementing them. We saw each other off and on back in Oakland. Ironically, he survived the years in India only to go home and contract an infectious disease that took his life making his wife a widow and his children fatherless.

Back in India, John's counterpart and successor had been Om Prakash. Om had the opposite personality. When he started his job, he was shy, diffident, and totally lacking in self-confidence. However, with John's training and encouragement, he too became a great supervisor and even the best man at my wedding. A few years later he was killed in an accident.

Phil was a volunteer who was stationed not far from my village. He often came over to eat at my house. Phil was one of the most upbeat and intentionally optimistic people I have ever met. He came from Alaska and had a hard time adjusting to the heat of summer, but he never complained. He went about his work cheerfully and was much respected by the villagers. He had climbed in the Himalayas with me, and I never saw someone so happy to be back in the snow. Later, he took a vacation alone out in the desert and had gotten meningitis. The local doctors misdiagnosed the illness and failed to administer antibiotics immediately. He went into a coma. The Peace Corps medevaced him to the best hospital in Delhi but it was too late. He died within three days.

Gary, my closest friend in the group, had survived India and returned home to Berkeley. He was not only an excellent volunteer, who had been allowed to extend a year, but he was also a brilliant improvisational musician, linguist, pre-med student, sociologist, and home grown philosopher. While we were struggling to learn Hindi and mastering simple sentences like "where is the bathroom," and "please give me back my passport." Gary was making up phrases like "I've been doing such and such since I came fresh from the womb." At one point in a discussion about proximate and long-range goals, he said, "Better here and now." We have been scratching our heads over that one ever since.

When he first visited me in my village, which for all practical purposes looked like most other villages, he said, "I hate to tell you, but you live in a slum." My pride in place and the effect of my own special presence, which presumably upgraded the neighborhood, was instantly deflated. Gary was not really disparaging the area; he was just stating the obvious and taking some of the pretension out of my grand designs for development.

Once, when a group of us were sitting around a table at Berry's Restaurant, we passed around a small bowl of bright red pickled onions that were a specialty of the house. Each guy picked the largest onion available. Gary was last, and as he popped the smallest onion in his mouth, he declared, "I have won a moral victory." Back in Berkeley, he became a street musician in San Francisco and often made enough money to pay for his transportation back and forth to Berkeley. He lived off a small stipend from a trust fund left to him by his deceased father. As an only child with no immediate family connections and few friends in the area, he became increasingly isolated and alienated. He gradually became paranoid and grandiose at the same time. I encouraged him to seek help but he resisted. The two of us visited fairly regularly, but one day when I was studying for some important exams, he dropped by to talk. I apologized and said that these tests were very important and that we would have to talk later. I never saw him again. Ten years later, I found out that he had jumped off an eight story building in San Francisco.

However, in spite of these losses, there were even bigger and stronger ghosts to wrestle with in Berry's restaurant. There was an immediate and palpable sense of grief and pain that was as inexplicable as it was totally unexpected. It was hard to breathe as I sat in the dark room somehow expecting to see my friends come through the door at any moment. At the same time, I was dreading that they would do so. If they came through the door, that might mean we were still volunteers and that we would only be enjoying a brief respite from the difficulties of being very young in a strange and alien culture 12,000 miles from home. We would never once be able to call home in those days. A letter took two weeks to go each way. We were always sick, and if someone had a solid shit, we had a party. All of us had lost about twenty percent of our body weight. We had voluntarily taken a vow of poverty and, since we were not allowed to date local girls, we became involuntary monks by default.

We faced many dangers. There were diseases, accidents, riots, and cobras. I kept my eye out for cobras. A volunteer got on a bus once with a highly agitated group of villagers who were yelling at the driver to get to the hospital right away. They had a woman with them who crawled into bed with a cobra and had been bitten six times. Cobras do not have fangs but many small sharp teeth that abrade the skin so that the poison can enter the blood stream. Not all bites are fatal but we never found out what happened to the woman. I used to walk from my house out to the village leader's farm about once a week on some errand or another. Sometimes I would eat there and come back in the dark. Every time I walked back, I would pass this one particular bush. On the last trip I saw a five foot cobra dive into a hole under that bush. It had always been living there and I could have stepped on it at any time.

Village food supplies were very seasonal. There was no refrigeration and almost no processed foods. We ate the same limited supply of fruits and vegetables for months until we were sick of that limited fare. After three months of tomatoes and onions, for example, using every conceivable recipe, you never wanted to see a tomato again. Then, with the next season, we ate eggplant and carrots for three months until we could not stand them anymore. We ate mangos until we overdosed on vitamin A and then could not get one for nine months.

Fall and spring were brief but delightful; however, the three major 'seasons' were occasions of death in the village. The elderly died of the cold, flu, and pneumonia during the winter. In the rainy season, the lack of sanitation facilities in homes allowed crap to wash into the wells that caused enteric diseases that killed a lot of kids and the weak. People died of the heat in the summer. Daily body counts were listed in the newspapers.

We were completely on our own in our work in the villages. Few of us could rely on our Indian coworkers or agricultural department officers for project suggestions. We had to come up with our own plans to experiment with crops or fertilizer or irrigation. We did come up with good ideas, but they were hard to implement. We had no funds, materials were scarce, transportation and communications were very difficult, our language skills were limited, and farmers were resistant to change.

We went everywhere on the cheapest one-speed bikes made in India that were in constant need of repair. Thorns in the sand would pop the tires. We usually threw away an inner tube after it had over twenty-five patches in it. We took longer trips on busses that frequently broke down. The seats often were wooden and there was often a bolt sticking out somewhere that would rip your pants. The busses were crowded with villagers. Guys would get up into the baggage racks and dangle their feet in your face. Many of the locals were not used to highway travel. I never met a volunteer who had not been thrown up on.

Indians often commented that westerners were not only war mongers but also very materialistic. They, on the other hand, considered themselves to be very spiritual people. I heard this over and over again and, in fact, there is much to substantiate this self-perception. There is a lot of religion in India—Hinduism, Buddhism, Islam, and Christianity, among other sects. Many are vegetarian out of principle and the extreme Jains would sweep the path in front of them to keep from stepping on a bug. Some people would not eat certain vegetables because they might accidentally boil an earwig. Gandhi, of course, was the ultimate symbol of non-violence and the use of moral force as it applied to politics.

However, there were times when people took other actions that were difficult for westerners to understand. Newspapers reported that some untouchables had been murdered because they turned their moustaches up in the fashion of the upper class. Parents murdered infant girls because boys are preferred. Not too many years before, the penalty in my village for getting an unmarried girl pregnant was to cut off a man's nose. This happened to a guy in my village. He had a large scar on his forehead where the doctors had cut his skin and pulled it down

to make a kind of make-shift nose that did not work very well. The man was a good farmer and family man and was a delight to work with, but it was always somewhat difficult to look at him.

My apartment was on the second story of the house, and I could look down on the courtyard of a house below. An eight-year-old girl living there had deformed legs and could not stand. She would get herself around the ground by digging one hand into the dirt and then pulling herself toward the foot. I immediately asked if there were an operation that would help her, but I was told that many doctors had been consulted and nothing could be done. I watched her crawling around for three years.

One day, after having been in the village for about four months, I climbed the highest hill in the area on a beautiful mild day and got my first overhead view of the plains and farms and fields spreading out as far as the eye could see. I had a kind of ecstatic experience as I felt that for the first time I got a comprehensive view of the scope and wonder that is India. However, I realized that there were a lot of problems down there, like 900 million of them, and that I could not solve very many of them.

When my group arrived in Udaipur District, India had just had to deal with a costly war with Pakistan and a Chinese invasion. The state of Rajasthan, where we were assigned to work, had experienced years of drought and full-fledged famine. Women on famine relief work projects sat on the side of the roads and broke rocks into gravel with hammers to make road base. The monsoon rains had come that year so hundreds of emaciated farmers with their even more depleted cows were walking hundreds of miles home from areas to which they had migrated to find better pasturage during the drought. Our job was to grow more food and that was about all we could handle.

Once we settled into our villages, many of us discovered needs and addictions that we never knew we had. At home I had loved to buy a different cheese every week experimenting with it in cooking and for lunch. At the time in India, there was only one cheese. It was a nice cheese. For an extreme cheese eater, it quickly got old. In the states, I had been hooked on classical music and was constantly borrowing records from the music library. In India, I had to go cold turkey.

Other things were disconcerting in India. Poverty impacted the lives of millions of people. Beggars with strange deformities populated the city streets and especially the bus and train station. The first time I went to Udaipur, I was confronted by a boy with a double hare lip and a cleft pallet. He would come up asking for money. If you did not give him any he would open his mouth and let you see into his head where the roof of his mouth was supposed to be.

Horrified, I gave him a few coins and vowed to avoid him in the future at all costs. The next time I came to town I had arranged to meet another volunteer at a certain building. While I was waiting, the kid saw me and hurried my way. There was no escape, so I decided that it was him or me. If he ruled the town,

I would have to give him money every time I went there. So, I did not budge but just sat and waited for him.

When he arrived, I gave him a big smile and a greeting. He gave me a moan and groan while asking for money. I said no and he got up into my face, opened his mouth and made weird gurgling sounds in his throat and stuck his tongue into what I supposed was his sinus cavities. I smiled again and apologized for not giving him any money. He looked really disappointed, not so much because he did not get the handout, but because I think that he had never been turned down before. He tried a few more tricks before mom spotted some rich Indians and sent him after them. They paid willingly, and so did many others. He was a cash cow for the family but never came after me again.

Perhaps, that is how I adapted to India, one inconvenience at a time. There was no TV, very limited radio, but one of the new discoveries in India was reading. Of course, I read in college but mostly for courses. Peace Corps lent us a book locker with about fifty books in it. You would read them all and them swap the locker with someone else and read another fifty.

At night in the village, it was so quiet I could hear the termites eating my table. I became interested in photography. I shot in black and white and used to get one good shot out of a roll. At first, I wanted to use my pictures as a record for others, focusing on the painful side of India. When I saw something ugly or disconcerting, I shot it. But something very strange would happen. When I developed the film, the pictures came out wonderful. The camera lied. I tried again and again, roll after roll, but failed.

One day, I saw a girl sticking her head out a window with a scabby rash all over her cheek. This was going to be a good one. This would show the world what I was up against. When I developed the photo, she had turned her head to her good side. The wind caught her hair and she was radiantly beautiful.

I gave up. The camera would not stop lying. Perhaps, it was showing me another side of India that I had difficulty seeing. I kept looking through my magic camera and it showed me more and more beauty. The architecture was rich in intersecting lines and arches and domes and carvings, and hanging staircases all of stone and plaster and brick hundreds of years old. There were temples, castles, forts, moats, palaces, walls, and gates. There were carved wooden doors with handsmithed hardware in iron, brass, and bronze. There were paintings and murals and tapestries and even the poorest house had elaborate finger painting designs in time sketched on the manure plastered mud walls. The traditional women's clothing consisted of the brightest reds, oranges, pinks, and yellows and from their ears and neck and wrists dangled an infinite variety of jewelry designs. The grace of a woman in a sari carrying water on her head cannot be equaled.

Having been raised in the Oakland Hills, I did not think I could adjust to flat land. I learned that late in the afternoon, there were long shadows and trees lit up from underneath. Sunsets were spectacular, and after nine months of clear blue skies, the monsoon filled the atmosphere with gigantic billowing clouds and storms and wind and rain. Mornings were fantastic year round. Even with frost on the ground in the winter, the sun would warm things quickly. I used to lie in bed until the sun shone through a high window at about seven o'clock. Then I would jump out of bed and throw open the double doors to let in the sun. In summer, the morning is always the coolest part of the day and good for moving about.

The topography of my district drew my interest with its endless variations. These were flat plains, steep hills, and mountains 5,000 feet high. There were arid salt flats, dense jungles, deserts, forests, and scrub lands. Wildlife was sparse but exciting. There were monkeys, giant cranes, camels, great flocks of vultures, foxes, rabbits, mongooses, hedge hogs, hoopie birds, and partridges.

The endless varieties of people provided their own form of entertainment. Along with beautiful women bathing half-naked in the irrigation canals, there were holy men and sadhus, transsexual actors, poets, priests, and peasants, tribal people from the hinterlands, artists, circus performers, and Anglo-Indians working at the railroad junctions. One man in the town nearby

used to stand in the middle of the street and talk to himself for most of the day. Once I had a long conversation with him that consisted of a series of totally discontinuous thoughts on both our parts. Some of the local shopkeepers saw me talking to him and asked about the conversation. I said that we got along fine and that I thought that he was not crazy, but that maybe the rest of us were. This really upset the shopkeepers, and they denied my claim adamantly.

Most of all, my relationship with my host family provided the greatest amount of satisfaction and joy. I had four brothers and two sisters, three uncles, a mother and grandmother, two great uncles and a grandfather. The village leader became my surrogate father. There were weddings, feasts, and quiet dinners. There were endless stories and lots of gossip, as well as long historical, cultural, and political discussions. For the next three-and-a-half decades, I would have at least one dream a month of returning to the village. When I mentioned this to my youngest Indian brother, then 12 and now 47, he pointed to the sky and said, "You see, God has brought you here!"

In the village, Nate and I stayed in my old room which had a niche in the wall filled with family photos including a faded black and white photo of me. We ate all of our meals with the family. One day, I mentioned to the village leader that Nate and I would go into town to use the internet and then stay for lunch because we did not want to inconvenience anyone. He replied, "It is not a problem of convenience; it is a question of love!" We stayed for lunch.

CHAPTER 13

Final Reflections

*Your purpose in life is to find your purpose in
life and to give your whole heart and soul to it.*
                                    Buddha

Our reflections in no way constitute a discursive narrative
describing our Peace Corps experience. They are a collage
of images, emotional reactions, lessons learned, innocence lost,
and scraps of memories shaped by four decades of subsequent
life experiences. Some of what we shared here is humorous,
some parts are sad, and other parts have become sources of
pride and comfort. Although some dimensions of our common
experience undoubtedly touch on a deeper sense of failure and
occasional regret, there clearly remain ample wellsprings of
joy, laughter, and irreplaceable experiences and human connections. In the end, these reflections are probably little more than
what we think we experienced, viewed through the prism of our
adult lives. Nevertheless, they are at the same time integral and
fundamental building blocks upon which our adult selves were
founded.

In many ways, therefore, our collective story is a tale of
personal change and growth born in large part out of perceived
failures, whether real or not, in the face of uncompromising
challenges. It is a narrative that confronts our own doubts and
demons with unflinching honesty and, in doing so, seeks a form
of redemption and self-awareness. Perhaps, in spots, we are also
looking for some forgiveness for our immaturity and naiveté
way back then. At the same time, we share some successes as

volunteers and have come to appreciate that our very concept of 'success' demands a more elastic and nuanced definition of the concept than is ordinarily the case. Indeed, we undoubtedly left small footprints in our villages and towns as witnessed by the few who have returned to their sites.

Who We Were...

For some, Peace Corps meant a spiritual search for meaning; for others, an almost comical struggle to survive. For virtually all of us, our reflections capture and encompass a string of reminiscences and feelings that sometimes haunt us and, at other times, still illuminate our lives some four decades later.

Each of us went to India for different reasons and with distinct expectations. Don Nordin, who grew up in the small, remote city of Cheyenne, Wyoming, far from the social turmoil sweeping America at the time, pondered his improbable route into Peace Corps as follows:

When I contemplate Peace Corps service through a filter of 43 years, one particular question still arises. Just how did Peace Corps choose who would be invited and who would ultimately be assigned? I forget now exactly what the statistics were but I recall something like out of a hundred applications, six were invited to train. Maybe half of the trainees are selected. Then another twenty percent or so of the selectees left for other reasons or from another round of de-selections. Several people terminated early, leaving very few of the original pool of applicants who actually finished two years in the field.

Don pondered how and why he made it through this gauntlet where few successfully tread. Like many others, some deeper spiritual and ethical factors tugged at him.

Perhaps it was Catholic school training that suggested a vocation in the missions. From early memories, fourth grade or earlier, I remember being extolled to admire those who left their homes in our comfortable "developed" land to live in "primitive" cultures and help people there acquire some of the comforts we enjoy as well as avoid the hunger or disease that we do

331

not experience. Did more Catholics apply to the Peace Corps? Was Catholicism a selection factor? ...I remember a night a bunch of us India 44ers were hanging out on George Wilson's roof in Nathadwara for a Diwali celebration. The subject came up and we realized that a very high percentage of 44-B had received a Catholic education. If early indoctrination toward missionary work was a factor, where were the Mormons or the Pentecostals? Perhaps one had to be a "lapsed" Catholic?

Of course, the reality is that we came from many diverse traditions and represented wildly distinct perspectives. Nancy Simuel was very different from Don Nordin. She was a young, black woman caught up in the racial struggles that dominated American cities in the 1960s. Her decision to become part of India 44-A was both an easy and a very complicated choice:

I don't remember what prompted me to join the Peace Corps. A recruiter came to my college campus, I went to hear what was being said, liked what I heard and the rest as they say is history. Race and civil rights were very much in the news and on the minds of Americans everywhere. I had experienced segregation first hand and here I was going off to another country with mostly white people to live for two years. Was I naïve, stupid, or what?

Shouldn't I remain home and carry on with the struggle? This was to be a cultural exchange for me in not only learning and living in India but also learning and living with whites. Leaving home at a time when our country was in such social and political and economic upheaval did give me pause but upon arrival in India I found the same conditions prevailed. But of course, we were not to involve ourselves in politics.

Others chose to sign up for India 44 for all kinds of idiosyncratic reasons. Bill Whitesell, a kid from a large Catholic family who would become a Yale scholarship student and role model for his siblings, sought a spiritual renewal which he thought India might offer. Gareth Loy, once he realized India was his destination, sought an intense cultural affinity through the art and music of the country which he came to appreciate so fully. Through India and the Peace Corps, Mary Jo Clark, then Dummer, sought more confidence and competence as she embarked on a career in nursing. Kathy Kelleher Sohn sought a form of escape from the provinciality and isolation that growing up

Nancy Simuel, India 44A B reunion, Oakland, CA 5-24-09

Catholic in the rural south imposed. For Haywood Turrentine, the road to India was a classic story of rags to riches, of growing up dirt poor in a tenant farmer home with apparently few prospects and limited ambitions. However, he found his way half way around the world with a diverse array of mostly privileged white kids who would remain part of his life. Mike Simonds seemingly stumbled out of a working class family seeking a foreign adventure hopefully in a country with beautiful women. For Tom Corbett, Peace Corps was a suitable venue for satisfying the thirst for social justice that had first taken him into a missionary Catholic order. For so many of us, Kennedy's exhortation to "...ask what you can do for your country" touched us in such personal ways.

Each of us came from a unique background and each of us found Peace Corps and India through our individual pathways. The group of kids that assembled at the University of Wisconsin-Milwaukee in the summer of 1966 was a diverse collection of people and stories, a weave of colorful motivations, backgrounds, and aspirations that could have created a wondrously rich and chaotic tapestry. It is amazing, however, how many of us can consciously recollect the Kennedy call for sacrifice, for giving back, for making the world a better place. There existed an indefinable quest for doing the right thing that cut across all of our individual journeys.

Don Nordin, in a set of partially completed recollections titled *Why Me*, noted that he "...remembered the training as being intense. We had all day, every day, except maybe Sunday, scheduled with classes and activities. All of the remaining time was spent socially with the same people involved in the same discussions about the same subjects. We slept in shared dormitory rooms and had little time alone."

I don't know if it had anything to do with India or not but we were also made to confront the meat industry as part of our training. Here on the high plain of South Dakota we were invited to participate in the inoculating, castrating, and branding of beef cattle. While some of the trainees watched, I felt bound by solidarity with the cattle producers because of my Wyoming

connection. Though I had lived in Cheyenne, a small city of 50,000, I had never before been involved in cattle roundups. But, by golly, I jumped right in there. I grabbed those doggies by the tail and held them while a brand was applied, shots were given, and their testicles were cut off. I didn't hesitate a bit in partaking of "Rocky Mountain Oysters" roasted up in the fire with a branding iron.

We ended that summer of training with everyone being given a slip of paper with instructions to go to room 101 or some other room. Those of us who were sent to room 101 were selected. Those sent to the other room were deselected. Deselection became a new word in our lexicon, one that had some pain and sadness attached to it.

By the time we left the United States, we had experienced so much and had grown in so many ways. We were a diverse lot, separated from one another by race, region, and culture. And yet, we had been bound together by the rigors of a long training period, by knowing we were one of the few that remained of the many who started out. We had little foresight or appreciation for just how challenging the next two years of our lives would be. Perhaps not surprisingly, each of us returned as a very different person. As our reflections reveal, sometimes through painful honesty and dark humor, the experience of India was personal, intense, and transformative. We left the U.S. as kids and returned as something more. Nancy Simuel put it this way, "Those two years of my life shaped me in many ways and that experience etched a lifelong desire to continue to help those in need and in poverty. I feel with certainty that I received more than I contributed."

Making Sense of It All

The 2009 reunion afforded us a venue through which interpersonal bonds might be cemented once again and for developing insights into what to make of our PC experience. It was a way to make some sense of the compelling and sometimes overwhelming character of that experience.

Most of us had gone home after our India tenure and simply lived with whatever lingering doubts, unresolved emotions, and feelings of failure remained within us. As returning combat veterans know all too well, and undoubtedly with more intensity, those who did not experience the same things as you cannot really comprehend. You can talk about it; they seem to listen; yet, at some level, you know that they do not really understand what you are talking about. Thus, we continued through life absent the opportunities to work out the residual emotional detritus we carried back with us.

In this context, as suggested earlier, the sharing at our reunion was redemptive and transformative. The need to seek further understanding, if not catharsis, though these confessional reflections became even more immediate and compelling. It became obvious that certain feelings of inadequacy and failure were not unique to us as individuals but rather universal throughout our group. Moreover, we began to unravel our often twisted emotional threads to make better sense of what we experienced and what we accomplished. Surely, some healing took place over that short weekend. Our private and now public struggles on paper are evidence of this.

Susan Krawiec Young talked about reconciling the complex contradictory feelings and emotions that welled inside her as she tried to make sense of her PC experience:

I have come to believe that some good came of the Peace Corps experience. Perhaps we gained the most. Yet the people who met and worked with us could not help but be influenced. Here were these people (U.S. volunteers) who visited the errand girl's mother and new-born brother in their mud walled home and ate their food. Here were people who would chat with the rickshaw-walla as readily as the landlord. This is one of my favorite over told stories. One day I was sewing with the handicrafts teacher and pricked my finger. As the red drop of blood pooled on my finger, Rukmini exclaimed, "Abbah! Your blood is red." "What color did you think it was?" I asked. "Pink, because you are light."

Living in India as volunteers made a big difference in our lives. We have this shared experience. I will never forget how angry and embarrassed I was one night soon after I arrived. I walked too rapidly into the kitchen and picked up a can of cocoa only to shriek at the large roach climbing up the side of the can towards my fingers. The worst part was that I was with volunteers who had been in country for a year. Bill Day (India-28) pointed at me, howling in laughter and screamed, "Culture shock!" I wanted to ring his neck. He lives today only because he outranked the "newbie."

Culture shock, that painful teacher, was the greatest gift of all. Culture shock blew open our heads. There was no going back. There was no undoing it. Culture shock unraveled me and began to teach what was me and what was just a reflection of my culture. Culture shock taught me about others, their culture, and how individuals and culture intertwine. Culture shock made me a better mother, a better Girl Scout leader, a better health educator.

In the end there is no substitute for living with folks in or close to their own circumstances.

Jerry Weis eloquently expresses how the experience of India subsequently shaped his thinking and how it still affected his reactions to events and challenges long after his return to the states:

I try to talk to people about the way village India is our common history. Poverty is the condition of the overwhelming majority of everyone who ever lived. Must be at least 95 percent of everyone who ever lived...

Not to put too fine a point on the matter, but even as a twenty-something kid from the suburbs in 1967—I understand that I am wealthy in this world. We sleep in a quiet bed; we worry about our love life, not about our meal tomorrow. We are fantastically wealthy by any historical standard for human beings.

We push a button or twist a faucet to produce water. It flows from the wall to a temperature of our own choosing. Like I said, I try to tell people about our common history. I try to tell people to imagine a world without electricity and without running water, where the doctor is someone who visits the nearby town twice a week.

Everything for Jerry, and for all of us, is filtered through those experiences halfway around the world in what seems like a lifetime ago. Think about a current issue in the States, healthcare reform, for example. What is necessary and what is obscene waste?

My 93-year old mother lived at home and had a heart attack. Her daughter (my sister) was with her at the time and called an ambulance. They took her to the hospital and kept her alive for four days at a cost of nearly $200,000.

Understood, I'm not objecting to keeping my mother alive for four days so the family could gather. (Although the actual sight of her connected to all the machinery was pretty gruesome.) I'm objecting to the cost being about $2,000 per hour. How can that be accepted as normal?

Truth be told, my mother would have preferred the $200,000 be given to a village health clinic, even if it meant dying on June 1 instead of June 5.

For Jerry Weiss, the very way he thinks about things is shaped by what he saw, experienced, and internalized in India. He is not alone in that regard.

Tom Corbett mused about the enduring significance of PC to his life in the following terms:

The meaning of PC to my life is subtle and nuanced. There were no grand lessons, piercing insights, great aha moments. As I tried to suggest at the beginning, doing PC seemed a given in light of my evolving world view. Nevertheless, there are sentiments and sensibilities that might well be traced to those days in the Rajasthani desert.

Sense of self. For a good deal of my life, I had a terrible sense of self. I had a classic case of 'imposter syndrome,' that I would be discovered as a fraud. India did not cure that and, in some ways, supported that appraisal. At the end of the day, though, dealing with the pressures and challenges pushed my limits and helped me appreciate some of my strengths. Perhaps I did have a personal core on which I could build.

Patience. We used to laugh at the stock Indian phrase, "it is just now coming," which in India could mean in five minutes, or hours, or days, or months. But not to worry, it is 'just now coming.' That different sense of pace in life helped me a lot in the policy world that I would operate in as an adult. Too many expect immediate results and assume failure when things do not immediately go their way. I, on the other hand, came to see life as more of a marathon, not a sprint. Life is both breathtakingly fast and immeasurably slow. You build change one brick at a time and you don't even know what the final edifice will look like.

Interconnectedness. India is a very complex place. The homily of the blind man interpreting the meaning of an elephant through touch seems an appropriate metaphorical device. Feel the trunk and the elephant is a fat snake, the body and it is a whale, the leg and it is a massive tree. India helped me appreciate that life has many portals to understanding. We will never peel back all the layers to get to truth, but we can sure enjoy the journey.

340

A Sense of Others. I also obtained a better sense of my shortcomings in India. I am sure that Randy Stoklas, who suffered as my site mate, would heartily agree that I was insufferable to live with. I struggled so hard with my own challenges, never fully appreciating what was going on with those around me. I learned, perhaps too late, that to focus on others is always a great lesson never to be overlooked. It really is not all about me. The 'others' in your life are what is really important.

Hopefully, we have captured here just a sampling of the impact that our Peace Corps experience had on us as individuals. To do justice to this question would push us far beyond our meager talents. Perhaps we will tackle the question more fully in another work. As a group, moreover, assessing the effects of our PC experience is even more difficult to measure. It remains difficult to assess the overall affects of our Peace Corps experience. Still, the 2009 reunion provided some clues to how we were changed as individuals and as a group. One undeniable effect is the creation of a special bond among us.

A Special Bond

It did not matter that our bodies sagged and drooped in awkward ways or that our faces were now lined with wrinkles. It did not matter what we had achieved in life, or not, although the professional track record of the group is striking indeed. It was clear that our feelings for one another were as intense as they had been some four decades earlier. Our love for one another had not diminished one bit. We were, in fact, a band of brothers and sisters whose ties had been forged in the crucible that was India.

Anyone who served in the military or went through some kind of arduous training or rite of passage, or endured some kind of intense and consequential experience, can relate to the PC experience. You know you have participated in something special, something that is set apart from the ordinary pace and substance of life. And once experienced, you are never quite the same. More than that, you have a shared and private place in your life that few others can enter or really appreciate.

Our singular connectedness endured despite, for most of us at least, decades of virtually no contact with others in our group. The words of Susan Young and Tom Corbett capture how most of us had lost touch with each other.

Susan (Krawiec) Young expressed her involvement as follows:

We did go to the 30th anniversary celebration in Washington and ran into some folks from India 28 (including Bill Day). We also met Dave Dell. We do get newsletters from an RPCV group called Friends of India and met some of them also in DC. Not so many folks from our training group had joined. There is also a Long Island group that we sometimes meet. Maybe after these conversations I will do more with them.

While Susan married early in her PC experience and served in southern India with another group entirely (India 28), she never lost the sense that India 44 was 'her group.' There was something about the early training experience that forged a sense of identity and belonging.

Tom Corbett lived in the Midwest whereas most members of India 44 resided on one coast or the other. He describes very infrequent interaction with other members of India 44.

I had very little contact with members of India 44 over the past four decades. As I mentioned, Don Nordin stopped by my parent's home just after I arrived but slept through most of his visit. I attended Bill Whitesell and Dale's wedding in 1975, but they were more focused on their wedding than visiting with me (how self- centered of them). Mike Simonds must have been there but I cannot even recall seeing him. David Dell called once about ten or fifteen or maybe twenty years ago I think. My wife answered the phone since I have few friends of my own as you can well imagine. So, I was shocked when I heard her say, "Oh, Tom will definitely want to talk to you." I never want to talk to anyone.

You probably have had the experience of running into some-one out of their usual context and, for this reason, have diffi-culty recognizing them. This is why I ask my wife to wear a name tag whenever she wanders into the kitchen by mistake. That is exactly what happened in this instance. I faked a conversation while my mind raced to figure out who the hell David Dell was. About three minutes into the conversation it hit, that David Dell, the India David Dell.

One day I was giving a talk in Milwaukee and a woman approached me asking if I was the Tom Corbett who served in the Peace Corps in India. Although my first reaction was to say, "Not me, I'm innocent," but then I recognized Nancy Simuel and we gave each other a big hug. She was the first India 44 volunteer I had seen in a very long time and I doubt I expressed to her just how great it was to see her.

A few I may never see again. A couple I know I will never again see. I think particularly of Gary Gruber, who died appar-ently of his own hand back in the 1970s. He always struck me as older than his years—wise and gentle and loving. He played the violin, I believe, and quite well. I always wanted to be more like him, with his kindness and his sweetness and his dry, sometimes enigmatic humor. Some things are merely inexplicable.

343

The sense of 'specialness' is found throughout the reflections just presented. For some, this experience was an awakening, exposing them to people and situations that greatly expanded their self-awareness, their confidence, and their appreciation of what they might accomplish. For others, as we have mentioned, they recall all too closely a sense of frustration, disappointment or even failure. Some of these memories are still with them after four decades and after full lives. Still others are yet able to relive the humor and irony of it all, a bunch of kids thrown into impossible situations with good intentions but questionable skills and preparation.

Of course, we all remember in singular ways and express those recollections in our own distinct manners. For Nancy Simuel, the PC experience came out in sharp, isolated memories:

Our training between my junior and senior years enabled me to have positive experiences with whites. Back then, it was a revelation to me that they were not all segregationists and/or bigots. I thought that all whites were just white until I learned that they each had different ethnic heritages and talked proudly about them.

Watching how some of the female volunteers watched and asked questions when I straightened my hair with a hot straightening comb.

Experiencing my first plane ride.

Being hustled out of the inner city where we were staying to the Sheraton-Schroeder Hotel downtown as riots were happening on Third and North streets in Milwaukee.

Being called names by two rickshaw drivers because I refused to pay their inflated fee.

The hustle, bustle, smells, overcrowding, and beggars of India. The beauty of India (Taj Mahal, Gateway to India, the Varnassi Caves, the people).

Learning to wrap and wear a sari; learning Marathi and becoming fluent.

Being welcomed in my village with curiosity and convincing them that I was from America and not Africa. The village children called me Kalichibai (black woman) and my site mate

Gorichibai (yellow woman). Carolyn is Japanese. No way could we have been Americans.

Receiving care packages from home that had been wrapped with love and lots of times opened by the Indian authorities.

Overnight rides on the Howrah Express in the 2nd or 3rd class ladies section.

Trips to Mumbai (Bombay) for medical check-ups and R&R and hanging out at the Trautmanns (the PC regional Director).

The monsoons and the heat.

Just missing stepping in cow dung; not missing the cow dung.

The giggles of our hosts when I got too hot and yet I insisted that the water be boiled before I would drink it.

Sometimes going to the Primary Health Center and being bored because there was nothing to do.

Becoming a bibliophile.

Establishing lasting friendships.

Village life (chai and biscuits, Cadbury chocolates, shopping in the bazaar, wedding invitations, the many festivals).

Being wowed that an Indian mother could give birth and the next day return to the fields to work.

Receiving the news of Dr. King's and Bobby Kennedy's assassinations from our neighbors.

Coming to grips with expectations that as much as the US government wanted us to live like the villagers in our site, the villagers didn't expect it and in some cases that was impossible to do.

For Don Nordin, his first exposures to Indian culture and challenges are embedded in his consciousness and are clearly a part of him now:

We were sent to a "training village." We were slowly immersing into our Peace Corps persona. Earlier Peace Corps programs had used the "parachute" method. The idea being that you just put a young, educated American into a pre-industrial village with instructions to develop it and waited to see what happened. What happened was a high rate of early terminations. India 44's advance training program was probably an adjust-

ment to the other side of the training spectrum. In any case, I joined Gareth Loy and Don Carter in a domicile in the village of Lakavlie a couple of miles from Udaipur.

Here we had to confront the realities of day to-day living. We had to find food and water, clean ourselves, and face the reality of homes with no sanitary facilities at all. This was a new challenge for people who had lived all of their lives with indoor plumbing. We had to squat on the ground to defecate in full view of whoever happened by and cleanse ourselves with our left hand and a little bit of water carried in a lota, just like the people of this village had been doing for millennia. For folks whose first social lessons as toddlers had been the proper use of the toilet, this was hard. Although I learned to adapt, having no toilet facilities for the first six months I lived in my village of Kathar, I was never comfortable with defecation as a social activity. Maybe it was early imprinting and twenty years of living with Western mores but defecation had always been a private matter, and I was right handed, damn it.

The training village also gave us exposure to exposure. We were freaks here and curiosities. I remember one evening, the three of us lying on our charpoys in a small room we used for sleeping. The room had two windows opposite one another. There were bars on the windows, but otherwise they were open. Each window had four or five boys on the outside shouting at us within. This must have been the life animals had in zoos before they became more humane. I think that that experience broke Don Carter. Shortly afterward he called it quits and went home.

After all this, one would think that I'd be thoroughly prepared to begin life as a Peace Corps volunteer. I was still shocked, however, when that day came a year and a quarter after I first began my association with Peace Corps. Lal, the Peace Corps driver, drove me out to Kathar, a small village in the mountains about twenty miles north of Udaipur. He unloaded my Peace Corps footlocker and a few other items in the middle of the road, said goodbye, and drove away. I was left standing in the road now surrounded by a crowd of curious villagers who had no idea who I was or why I was there. They mostly spoke Mewari, a dialect different enough from the Hindi that I had been taught so that I found it unintelligible. Of course there were no living quarters that I had been led to expect and the sun was going down. This moment was the end of training and remains vivid in my memory to this day.

Whether we expressed ourselves in a list, an evocative allegorical statement, or a long discursive narrative, the very act of remembering and expressing has been a welcome purgative, a way of cleansing the stuff we brought back with us.

And so, Nancy's list, Don's vivid memories, and Susan's recollections are no less profound than the longest chapter and still communicate the enduring and profound character of the India experience. It is touching that part of Nancy's PC experience was learning more about the caucasian community in her own country. That reflects a learning opportunity that all of us were fortunate to experience. If you read the reflections carefully, you see how many were being thrown together with other kids outside their familiar cultural milieu for the first time, and in a situation of extraordinary stress.

A kind of cleansing

Despite the variation in what was expressed in each reflection, or how it was expressed, there are critical commonalities. The very act of articulating individual experiences proved to be a healing balm. Sentiments and fears carried within for so many years were divulged and shared. Doubts and anxieties, once revealed, appeared a bit less daunting and much more manageable.

In some cases, long-held misperceptions were erased. Many of us felt that we as individuals had failed while our colleagues had managed the challenges much better. It was illuminating to find that we all lived with this sense of falling short. Others, some of those who had not completed the two full years, had been reluctant to attend the reunion or to write a reflection. They soon realized that they were as much a part of our little band of sisters and brothers as those who endured to the bitter end. They were no less talented or able than the others. Their experiences

347

and perceptions were no less valid. We all had something to share and contribute. As Susan Young notes ...

All this time I imagined that you all had more structured sites and tasks. I thought you, especially the nurses who had some real expertise as opposed to a broad liberal education, had done so much more than we had.

Uncle Sam, it seems, just dropped us all off among a bunch of folks who shared our lack of any idea of what was supposed to happen. In some cases they didn't know we were coming.

We "worked" at Bal Bhavan, a children's center in Hyderabad. Most of the time I felt like we were just hanging out and not accomplishing much. Because we were in the city, I always felt a little guilty that it wasn't real Peace Corps—like in a village. When people ask, I kind of soft peddle what we did. It is soothing to know that others have had the same feeling of shame.

Perhaps, at long last, we are coming to terms with our PC experience, with India, and with ourselves. Don Nordin captures some of our collective thinking in the following observation:

Manifest destiny was a nineteenth century idea and American exceptionalism was not a current phrase. Yet somehow ... somehow there was a notion that we had something to offer to the people of India as young, educated Americans. Perhaps it was just hubris. Perhaps it was a core of that which would make us effective in whatever we might have been.

Some had traveled back to India and to their sites. The experiences were complex, if not bittersweet. The immediacy of being back there brought memories to the forefront, some good and some bad. But for many of us, we might now be ready for the journey we have so long avoided. As Tom Corbett observed...

For many years, periodically I would dream about my village in India. I could never quite recall how the villagers responded to my nocturnal return. That was probably a good thing, the image of an angry mob running me out of town probably would have woken me in a cold sweat—"my god, the crazy American is back." The Salumbar of my dreams now had suburbs. Where the desert greeted my daily review of the terrain fronting our house, now an American type utopia lay before me. Surely, the village has not changed that much but precisely how much of contemporary India I would recognize is an intriguing question.

Over the years, Mary (my spouse) periodically asked whether I was interested in returning to India, or my village. Curious, yes, but I had never felt any compelling need to return. Perhaps I never quite got over a lingering sense of guilt. Like a lot of volunteers, I could not shake that feeling that I took far more than I gave. We were young, naïve, and lacking in appreciable skills. What were we thinking back then? Where did our arrogance and hubris end that we thought we had something to offer? What would I say to those who might possibly recognize me? Yes, I was that tall, skinny kid who stumbled around the fields here looking totally helpless, hopeless, and surely hapless. But at least I left you with a few laughs...

In the end, this is truly a group effort. This is a work where the whole is very much greater than the sum of the parts. Each reflection has a refracted quality to it where truth is shaped and directed by the individual author. Yet, the whole is a reflection of the group experience and captures some elemental realities of the Peace Corps experience absent the romantic veneer we too often use to gloss over the harsher aspects of reality.

As we shared our lives with one another in the Bay Area in May of 2009, it became quite apparent that this was a special group of folk. As noted, many had gone on to careers that would have been considered successful and even prestigious by the ordinary metrics used by society to calculate professional and personal success. However, it was apparent that all of us considered our youthful foray into Peace Corps to be a very special and irreplaceable part of our lives. More importantly, we realized that we might never replicate that special bond with one another forged by our shared experience of Mother India. One of our group put their thoughts on the meaning of the reunion as follows:

The 40th reunion, however, has possibly proved to be an important epiphany in a way. I had never gone to a reunion before. Well, not quite true, my dear spouse did drag me to her grade school reunion. Yes, that's right, a grade school reunion! I mean, who remembers grade school? It actually makes sense if you knew the tight knit community in which she was raised. But I had never been to one of mine, at any level. As soon as we all talked and began to share, my sense of failure did not seem so personal, or so unique. More or less, we all shared that sense of limitation, a harsh introspection born of unrealistic expectations. In the end, we could have done better, but we probably did ok.

An idea that has not died

Presumably, as with many significant ideas, the concept of Peace Corps came about almost by accident. Then Presidential candidate John F. Kennedy, dead tired from the constant campaigning, drifted from his stock stump speech before students at the University of Michigan in October of 1960. He posed a challenge to the students in the audience, would they be willing

to volunteer to spend time in undeveloped countries to impart what they were learning to make this a better and hopefully more peaceful world?

Some in his audience were electrified by the thought and considered it a challenge and not merely a campaign speech throwaway line. They treated the concept seriously and began lobbying for just such opportunities. Just months later, on March 1, 1961, Peace Corps was created through an executive order. Last year, almost a half century later, some 13,500 candidates applied for some 4,000 volunteer slots. The Peace Corps ideal endures.

It was not the concept that determined whatever success has been achieved. It was not the 'spirit of the 60s' nor Kennedy's vision, nor even Sargent Shriver's energy, though all those were important. Ultimately, it was the quality and sacrifice of the 200,000 plus individuals who, over the past half century, gave part of their lives to the simple notion that sacrifice and giving of oneself is simply a good thing to do. It is not easy nor does it always turn out as anticipated or like the feel-good dramatic effect of the movie *Slum Dog Millionaire*. If given the choice, most of us in India 44 would probably do the same thing again. Undoubtedly, we are better human beings for the experience. Perhaps more than that, we belonged to something special.

At our reunion, Haywood Turrentine looked around the room and exclaimed what a great group this was. He noted that no one cared if you were rich or poor, successful or not, good looking or not. You just knew you were going to be accepted and loved because you were one of a group that had experienced something intense and special together. Some of us, such as Gary Gruber and Bob Proffit, will never join us again. But they will not be forgotten. They were members of India 44. We all were members of India 44.

Yes, we were, in fact, a band of brothers and sisters, with a connection that was forged half way around the world a lifetime ago, and yet which endures to this day.

We are very fortunate indeed.

Postscript

Carolyn (Watanabe) Adler

India!?
India!?

That was my mother's response when I informed her over the phone of my acceptance into the Peace Corps Advanced Training Program scheduled to start that June of 1966. My dad was a bit more enthusiastic, if not a touch pragmatic, with his response, "at least my tax dollars will be well spent." However, the most asked question by family and peers was "why the Peace Corps?" At the time my answer was simple. When President Kennedy was assassinated during my freshman year of college, I felt the need to help secure some fulfillment of the spirit of hope he inspired and to help see his dream of a better world come to fruition. In retrospect, his inspiration probably motivated me to pursue a promise to myself to not let that dream simply fade from sight. A close second reason would have to be the prospect of a grand adventure and a grand adventure it was!

Who would have guessed a group of lifelong friendships would have been started and lasting impressions born of the Indian experience would creep into all my subsequent life choices? Who would have guessed I would find my life partner and soul mate in the incongruence of beauty and cacophony that was India?

As with many Peace Corps volunteers, a deeper appreciation of what our country offered us in terms of creature comforts (running piped water, flush toilets, electricity, etc.) and the ability to mold our lives without fear of reprisal (cultural and/ or political) was brought home to me. In addition, the gift of

353

growing self-confidence came upon me in the realization that one did not have to be an expert with all the academic trappings in order to be somewhat effective in one's village. My site mate, Nancy Simuel, and I had on-the-job training giving shots (including IVs), mixing and distributing medications, and so many other necessary tasks. These are things we could not have done in the states with our degrees in education and social work. I also learned to live without so many things (T.V., radio, a stove, or any of the appliances) that make life so easy here. I had to depend upon myself to keep entertained, and even to grow as a person, during those long and lonely days.

Without even knowing it I had found myself. So, to answer my mom's question and ambivalence:

India!?

Yes, India! It was the best of times, it was the … (well, you probably recall the rest.)

ABOUT THE AUTHORS

Mary Jo (Dummer) Clark earned a Bachelor's Degree in Nursing from the University of San Francisco, a Master of Science in Nursing from Texas Women's University and a PhD in nursing from the University of Texas at Austin. After her return from India, she worked for several years as a public health nurse for Los Angeles County Health Department and then turned to teaching nursing. She has held faculty and administrative positions at East Tennessee State University, the Medical College of Georgia, and the University of San Diego. She currently teaches in the masters, PhD, and Doctor of Nursing Practice programs at the Hahn School of Nursing and Health Science, University of San Diego. In addition, she serves on the Board of Commissioners and Accreditation Review Committee of the Commission on Collegiate Nursing Education (CCNE), the accrediting body for baccalaureate and graduate nursing education programs. She is married to former nurse Phil Clark and has one son and a daughter-in-law, but no grandchildren (yet). In her spare time, she conducts research on breast cancer screening among the Thai population of southern California. Her internationally acclaimed population health nursing textbook is entering its 7th edition.

Thomas Corbett holds a Doctorate in Social Welfare from the University of Wisconsin-Madison (UW). For many years, he was a Senior Scientist and Associate Director of the Institute for Research on Poverty, a national think tank on poverty and welfare issues located at the UW. He also taught policy courses to undergraduate and graduate students in the School of Social Work. He spent a great deal of time working with government at the local, state, and national level focusing, among many other things, on welfare reform and the design of human service systems. He served on a National Academy of Sciences expert panel on evaluating national welfare reform, spent a year on leave from the University working in Washington D.C. on President Clinton's welfare reform bill, and most recently co-authored (with Karen Bogenschneider) a book titled *Evidence-Based Policymaking: Insights from Policy-Minded Researchers and Research-Minded Policymakers*. Now retired, he splits his time between Madison, Wisconsin and Hudson, Florida with his wife, Mary Rider, and the best dog in the world, Ernie.

Michael Simonds received a Bachelors Degree in Interdisciplinary Social Science from San Francisco State University, and a Masters Degree in Library Science from Drexel University. After working for the Van Pelt Library of the University of Pennsylvania and the Norwalk Public Library in Connecticut, he became the Chief Executive Officer of Bibliomation, Inc. a non-profit consortium of 48 public libraries located throughout Connecticut. He served as President of the Connecticut Library Association (1983-84) and has been a speaker at the American Library Association National Conference and the national Computers in Libraries Conference. Mike has two beautiful grown daughters and lives in Milford Connecticut where he continues his work in library automation.

Haywood Turrentine holds a Bachelors Degree in American History from North Carolina Central University, Durham, North Carolina, a Masters Degree in Urban Geography from the University of Cincinnati, and a Doctor of Divinity Degree from the Cambridge Theological Seminary. He is retired from the Laborers Training Trust Fund of the Laborers International Union of North America where he worked on the design and implementation of health, safety and skills training programs. While with the Laborers, he was appointed, by the General President to serve on the National Environmental Justice Advisory Council, a National Advisory Committee to the United States EPA. During his tenure on the Council, he served on a subcommittee that developed a Model Plan for Public Participation in the permitting and siting of waste facilities under the Clean Air and Water Acts. The Council elected him as the Chairman of the NEJAC, and he served in that capacity for four years, providing advice to then EPA Administrator, Carol Browner. He is retired and spends much of his time writing and volunteering at his church. He recently authored his first book entitled *The Invisible Chain That Enslaves Us: The Clergy's Misuse of the King James' Version of the Bible*. He lives in the greater Birmingham, Alabama area with his lovely wife of 32 years, Lelani. They have one son, James Lynwood.

CHAPTER NOTES

1 To the best of our recollection, these are the people who flew into India as part of India 44 in the summer of 1967.

Notes for chapter 1.
2 See The New York Times, September 20, 2010, *Moynihan in His Own Words,* by Sam Roberts, p. A25.

Notes for chapter 10.
3 Personal communication from Mike Simonds

4 This problem was eventually addressed when Union Carbide built a big fertilizer plant in Bophal in the late 1970's, however, this plant famously exposed half a million people to poison gas in 1984, and killed at least thousands.

5 Why didn't the Peace Corps just start over and hybridize using a local Indian grain? As it turned out, long after our program ended, something like this eventually did happen in India. Mike Simonds told me recently, "What happened [ultimately] was that the Indian government took the Sonora 64, and blended it with a number of other varieties to come up with one that worked in India, and was more in keeping with Indian tastes. It was this hybrid (which was based, in part, on Sonora 64) that led the Green Revolution in the country." India's Green Revolution eventually made India self-sufficient in food production; now India competes in world markets for grain exports. More recently still, excessive use of government-subsidized urea fertilizer is starting to ruin the fertility of some Indian farmland. See the Wall Street Journal, "Green Revolution in India Wilts as Subsidies Backfire", Feb. 22, 2010.

6 A Sony 800 portable 5" reel recorder, that incorporated the first hysteresis-synchronous motor to appear in a battery-operated portable recorder; I still have the excellent field recordings I made there.

7 Yes, it's true, people used to smoke on airplanes. Can you imagine? How strange...

8 http://www.sfgate.com/cgi-bin/article.cgi?f=/c/a/2005/06/13/ DDGQ4D6R M51.DTL&#ixzz0SLSp6JOS

9 "Semiprofessional" means they paid me, but not enough to live.

10 Saying #70 from the translation by Thomas O. Lambdin. I don't think this is the translation in the book that I had in those days, but I like this version better anyway.

CPSIA information can be obtained at www.ICGtesting.com
Printed in the USA
LVOW080251280112

265811LV00004B/12/P